Academic Writing and Genre

Also available from Continuum:

Academic Writing and Plagiarism, Diane Pecorari
Academic Writing: At the Interface of Corpus and Discourse, Maggie Charles, Susan Hunston and Diane Pecorari
Academic Writing in Context, Martin Hewings
Analysing Academic Writing, Louise Ravelli and Robert Ellis
Teaching Academic Writing, Patricia Friedrich

Forthcoming:

Academic Writing in a Second or Foreign Language, Ramona Tang

Academic Writing and Genre

A Systematic Analysis

Ian Bruce

continuum

Continuum International Publishing Group

The Tower Building
11 York Road
London SE1 7NX

80 Maiden Lane, Suite 704
New York
NY 10038

www.continuumbooks.com

First published 2008. Paperback edition published 2010.

British Library Cataloguing-in-Publication Data
A catalogue record for this book is available from the British Library.

ISBN: 9780826498441 (hardback) 9781441103086 (paperback)

Library of Congress Cataloging-in-Publication Data
A catalog record for this book is available from the Library of Congress.

Typeset by Data Standards Ltd, Frome, Somerset, UK.

Contents

List of Figures and Tables		vii
Acknowledgements		vii
Chapter 1:	The teaching of academic writing	1
1.0	Introduction	1
1.1	The notion of discourse competence	2
1.2	Genre-based approaches to developing discourse competence in writing	5
1.3	Genre-based teaching: critical or accommodationist	9
Chapter 2:	From social genre towards pedagogy	13
2.0	Overview	13
2.1	Relating genre to language learning	13
2.2	The approach to genre influenced by systemic functional linguistics	14
2.3	The systemic functional approach to genre: summary	19
2.4	Discussion: the systemic functional approach to genre as a discourse-categorizing construct	19
2.5	Conclusion	25
2.6	The approach to genre of the English for Specific Purposes movement	26
2.7	Genre as a means of analysis of ESP texts	29
2.8	An ESP framework for genres	32
2.9	ESP approaches to the analysis of texts: summary	33
2.10	The two pedagogic approaches to genre: discussion	34
Chapter 3:	Constraints on a cognitive genre construct	39
3.0	Introduction	39
3.1	Fundamental notions in cognitive approaches to categorization: prototype and hierarchy	40
3.2	Theories of underlying patterns employed in the organization of knowledge relating to specific domains	47
3.3	Other schematic constructs: scripts, plans, goals, frames and scenarios	52
3.4	Theories relating to procedural knowledge	64
3.5	Discussion: implications of categorization theories for discourse creation	73
Chapter 4:	Operationalizing cognitive genres in academic writing	79
4.0	Introduction	79
4.1	Some observations on the cognitive structuring of discourse	80
4.2	Cognitive genres and young learners	85
4.3	Cognitive genres and academic writing in university contexts	87

4.4 Towards a cognitive genre construct for academic writing 91
4.5 A model for cognitive genres in academic discourse 94
4.6 Study 1: A corpus investigation of the use of cognitive genres in academic texts 99
4.7 Study 2: Use of the features of the cognitive genres by three groups of writers 101
4.8 Conclusion 106
Chapter 5: Relating cognitive genres to the teaching and learning of writing 109
5.0 Introduction 109
5.1 Cognitive genres and language learning theory 109
5.2 Principles of curriculum design for general EAP courses 112
5.3 Relating cognitive genres to a syllabus design 117
5.4 A general EAP syllabus unit based on the report cognitive genre 121
5.5 Conclusion 126
Chapter 6: The scope of social genre knowledge 129
6.0 Introduction 129
6.1 Towards a construct for social genres 129
6.2 Social genres and context 132
6.3 Social genres and epistemology 133
6.4 Social genres and writer stance 136
6.5 Social genres and the staging of content 138
6.6 Social genres and cognitive genres 140
6.7 Summary of social genre knowledge 140
6.8 Relating social and cognitive genre knowledge to EAP writing courses 142
6.9 Conclusion 150
Chapter 7: Teaching genre knowledge in an advanced writing course 151
7.0 Introduction 151
7.1 The sample course unit: syllabus 152
7.2 Results sections: social genre focus 153
7.3 Results sections: cognitive genre focus 159
7.4 Conclusion 167

References 171
Appendix 1 Crombies interpropositional relations 185
Appendix 2 Corpus study: selection method, population and sample 186
Appendix 3 Instructions for the administration of the four writing tasks 188
Appendix 4 Example of an analysed script from Study 2 189
Appendix 5 Results sections corpus 190
Index 191

List of Figures and Tables

Figure 4.1	The relationship between social genres and cognitive genres	95
Table 1.1	Diversity of approaches to text classification	7
Table 4.1	Summary of Quinns taxonomy of text types for EAP courses	92
Table 4.2	Comparison of Biber's and Quinns text types for academic prose	93
Table 4.3	Proposed cognitive genre model	97
Table 4.4	Cognitive genre corpus	99
Table 4.5	The cognitive genre model incorporating the corpus findings	100
Table 4.6	The sample	102
Table 4.7	Total overall prototypicality ratings for each sample	104
Table 4.8	Comparison of the overall prototypicality ratings of teachers and native-speaker students	105
Table 4.9	Comparison of prototypicality ratings of native-speaker (NS) students and non-native-speaker (NNS) students	106
Table 5.1	Proposal for a general EAP writing syllabus	119
Table 5.2	Sample general EAP syllabus unit	122
Table 5.3	Report cognitive genre – sample text	124
Table 5.4	Examples of interpropositional relations from the sample text	126
Table 6.1	Hyland's interpersonal model of metadiscourse	137
Table 6.2	Framework for analysing social genres	141
Table 6.3	Analytical marking guide for report cognitive genre	149
Table 7.1	Postgraduate level writing course: unit topics	151
Table 7.2	Unit 6 syllabus: reporting Results in research	154
Table 7.3	Results section study	160
Table 7.4	The use of cognitive genres in results sections	162
Table 7.5	Defining the amplification relation	162
Table 7.6	Results corpus wordlist	163

Acknowledgements

In relation to the approach to cognitive genre that I put forward in this book, I wish to acknowledge the central influence of Winifred Crombie and her work on interpropositional relations. This theory is a significant element in the genre model that I propose. I would like to thank my wife Carolyn for her support and assistance in preparing the manuscript. Also, I would like to thank Colleen Coalter from Continuum for her willing assistance and guidance.

Chapter 1: The teaching of academic writing

1.0 Introduction

During the last few decades, the worldwide phenomenon of the increasing use of English as an international language, and the accompanying demand to learn English as an additional language (hereafter EAL), have given rise to exponential growth in the activities of language teaching, materials publishing, and research that further informs these activities. Increasingly, the motivation of students to learn English is for the purpose of participation in higher education at English-medium universities. Thus, for many teachers, a major focus of their work is on preparing learners to cope with the language requirements and, in particular, the writing requirements of university courses.

Central to the mastery of academic writing is the novice writers' development of *discourse competence,* particularly in relation to academic prose. This involves writers developing the ability to integrate a wide range of different types of knowledge in order to create extended written discourse that is both linguistically accurate and socially appropriate. In the first part of this chapter, approaches to this underlying construct of discourse competence are reviewed and discussed, in terms of their commonalities and the issues they raise in relation to the teaching and learning of academic writing.

Given the centrality of the development of a discourse competence to the aims of academic writing courses, it is evident that the object of teaching and learning in such courses will be extended units of written discourse. Teachers, therefore, need to develop ways of systematically classifying and deconstructing such larger language entities. In relation to this need, genre-based approaches to language teaching (and particularly the teaching of writing) continue to attract considerable interest from language teachers who are looking for frameworks around which they can organize their courses in order to promote the development of the discourse competence of their learners. The second part of this chapter reviews the idea of a genre-based approach to the teaching of writing, along with approaches to discourse classification and notions of genre. This section also considers the problem of the current multiplicity of approaches to discourse classification and, as a way of resolving this issue, proposes two broad categories of genre, those of *cognitive genre* and *social genre.* These two categories form the basis for the modelling, model testing and approaches to writing pedagogy presented in subsequent chapters.

The third section of this chapter briefly reviews the ideological debate that surrounds second language pedagogy (including writing pedagogy) about whether it should be *accommodationist* or *critical* in respect of the ways in which teachers introduce learners to second language knowledge. This section outlines the philosophical position that this book takes in relation to this particular debate.

Thus, the central focus of the chapters of this book is on the types of knowledge that constitute a discourse competence, and the operationalization of this knowledge in terms of genres and genre-based approaches for the purposes of teaching academic writing.

1.1 The notion of discourse competence

To develop the writing skill of EAL learners, it is now acknowledged by many that approaches to language teaching that focus on atomized units of language merely at sentence or clause level (and below) are not only inadequate but also possibly misleading. This is evident in the language outcomes that can potentially result when learners who are taught atomized knowledge are then faced with the task of writing extended prose in academic settings. Thus, rather than teaching and learning discrete linguistic items, such as features of morphology, lexis, grammar and syntax, there needs to be an integration of these aspects of linguistic knowledge with pragmatic knowledge and conventionalized forms of communication, in order that language learners have the means to be able to write extended prose that is both accurate and appropriate. The ability to use these knowledge systems and forms in this integrated way in order to process and create extended discourse is referred to as *discourse competence*. In the range of models that have been put forward to describe the overall concept of *communicative competence* in a language, discourse competence has always been included as an essential component in each case.

Hymes (1972) first proposed the concept of communicative competence as a way of describing the different areas of human knowledge that would need to be investigated in order to fully account for the language ability of a competent language user within a specific setting. Hymes' proposal was a reaction to the narrowly grammatical approach proposed by Chomsky to describe the types of knowledge that a language user draws upon. Hymes proposes that communicative competence is divided into linguistic knowledge and pragmatic knowledge. The linguistic aspects include phonology and orthography, grammar, vocabulary and discourse, while the pragmatic aspects involve functions, variations, interactional skills and cultural frameworks. However, from the outset it must be emphasized that Hymes' approach to communicative competence (an approach that included discourse knowledge) was not put forward as a basis for pedagogy, but rather to be used in ethnographic research that aimed to account for the range of different types of knowledge that contribute to an individual's competence to communicate effectively within a language.

Drawing upon Hymes' ideas, Canale and Swain's (1980) proposal for communicative competence included discourse competence, which was seen as encompassing grammatical competence as well as other types of knowledge. The knowledge specification of Canale and Swain's communicative competence model was for the purpose of informing language teaching and learning and thus had a pedagogical agenda that was not part of Hymes' original proposal. As the idea of discourse competence was clearly new territory, Canale and Swain (1980) were quite cautious in their descriptions of the types of knowledge that this may entail, stating:

> until more clear-cut theoretical statements about rules of discourse emerge, it is perhaps most useful to think of these rules in terms of the cohesion (i.e. grammatical links) and coherence (i.e. appropriate combination of communicative functions) of groups of utterance. (1980, p. 30)

In many ways confining descriptions of discourse competence within these two areas of cohesion and coherence set the agenda for proposals for discourse competence in subsequent communicative competence models. For example, Canale (1983), in a slightly adapted version of the Canale and Swain model, defines discourse competence as 'mastery of how to combine and interpret meanings and forms to achieve unified text in different modes by using (a) cohesion devices to relate forms and (b) coherence rules to organize meanings' (p. 339). Similarly, in discussing a model relating to language assessment, Bachman (1990) includes within the domain of communicative competence what he refers to as 'textual competence', involving both cohesion and rhetorical organization:

> Cohesion comprises ways of explicitly marking semantic relationships such as reference, substitution, ellipsis, conjunction and lexical cohesion, as well as conventions such as those governing the ordering of old and new information in discourse. Rhetorical organisation pertains to the overall conceptual structure of a text, and is related to the effect of the text on the language user. (1990, p. 88)

Celce-Murcia and Dornyei (1995), in developing a communicative competence model for pedagogical purposes, also include discourse competence as one of the five components of their model. Within the domain of discourse competence they include 'cohesion, deixis, coherence, generic structure and conversational structure inherent to the turn-taking system in conversation' (1995, p. 13). Discourse competence is also included as part of a broader category of pragmatic competence in the Council of Europe's *Common European Framework of Reference for Languages*, where it is stated that discourse competence is:

> the ability of a user/learner to arrange sentences in sequence so as to produce coherent stretches of language. It includes knowledge of and ability to control the ordering of sentences in terms of:
>
> - topic/focus;
> - given/new;
> - 'natural' sequence e.g. temporal ...
> - cause/effect (invertible) ...
> - ability to structure and manage discourse in terms of: thematic organisation; coherence and cohesion; logical ordering; style and register; rhetorical effectiveness the 'co-operative principle' (Grice 1975) (Council of Europe, 2001, p. 123);

Common to the concept of discourse competence as it appears in the various communicative competence models is the idea that it relates to the appropriate arrangement of both content information and language in order to create extended spoken or written discourse. In relation to the informational element of the fusion, what is frequently emphasized is the representational ordering and structuring of content information in ways that make it comprehensible – the aspect of discourse structuring originally referred to by Hymes as 'coherence'. In relation to the organization of the language system to create extended discourse, there is an emphasis on the use of various connective devices that combine to create extended stretches of language in ways that are comprehensible and promote coherence. This aspect of the linguistic features of discourse organization is often referred to as 'cohesion'. Thus, the various proposals for what comprises discourse competence agree that it is a central component of communicative competence in a language and that it involves a number of elements, often grouped under terms such as cohesion and coherence, reference and rhetorical organization, all of which relate to creating or interpreting connected, functioning, extended units of language.

The notion of the construct of discourse competence, as it is proposed in the communicative competence models, has two major implications for the planning of language teaching and learning, and especially for the teaching of writing extended discourse. In effect, these implications should operate as important constraints on the planning and implementation of any academic writing course.

The first major implication relates to the content of academic writing courses. Course designers, materials writers and teachers need to consider the range of types of knowledge that the exercise of a discourse competence draws upon, and the ways in which these different types of knowledge can form part of an academic writing course. (It will, for example, be unsatisfactory to focus solely on discrete aspects of linguistic knowledge in a course that claims to teach academic writing.) The second implication relates to pedagogical processes. This stems from the fact that the exercise of the range of types of knowledge (that relate to a discourse competence) is an integrated operation, and the fact that any pedagogical approach to deconstructing and teaching these types of knowledge, while involving analysis, must also involve principles of synthesis to support the integrative nature of the development and exercise of a discourse competence by novice writers. This second implication, therefore, has implications for the cycles of learning that take place in the process of academic writing.

1.2 Genre-based approaches to developing discourse competence in writing

Thus it now appears to be accepted that the development of discourse competence is a key element of an individual's overall communicative competence in a language, and that this element is particularly important for learners who need to develop skills in academic writing. Therefore, the issue that confronts the teacher is how to develop a clear understanding of the types of knowledge and process that need to be integrated into syllabus, pedagogy and teaching materials in order to support the development of this area of language knowledge. From the theorizing that has given rise to the notion of discourse competence, it seems that pedagogy to develop the discourse competence sub-skill should be guided by two key principles:

- discourse competence involves a range of different types of knowledge, including both linguistic and non-linguistic knowledge;
- pedagogy that develops discourse competence, in novice writers for example, needs to be able to integrate the full range of the different types of knowledge that discourse competence draws upon.

In order to meet the requirements of these two principles, many turn to what are often referred to as *genre-based approaches* as an appropriate basis for teaching the writing skill and, thereby, developing a discourse competence in language learners. However, defining what is meant by the terms 'genre' or 'genre-based approaches' when discussing the teaching of writing can be problematic as both the literature on the subject and the related terminology is extremely diverse and potentially somewhat confusing, and this is particularly the case for new teacher-practitioners. Thus, this section begins by providing a brief preliminary, a 'rule of thumb' explanation of 'genre-based teaching' as a precursor to the issue being addressed in more detail in Chapters 5 and 7. Following this explanation, the present section addresses the problem of defining what genres actually are. The definitions presented here will be used throughout the following chapters as a framework for reviewing genre theory, and for proposing genre models and their incorporation into the teaching of writing.

The French word genre, meaning 'type' or 'kind', when applied to English literature, has been used to denote literary categories (such as types of novel, or short story) involving categorization of texts in terms of a range of structural and stylistic features. Subsequently other non-print media, such as film, stage drama and graphic art have appropriated the term genre as a categorizer of creative outputs. In the last few decades, genre has also been applied to categories of non-literary written texts, sometimes for the purpose of characterizing the features of such texts for the teaching of writing. For example, newspaper editorials, letters, obituaries and different types of academic texts have also been identified as genres. These are often characterized in terms of similarities of content, the staging of the content, and the linguistic resources employed.

Taken in its widest sense, a genre-based approach to language teaching refers to pedagogy that involves examining and deconstructing examples of genres (categories of texts). For example, using a sample text (an example of a particular genre), learners engage with tasks that focus on the organization and constituent features of the text in order to acquire the types of knowledge necessary for creating their own examples of the same genre. Often the outcome of the learning cycle will be tasks that require students to use the target genre knowledge (which they have been analysing and practising) to create new examples of the same genre.

For the teaching of the writing skill, it seems that genre-based courses have three major strengths: firstly, they make it possible to focus on larger units of language; secondly, they can provide a focus on the organizational or procedural elements of written discourse; and thirdly, they make it possible to retain linguistic components as functioning features of a larger unit of discourse, thereby avoiding atomistic approaches to language teaching. As Paltridge (2001) observes:

> [a] genre-based approach to language program development aims to incorporate discourse and contextual aspects of language use that are often underattended to in programs based only on the lower-level organizational units of language, such as structures, functions, or vocabulary. (p. 6)

While many now may claim that there is much value in using a genre-based, discourse-focused approach as a basis for teaching the writing skill (and, thereby, developing a discourse competence in language learners), a central problem with implementing this approach is that there is still a considerable diversity of views about how genre should be defined. For pedagogy, therefore, this raises questions about which genres should be selected and how they should be used for the teaching of writing at different levels of learner need. The lists in Table 1.1 following provide some indication of the range of terminology and variety of approaches to discourse classification that have been proposed. The separation into two different columns is to contrast terms used to classify whole discourses and those used to classify parts of discourses.

Table 1.1: Diversity of approaches to text classification

Whole texts	Parts of texts
genre (Hasan, 1989; Swales, 1990; Bhatia, 1993; Fowler, 1982) **text genre** (Pilegaard and Frandsen, 1996; Werlich, 1976) **macro-genres** (Martin, 1994, 1995, 1997) **discourse types** (Virtanen, 1992)	**genre** (Swales, 1990) **elemental genre** (Feez, 2002) **text type** (Biber, 1989; Pilegaard and Frandsen, 1996; Werlich, 1976; Virtanen, 1992) **rhetorical functions** (Lackstrom, Selinker and Trimble, 1973; Jordan 1997) **rhetorical modes** (Silva, 1990) **macro-functions** (Council of Europe, 2001) **macro-genres** (Grabe, 2002) **séquences** (Adam, 1985, 1992) **discourse patterns** (Hoey, 1979, 1983, 1994, 2001) **macrostructures** (Van Dijk, 1980) **generic values** (Bhatia, 2002, 2004) **language styles** (Bloor, 1998)

A consequence of this diversity of approach is also the wide diversity of types of knowledge that constitute genres in these various proposals. While earlier approaches to genre focused mainly on textual analyses, it is now suggested that the scope of knowledge to be taken into account in genre analyses includes an ethnographic as well as a textual perspective (Bhatia, 2004) and metadiscoursal as well as propositional knowledge (Hyland, 2005).

Thus, any review of theory or research related to classifying texts in terms of such categories as 'genre' and 'text type' needs to address the fact that terminology is used in very different ways by different writers. This is not just a terminological problem of naming or designation. It is also a problem that arises out of fundamental disagreement about the very nature of the object of enquiry, what it is that is being investigated and classified. For this reason, different readers may have different expectations in relation to the use of these terms. For some, discourse classification is largely a social phenomenon, something directly reflected in the overall conventionally recognized purpose and conscious organization of texts: for example editorials, postcards, or research articles. For others, discourse classification is a communicatively or rhetorically motivated, cognitive phenomenon: for example discourse categories such as argument, explanation, recounting and description. In this case, the phenomenon is reflected only indirectly, if at all, in the overall structure of whole texts.

As a basis for resolving the problem of the social/cognitive dichotomy in the different approaches, it is proposed that the existing approaches to discourse classification generally fall within one of two categories, either the category of *social genre* or that of *cognitive genre.* These are benchmark terms in this book, and will be defined here and used in the following chapters as a basis for the review of literature and as a framework for the genre construct proposals that are presented in the following chapters.

Social genres are similar in type to the category of *text genre* proposed by Pilegaard and Frandsen (1996), referring to socially recognized constructs according to which whole texts are classified in terms of their overall social purpose. Thus, for example, personal letters, novels and academic articles are examples of different social genres, which are created to fulfil different types of socially recognized and understood purpose. Although a specific example of a particular social genre may exhibit features of a single cognitive genre (see below), it is more common for examples of social genres to exhibit features of more than one cognitive genre.

The term cognitive genre is used to refer to what Pilegaard and Frandsen (1996) label *text type.* As examples, they cite: 'narrative, expository, descriptive, argumentative or instructional text types' (Pilegaard and Frandsen, 1996, p. 3). Cognitive genres can, therefore, be aligned with macrofunctions as described by the Council of Europe's Common Framework of Reference. Macrofunctions are 'categories for the functional use of spoken discourse or written text consisting of a (sometimes extended) sequence of sentences e.g. description, narration, commentary, exposition, exegesis, explanation, demonstration, instruction, argumentation, persuasion' (Council of Europe, 2001, p. 126). The term cognitive genre is used here to refer to the overall cognitive orientation of a piece of writing in terms of its realization of a particular rhetorical purpose, something that is reflected in the way in which information is internally organized and related. Different types of rhetorical purpose (such as: to recount sequenced events, to explain a process, to argue a point of view) instantiate different cognitive genres. A particular example of a social genre (e.g. a personal letter) may draw upon a range of different cognitive genres in relation to the different rhetorical purpose [illegible] acterize different sections of the overall message, for exa[illegible] an argument or providing an explanation.

Whol[illegible] different social genres (such as, for example, scientif[illegible] lly combine and frame a range of cognitive genres. In addi[illegible] ocial genres are characterized by different framing feature[illegible] xample, an introductory salutation and greeting in the cas[illegible] ell as by different introductory and linking features (ways [illegible] nd linking different cognitive genres). However, some [illegible] h as, for example, instruction manuals, may be associa[illegible] cognitive genre by virtue of the fact that they have a sing[illegible] urpose. It may be for this reason that there is consid[illegible] nent about terminology in the research literature. Thus, [illegible] to here as social genre may be referred to in the resear[illegible] either genre or text type.

In [illegible] to the issue of assisting EAL learners to develop a disco[illegible] e in academic writing, there appear to be two fundamental questions that need to be addressed by syllabus and course designers, materials writers and teachers:

- What are the genres that occur in academic discourse that need to be taught?
- How do we teach them?

Chapters 2 to 4 address the first question. Chapter 2 critically reviews the two main pedagogic approaches to social genre: that of educators influenced by systemic-functional linguistics, and that of the English for Academic Purposes movement. Drawing on categorization theory and cognitive psychology, Chapter 3 reviews the constraints that should operate on any theory of cognitive genre, and Chapter 4 proposes a model for the cognitive genres that occur in academic prose. Also, as a response to the first question, Chapter 6 presents a framework for examining social genre knowledge in academic discourse. Chapters 5 and 7 address the second question by exemplifying approaches to deconstructing and understanding social and cognitive genres in syllabus units of courses designed to teach academic writing. Chapter 5 focuses on a pre-university writing syllabus unit based mainly on cognitive genres, and Chapter 7 examines a syllabus unit from a postgraduate writing course that incorporates cognitive and social genre knowledge.

1.3 Genre-based teaching: critical or accommodationist

For some time, there has been an ongoing debate about whether the teaching of second language (hereafter L2) knowledge, such as in an academic writing course, should proceed on the basis of an *accommoda-*

tionist (sometimes referred to as *assimilative* or *pragmatic*) pedagogy, which assists students to master the conventions and values of academic writing in an uncritical way, or whether it should follow the course of a *critical* pedagogy that encourages the questioning and challenging of such norms and values (see Benesch, 2001). This book puts forward a systematic and detailed proposal for approaches to genre analysis in order to identify and teach different types of knowledge that L2 writers require in order to exercise a discourse competence appropriately in an academic setting. Therefore, it is possible that some readers will see the approaches proposed here as falling solidly within the accommodationist camp. From the outset, therefore, it is important to address this debate, and to state the philosophical position taken towards the teaching of academic writing through the genre-analytical approaches proposed here.

Educational debates that are carried out in terms of simple binaries, such as accommodationist versus critical, have the value of highlighting pedagogical issues and promoting awareness and discussion of such issues. However, at the same time, the actual act of carrying out such debates in terms of simple binaries is problematic in that it may not necessarily lead to practical solutions to the multiplicity of issues faced by teachers in everyday teaching situations, where they are required to tailor pedagogy to learner need as well as to meet the expectations of a range of other stakeholders in the teaching and learning process. Such stakeholders, apart from novice writers themselves, may include funders of their education (such as parents and scholarship providers), teachers, school authorities, testing organizations, and the disciplinary discourse communities that novice writers aspire to join. The view taken in this book is that effective writing pedagogy that uses a genre-based approach (as a means for developing novice writers' discourse competence) has to be both accommodationist and critical at the same time. *Accommodationist* here is taken to mean exercising a discourse competence by being able to understand and appropriately draw on the various types of systemic knowledge necessary for producing discoursal outputs. *Critical* here is taken to mean a novice writer being able to exercise an authorial voice by individuated and innovative use of the various aspects of discourse knowledge at his/her disposal.

Following the approach of Johns (1997, 2001), the proposal here is that novice writers need to be trained as discourse analysts in order to develop heuristic processes and frameworks to analyse the discourses of their subject areas, and thereby develop understandings of linguistic, procedural and socially situated knowledge in order to construct their own texts competently. Johns proposes that disadvantaged undergraduates need to become ethnographers in their fields in order to demystify academic practices. The approach taken here does not disagree with Johns, and Chapter 6 proposes approaches to learner ethnographic enquiries in order to come to terms with disciplinary social genres. (Chapter 7 aims to provide a practical example of how this approach may be implemented.) However, this book proposes that novice writers also need to develop approaches to textual and procedural knowledge, and to understand how these areas of knowledge underpin overall genre knowledge, and it is these areas that are the focus of Chapters 4 and 5.

Chapter 2: From social genre towards pedagogy

2.0 Overview

In this chapter, two approaches to defining and analysing social genre that have had an influential effect on pedagogy are examined. These approaches include the work of:

- linguists influenced by the *systemic functional* school of linguistics, e.g. Eggins (1994), Hasan (1985/1989), Martin (1986, 1992, 1997, 2000), and Ventola (1985);
- linguists working in the field of *English for Specific/Specifiable Purposes* (ESP), e.g. Dudley-Evans (1986, 1989, 1994), Swales (1981, 1990, 1998, 2004), Bhatia (1993, 1998, 2004), and Johns (1997, 2001).

In each case, the overall genre approach is presented and discussed in some detail. At the end of the chapter, a concluding discussion reviews the commonalities of the two approaches and questions the tendency of both approaches to define genre in terms of a relationship between conventionalized structuring of the content of texts and their linguistic features.

2.1 Relating genre to language learning

The construct of genre identified by linguists working in the context of the systemic functional approach began to be applied to the teaching of writing in schools from the 1980s in Australia (see, for example, Macken, Kalantzis, Kress, Martin, Cope, and Rothery, 1989; Martin, 1989; Derewianka, 1990; Christie, 1990; Knapp and Watkins, 1994; Butt, Fahey, Feez, Spinks and Yallop, 2000; and Martin, 2000). This approach to genre typically describes texts in terms of:

- *schematic structure*: described by Eggins (1994) as the 'staged, step-by-step organisation of the genre' (p. 36);
- *linguistic* (lexico-grammatical) *features*: such as syntax, lexis, types of cohesion and reference (which relate to the elements of the schematic structure).

Within the context of this approach, although some theorists focus on social genres, such as, for example, service encounters (Hasan, 1978, 1989;

Ventola, 1984), attempts to generalize for pedagogic purposes have tended to result in a more rhetorically motivated classification in which the focus moves to cognitive genres, such as recounting, instruction, exposition/argument, narrative, report, or explanation (Derewianka, 1990), and instructing, arguing, narrating, explaining, or describing (Knapp and Watkins, 1994).

In another approach to genre, linguists working in the field of English for Specific Purposes largely confine their description to English texts used in academic and professional contexts, such as introductions to research articles (Swales, 1981, 1990, 2002, 2004), introduction and discussion sections of dissertations (Dudley-Evans 1986; Hopkins and Dudley-Evans, 1988), and medical, legal or business documents. The focus of the (social) genre construct in this type of analysis is on specialized types of writing that may be inaccessible to non-specialized language users as well as to second language users who are unfamiliar with the rhetorical patterns of academic or professionally related fields. Analysis of genre in this tradition involves examining the organization of the conventionally recognized stages of a text in terms of *moves* and *steps*. This knowledge is then used as a basis for teaching the language and rhetorical patterns of the genres identified.

2.2 The approach to genre influenced by systemic functional linguistics

The systemic functional approach to classifying texts in relation to social context derives from the ideas of the social anthropologist Bronislaw Malinowski (1923, 1935). Based on his experience of studying an unwritten Melanesian language, that of the Trobriand Islanders of Eastern New Guinea, he proposed the idea that understanding language involves understanding the local situation and the wider culture in which the language occurs. In order to develop a working understanding of the language of the Trobriand Islanders, Malinowski emphasized the need to understand their culture (*context of culture*), stating that 'language is essentially rooted in the reality of the culture, the tribal life and customs of a people, and that it cannot be explained without constant reference to these broader contexts of verbal utterance' (Malinowski, 1923, p. 305). In relation to the development of a clear understanding of individual words and phrases, especially in order to translate them accurately, Malinowski also emphasized the need to take account of context (*context of situation*): 'the meaning of any single word is to a very high degree dependent on its context ... [it] becomes only intelligible when it is placed within its context of situation' (Malinowski, 1923, p. 306).

As Widdowson (2004) points out, Malinowski's ethnographic observations provided interesting insights that were later taken up by linguists, but do not, of themselves, constitute a linguistic theory able to incorporate the notion of context, since 'it is not entirely clear how the concepts of context, situation and context of situation are to be distinguished. The terms are often used interchangeably' (p. 38). However, a linguist who did attempt to develop the idea of context of situation was J. R. Firth (1957, 1957/1968) who put forward a possible framework including:

1. The participants: persons, personalities and relevant features of these:
   a. The verbal action of the participants;
   b. The non-verbal action of the participants;
2. The relevant objects and non-verbal and non-personal events;
3. The effect of the verbal action (Firth, 1957/1968, p. 177).

Yet again, beyond the initial framework, Firth did not demonstrate how his framework could be used for analysis. Thus, no illustrative approach was offered to performing the type of analysis of the elements of context that he proposed.

Halliday (1978) continued to develop the idea of context of situation, emphasising that the *social-semiotic* nature of language involved reference to the total meaning potential that people have as members of a society. Although a single individual may not achieve the full meaning potential of a society, typical social situations or contexts (the semiotic organization of our social system) may be systematically correlated with the linguistic system. The operation of language within a certain context of situation is what Halliday refers to as *register*. In discussing Halliday's approach to register, Martin (1992) notes that 'the socio-semantic organisation of context has to be considered from a number of angles if it is to give a comprehensive account of the ways in which meanings configure texts' (p. 494). Halliday proposes that the 'different angles' from which to analyse register are:

> *[T]he Field of Discourse* [which] refers to what is happening, the nature of the social action that is taking place: what is it that the participants are engaged in, in which the language figures as some essential component?
> *[T]he Tenor of Discourse* [which] refers to who is taking part, to the nature of the participants, their statuses and roles: what kinds of role relationship obtain among the participants, including permanent and temporary relationships of one kind or another, both the types of speech role that they are taking on in the dialogue and the whole cluster of socially significant relationships in which they are involved?
> *[T]he Mode of the Discourse* [which] refers to what part language is playing, what it is that the participants are expecting the language to do for them in the situation: the symbolic organization of the text, the status that it has, and its function in the context, including the channel (is it spoken or written or some combination of the two?) and also the rhetorical

> mode, what is being achieved by the text in terms of such categories as persuasive, expository, didactic, and the like. (Halliday, 1975, in Halliday and Hasan, 1975/1989, p. 12)

Halliday proposes that each semiotic variable of a text (field, tenor, mode) relates to a specific component of the semantic structure, and thereby to the systems of the lexico-grammatical features of a text. A register is 'the semantic variety of which a text may be regarded as an instance ... [and which] can be defined as the configuration of semantic resources that the member of a culture typically associates with a situation type' (1978, pp. 110–11). Martin (2001) emphasizes that register, as a meaning-making semiotic system,

> differs from semiotic systems such as language, music, dance, image and so on. This is because it is a kind of parasite. It has no phonology of its own. The only way it can make meaning is by using the words and structures of the semiotic we call language. (p. 155)

For linguists working within the context of a systemic functional approach, genre (as distinct from register) involves the context of culture within which a text occurs. Martin defines genre as 'a staged, goal oriented, purposeful activity in which speakers engage as members of our culture' (1984, p. 25). Hasan says: 'Genre bears a logical relation to CC [contextual configuration], being its verbal expression. If CC is a class of situation type, then genre is language doing the job appropriate to that class of social happenings' (Hasan, 1985/1989, p. 108). Later, a similar definition is proposed by Eggins and Martin (1997): 'different genres are different ways of using language to achieve different culturally established tasks, and texts of different genres are texts which are achieving different purposes in the culture' (p. 236). In describing the relationship between register and genre, Eggins (1994) says:

> genre and register are at two different levels of abstraction. Genre, or context of culture, can be seen as more abstract, more general – we can recognize a particular genre even if we are not sure exactly what the situational context is. (p. 32)

Eggins sees register as filling in the 'specifics relevant to a particular situation of use of a genre' (2004, p. 111).

The stages or steps that are conventionally followed in the typical organization of the content of a genre are called the *schematic structure*. These are also sometimes referred to as its *functional stages*, defined as 'those turns or groups of turns that fulfil a function relative to the whole. We therefore only call something a stage if we can assign to it a functional label' (Eggins, 1994, p. 38). As an example of a schematic structure, Hasan

(1985/1989, p. 64) describes the essential functional stages of a sales encounter as:

Greeting ⟶ *Sales Initiation*
Sales Inquiry *Sales Request*
Sales Compliance *Sale*
Purchase *Purchase Closure*
Finis

Hasan (1985/1989, pp. 64–5) proposes the idea that the functional stages (or schematic structure) of a genre are what characterize it as a category of texts. She distinguishes between the *actual generic structure* of a particular text and the *generic structure potential* of the genre to which the text belongs. The actual generic structure of a text is the actual series of functional stages which appear in that text while the generic structure potential (GSP) is the whole potential range of structures for a particular genre, not all of which, presumably, are likely to appear in one particular example of a genre. From the GSP, she further identifies *obligatory elements* – those functional stages which are necessary for a text to be identified as an example of a certain genre. They are the genre-defining functional stages that cannot be left out. Hasan (1985/1989) claims that the obligatory elements place restrictions on the types of semantic values which may be selected as the language which operates within that genre: 'One need not know all the details of a particular situation in order to be able to say what the overall structure of the message should be' (p. 105). Hasan terms this restriction which operates on semantic choices within a genre *genre-specific semantic potential*. She allows that, within one type of genre, texts can exhibit a variety of structures, although certain semantic elements are obligatory: 'the one respect in which they cannot vary without consequence to their genre-allocation is the obligatory elements and dispositions of the GSP' (1985/1989, p. 108). Hasan defines the obligatory elements which constitute a genre in terms of semantic rather than lexico-grammatical terms:

> the statement of genre-specific 'language' is best given in terms of the semantic categories, rather than the lexico-grammatical ones, since (1) the range of meanings have variant realisation; and (2) the more delicate choices within the general area is not a matter of generic ambience. (Hasan, 1985/1989, p. 113)

Martin (1986) describes genre as 'a staged, goal-orientated social process' (p. 33), and argues that not all language follows genre patterns. In cases where language accompanies (is ancillary to) actions, such as in a tennis commentary, Martin says that field and genre are indistinct. However, as the mode of a text becomes more abstract (such as in extended written texts where the sender and the receiver of the message of the text are separated), 'the grammar of the text becomes less iconic – it mirrors less closely the structure of the activity sequences to which it refers' (Martin, 1986, p. 33). In those cases where language plays a larger role, and more and more constitutes the action of the text, there is a need to distinguish between field and genre. Similarly, Hasan (1985/1989) suggests that in a genre-structured text 'the role of language is not ancillary but defining: all of the significant activity is manifestable only through language' (Hasan, 1985/1989, p. 113).

Among those whose approach to genre is influenced by systemic functional linguistics, there are stronger and weaker forms of the view that there is a specifiable relationship between genre (and register) and language. The stronger, deterministic, view involves the belief that 'Both the context of culture (via genre) and the context of situation (via register) determine the kind of language used to create a text' (Macken *et al.*, 1989, pp. 5, 18). A similar view is expressed by Eggins (1994), who argues that:

> both register and genre are realized through language. This means that we only know that we have a particular genre or register by looking at the way language gets used. It is through the patterns of meanings, words and structures, and of course sounds of language, that these contextual dimensions are expressed. (p. 36)

Knapp and Watkins (1994) also suggest that the structure and grammar of a text are determined by its genre: 'the generic features (structure and grammar) of the genre of *describing*, for example, remain constant for all writers, from the experiential descriptions of early writers, to the scientific descriptions of senior secondary students' (p. 20).

A weaker form of the systemic functional view describes the relationship between genre and language as *probabilistic* rather than *deterministic*:

> Genre theory suggests that texts which are doing different jobs in the culture will unfold in different ways, working through different stages or steps. Again, this relationship between context and text is theorized as probabilistic, not deterministic: an interactant setting out to achieve a particular cultural goal is most likely to initiate a text of a particular genre, and that text is most likely to unfold in a particular way – but the potential for alternative is inherent in the dialogic relationship between language and context. (Eggins and Martin, 1997, p. 236)

2.3 The systemic functional approach to genre: summary

The construct of genre proposed by systemic functional linguists relates to what is referred to in Chapter 1 here as social genre. It refers to socially recognized constructs according to which whole texts are classified in terms of their overall social purpose(s). In their approach to defining genre, systemic functional linguists claim that genres are identifiable in terms of:

- schematic structure: commonly occurring functional stages which Hasan (1985/1989) claims can be reduced to a group of genre-defining obligatory elements drawn from the generic structure potential (GSP) or range of elements that can potentially occur in a particular genre;
- lexico-grammatical features which systematically correlate with the genre-defining functional elements of the schematic structure or GSP realized through the related register variables of field, tenor and mode.

2.4 Discussion: the systemic functional approach to genre as a discourse-categorizing construct

The systemic functional approach to the construct of genre raises a number of issues, including:

- the nature of the relationship between different types of content knowledge and the genre paradigm influenced by systemic functional linguistics;
- the relationship between genre, generic structure potential, and text structure;
- the ways in which texts are classified in terms of genres;
- the relationship between genres and lexico-grammatical features of texts.

Content knowledge and the systemic functional approach to genre

In the systemic functional approach, emphasis is placed on the social use of language in context in the creation of a text and its interpretation as discourse. Language is seen as a social-semiotic, a system capable of expressing the entire range of potential meaning employed by society. It is seen as operating within a functional/structural type of syntagmatic and paradigmatic system. The functional or syntagmatic element involves the types of social use to which the language is put (such as a sales request in a shop or placing a bet). The structural or paradigmatic element refers to the choices from the semantic and lexico-grammatical systems of the language which are employed in social situations.

In the systemic functional approach, the content knowledge (*ideational content*) relates to the field variable. This includes not only the subject matter but also the nature of the speaker's or writer's participation in a social setting. Field, it is argued, influences the *transitivity* (case and syntactic) systems of the language. Eggins suggests that lexico-grammatical variation is influenced by field in terms of the degree of technicality from 'technical specialized to commonsense (everyday). Technicality is not only encoded in the lexis, however, technical texts frequently use abbreviated, non-standard syntax' (Eggins, 1994, p. 74).

The construct of field is seen as being susceptible to the influence of social action and the degree of technicality of subject matter. However, it does not appear to take account of the fact that different types of content knowledge (such as knowledge about real-world entities, empirical data expressed in statistical number abstractions, or abstract ideas or theories) may each be cognitively organized and categorized in different ways. Nor does it appear to involve any acknowledgement of the view that patterns of human categorization and structuring of different types of knowledge may exert an influence on the representation of such knowledge in discourse (Carrell, 1981, 1988; Johnson, 1987; Lakoff, 1987; Oller, 1995; Sanford and Garrod, 1981). Beyond the proposed connection between the degree of technicality of field and its influence on the lexico-grammar, types of content knowledge and their cognitive systems of categorization and internal, structuring are not seen as particular influences on the higher-level internal organization of a text. Rather, it is the social purposes to which such knowledge is put that are seen as the primary influence on the organization of patterns of language.

In the systemic functional approach, whatever effect the extra-linguistic content of field has on discourse also has to be considered in combination with the other register meta-functions of tenor and mode. While the field-tenor-mode paradigm may provide a useful approach for the analysis of transactional discourse (where the social and interactive element of the discourse is in the foreground and changing), it seems less appropriate for the analysis of extended, monologic, written discourse (such as certain types of academic writing), in which particular types of knowledge (and their related patterns of categorization and internal schematic organization) may influence overall structuring. In extended monologic texts, tenor and mode may provide relatively stable background influences, with the content-internal categorization systems of field (the ideational content of the text) playing a more foregrounded, structuring role, which has an influence on the ways in which such knowledge is represented. This is suggested in some of the cognitive approaches to the organization of knowledge which are reviewed in Chapter 4. To admit such a role would require that less primacy be given to social process, especially in relation to the creation of extended written discourse, than the systemic functional approach would appear to allow. Recognising that monologic texts may also be influenced in their organization by cognitive patterns routinely related to the rhetorical goal of representing certain types of knowledge (alongside the influences of social contexts of culture and situation) presents a challenge to any conceptualization of genre that is primarily socially orientated.

Genre structure: the schematic structure or GSP

In both the ESP (Swales, 1990; Askhave and Swales, 2001) and systemic functional (Martin, 1992) approaches to genre, *purpose* is seen as what distinguishes different genres. Where the two approaches differ is in how purpose is conceived. The approach to genre influenced by systemic functional linguistics sees genre as the result of a social process, working towards a goal, and this is manifested in the language choices of a text. The schematic structure drawn from the generic structure potential involves a series of functional stages, the sum of which fulfils the underlying objective of the social process of the text (such as, for example, writing a scientific article).

If, however, in extended, written, monologic texts, the social purpose/function is a relatively stable background element, and it is admitted that the cognitive organization of the content knowledge may also exercise some kind of influence, then a different approach to the issue of text purpose is required. Such an approach may need to take account of both the overall social purpose of a text (e.g. writing a scientific article) and the local *rhetorical* purpose of all or part of a piece of discourse (e.g. reporting, explaining, arguing) that is involved in the representation of a certain type of knowledge. This will also include the internal cognitive organization of the knowledge type involved.

In many respects, this issue is prefigured in the *iconic* and *non-iconic* distinction between texts which Martin proposes: '[t]exts can then be divided into those organised primarily with respect to activity sequence (iconic texts) and those organised along different lines (non-iconic texts)' (Martin, 1992, p. 517). Martin calls *non-iconic* texts *genre-structured* texts and makes a further distinction among the types of non-iconic (genre-structured) texts:

> Genre-structured texts are divided into those which review field-structured texts (e.g. movie reviews), and so are partially determined by their activity sequences, and theoretical texts which are not organised around a sequence of events in any respect (e.g. editorials). This scale arranges text with respect to iconicity and the amount of ideational meaning that needs to be made explicit to realise the field. (Martin, 1992, p. 518)

In the case of texts which Martin refers to as *theoretical* (in terms of their content), a socially constructed schematic structure (Martin, 1984) or Genre Structure Potential (Hasan, 1985/1989), may not necessarily account for all of the organizational patterns involved in content representation. Some evidence for this is offered by Paltridge (1993a, 1997), who examined twelve introductions to research reports relating to an environmental issue, and attempted to establish a generic structure potential, such as that proposed by Hasan (1985/1989), for his sample of research report introductions. In the introductions to the twelve research reports, Paltridge identified the following components of discourse (structure) elements: *background information, indicating a gap, question raising, previous research, purpose of study, materials, results, conclusions.* However, he found that:

> only two structure elements emerged as being essential to the Introduction sections of the text; that is, Previous Research (PR) and Purpose of Study (PS) ... Also, only one element, Purpose of Study (PS), occurred in the same position in all the texts, that is, in the final position. Beyond that, the analysis revealed a wide range of flexibility as regards sequencing of elements. (Paltridge, 1993a, p. 79)

On the other hand, in examining the same texts using a *macro-structural* analysis[1] (a cognitive, rather than social approach to text organization), Paltridge found that the following pattern applied to most of the texts with only slight variation in the order of the stages:

> Introduction ^ (followed by) ^ Materials and Methods ^ Results ^ Discussion. (Paltridge, 1993a, p. 177)

The constructs of *schematic structure* (Martin, 1984) and *generic structure potential* (Hasan, 1985/1989) are clearly important in terms of identifying certain instances of social genre. They do not, however, account for the role of different types of content knowledge in influencing internal patterns of organization. Furthermore, the research of Paltridge (1993a, 1997) appears to suggest that schematic structures may not prove to be stable, genre-identifying categories when examined in relation to certain social genres.

The approach of Hasan, which requires an instance of a social genre to contain certain *obligatory* elements, also raises the issue of the type of categorizing judgements which must be made in order to identify genres. In the following section, the difference between the systemic functional approach to categorizing social genres and cognitive approaches to categorization are discussed.

Identifying a genre

Hasan's generic structure potential (GSP) appears to rest on a type of criterial attribute categorization:

> The GSP becomes pivotal in any discussion of the identity of a CC

1 'higher level semantic and conceptual structures that organize the "local" macrostructures of discourse interaction and their cognitive processing' (Van Dijk, 1980, p. v).

> [contextual configuration] and we may claim that *only those values of field, tenor, and mode are defining for the identity of the CC that are motivationally related to the elements of its GSP* [my emphasis]. If the CC has these values, then these elements will appear in any text embedded in this CC; if these elements appear in any text, these values of the CC can be inferred from it. (Hasan, 1989, p. 103)

This type of criterial attribute categorization of genre in terms of values associated with field, tenor and mode may be successful in identifying prototypical instances of a genre in terms of those values. However, it may be less successful in identifying less prototypical (peripheral) members of the same genre category, since a text lacking one of the genre-defining GSP attributes would presumably be excluded from a particular category of genre.

Research on human categorization, such as that of Rosch (1973, 1975) and Rosch and Mervis (1975), suggests that human categorization allows for prototypical and less prototypical categories in a range of knowledge types. In terms of category-defining attributes or features, Rosch and Mervis (1975) note:

> The basic hypothesis was that members of a category come to be viewed as prototypical of a category as a whole in proportion to the extent to which they bear a family resemblance to (have attributes which overlap those of) other members of the category. (p. 575)

Rather than an item being either 'in' or 'out' of a category on the basis of one or more defining attributes, Rosch and Mervis argue for a categorizing approach that is closer to Reed's (1972) *cue validity* processing model whereby the validity of a cue as a characteristic of a category depends on its 'total frequency within a category and its proportional frequency in that category relative to contrasting categories' (Rosch and Mervis, 1975, p. 575). Rosch and Mervis prefer the term *family resemblance* (see Wittgenstein, 1953) to *cue validity* because their focus is on the structural principles of categories rather than the development of a processing model for categorization. The *cue validity* or *family resemblance* approach appears to offer a way of approaching grading that is likely to have important implications for the complex phenomenon of extended text in that it allows for prototypical or central examples, as well as peripheral or less central examples.

Interestingly, Fowler (1982) in identifying examples of literary genres, while not basing his argument directly on cognitive psychology, also argues for the *family resemblance* type of categorization that is based on Wittgenstein's (1953) approach. In the English for Specific Purposes approach to defining genre, Swales (1990, p. 52) proposes 'communicative purpose ... as the *privileged* property of genre. Other properties, such as form, structure and audience expectations operate to identify the extent to which an exemplar is *prototypical* of a particular genre'. Similarly, Paltridge (1997) suggests that peripheral or less typical cases of a genre may still be included in a genre category if a *family resemblance* approach to genre categorization is employed: 'A prototypical theory of categorisation allows for the inclusion of such cases within the umbrella of the one single genre rather than the much less flexible approach held in classical theories of categorisation' (p. 55).

Genre: the linguistic elements

The systemic functional approach to genre identifies genre in terms of the structural (*schematic structure*) elements of exemplar texts, and their sequencing and recursion. Schematic structure is then described in terms of register and the semantic values which are required to realize each of the structural elements in language. A stronger version of the connection between genre and register holds that the combination of the two actually determines the language which will be used (Hasan, 1989; Macken *et al.*, 1989; Eggins, 1994; Knapp and Watkins, 1994). At the lexico-grammatical level, three co-occurring aspects of language organization – *transitivity*, *theme* and *mood* – are recognized.

The *transitivity* system involves language which is 'associated with the realization of experiential meanings [field]' (Eggins, 1994, p.78). Halliday (1985) says:

> Transitivity specifies the different types of process that are recognized in the language, and the structures by which they are expressed. The basic system for the representation of processes is very simple. A process consists potentially of three components:
>
> (i) the process itself;
> (ii) the participants in the process;
> (iii) the circumstances associated with the process. (p. 101)

Theme involves aspects of the grammatical system of language which are used to produce 'patterns of foregrounding and continuity in the organization of the clause' (Eggins, 1994, p. 78). Halliday (1985) defines *theme* as follows:

> The theme is one element in a particular structural configuration which, taken as a whole, organizes the clause as a message; this is the configuration Theme + Rheme ... the Theme is the starting-point for the message: it is what the clause is going to be about. (p. 39)

Mood is language which is 'associated with the realization of interpersonal meanings [tenor]' (Eggins, 1994, p. 78). Mood is expressed through such verbal systems as indicative, subjunctive, declarative, interrogative, and modality.

Paltridge (1993a, 1997), in examining the introductions to twelve research articles which related to a specific environmental issue (that of the influence of air pollution on grain crops), examined a sample of texts attempting to identify examples of genre-specific language in terms of transitivity systems of the lexico-grammatical patternings for one structural element, that of *background information* and one semantic value for this element, that of *quantity*. The rationale for examining this component of the lexico-grammar was twofold:

> 1. [the transitivity structure of the clause, associated group structures and logico-semantic relations], in systemic functional terms, carry the maximum semantic load in terms of the ideational content of the text;
> 2. it is also a commonly examined aspect of lexico-grammatical patterning in other systemic functional genre studies. (Paltridge, 1997, p. 74)

The results of Paltridge's research indicated that none of the three aspects of the transitivity systems of the texts examined yielded any clear preponderance of lexico-grammatical structures which could be considered to be genre-defining:

> The analysis revealed that no particular process type would always occur at specific points in the text. It also demonstrated [that] a narrow range of verbal or nominal group structures might not necessarily occur in written research reports of the kind that were examined here. (Paltridge, 1997, p. 81)

In fact, in examining the sample of texts in terms of one structural element (background information) and one semantic attribute (quantity), Paltridge found that a 'wide range of language resources and structure are possible in the texts of the kind examined' (Paltridge, 1997, p. 81).

2.5 Conclusion

A review of the approach to genre which emerges out of systemic functional linguistics highlights a number of issues relating to the nature of genre categorization, issues which are particularly significant in relation to the categorization of extended monologic texts.

Firstly, attempting to assign texts to specific genres in relation to schematic structure or GSP will not necessarily adequately accommodate peripheral (as opposed to prototypical) examples, as indicated by the wide variety of functional elements and their orderings which may occur within examples of one type of genre (Paltridge, 1993a). In the case of non-iconic texts (such as extended monologic texts), a consideration of the socially recognized textual conventions (for example the sections of an article reporting research) may need to be supplemented by a consideration of a cognitively based approach to rhetorical organization.

Secondly, a *criterial attribute* approach to the categorization of a genre on the basis of a GSP (if, in fact, one can be clearly identified) may be insufficiently inclusive to categorize a range of texts within one genre. Given the wide range of discourse elements that Paltridge (1993a) found possible, and the difficulty of setting up a GSP (only two elements in his research), the usefulness of this for the construction of a broad category for something as complex as extended written discourse (social genre) would appear to be questionable.

Thirdly, it appears that it may not be possible to define a social genre in terms of lexico-grammatical characteristics. Paltridge (1993a, 1997) finds no basis for identifying actual examples of genre-specific language (in his sample of introductions to published, scientific research reports in one field) in terms of recurrent lexico-grammatical patterns. In fact, his analysis of the elements of the transitivity systems of his sample texts serve to underline the wide variety of lexico-grammatical resources which can occur within a very restricted sample of texts.

While the systemic functional approach to genre may offer a useful way of categorizing discourse which involves interpersonal transaction (in that it takes into account the social and attitudinal elements as well as the content of the discourse), it appears to be considerably more difficult to apply meaningfully to what Martin (1992) refers to as non-iconic texts.

2.6 The approach to genre of the English for Specific Purposes movement

Richards, Platt and Platt define English for Specific Purposes (hereafter ESP) as 'the role of English in a language course or programme of instruction in which the *content* and *aims* of the course are fixed by the specific needs of a particular learner group' (1992, p. 94). ESP courses are, therefore, courses, which in their formation are designed to take account of the needs and interests of particular groups of learners. According to Hutchinson and Waters (1987):

> ESP must be seen as an approach, not as a product; ESP is not a particular kind of language or methodology, nor does it consist of a particular type of teaching material. Understood properly, it is an approach to language learning which is based on learner need. (p. 19)

In the 1960s and early 1970s, ESP courses appeared to be based on the assumption that there were specific *varieties* or *registers* of English used in specialized areas, such as certain branches of science, technology or medicine. According to this view, ESP courses were not only for specific groups of learners, but also involved specialized types of English, a view that is now generally regarded as unsustainable. Hutchinson and Waters (1987) note that 'the assumption that language variation implies the existence of identifiable varieties of language related to specific contexts of use has, in effect, proved to be unfounded' (p. 31). Similarly, Corbluth (1975) states:

> Different fields of study in English do not have sufficiently different grammatical features to justify the preparation of courses appreciably dissimilar in these respects. Phonetic and phonological differences hardly apply either. Lexis, however, varies widely and courses will include the vocabulary essential to the subject or range of subjects where learners are studying the language of known specific purposes ... To extract certain syntactical features from the grammatical common core on a superficial acquaintance with a limited number of scientific or technical texts, and to emphasize them in teaching to the detriment of the whole body of common English structures and patterns, could be irresponsible and dangerous. (p. 280)

Therefore, the general consensus in the definitions of ESP by most writers is that it is the target group of learners rather than the variety of English which is specific:

> Given the great variety of contexts and of ESP courses around the world today, perhaps what we are really involved in as ESP practitioners is not so much teaching English for specific purposes but teaching English to specified people. (Robinson, 1991, p. 5)

However, an exception to the view that there are not specific varieties and registers of language is proposed by Dudley-Evans and St John (1998), who define ESP in terms of *absolute* and *variable characteristics*. In relation to absolute characteristics, they say that 'ESP makes use of the underlying methodology and activities of the discipline it serves; [and] ESP is centred on the language (grammar, lexis, register), skills, discourse and genres appropriate to these activities' (p. 4). While not claiming discipline-specific registers, they seem to be relating features of language at different organizational levels to the *activities* that occur within a particular discipline.

An attempt to characterize discipline-specific registers using corpus-based analysis of research articles from two disciplines (biology and history) by Biber, Conrad and Reppen (1994) showed inter-disciplinary variation in terms of the two dimensions examined (narrative versus non-narrative concerns, and impersonal versus non-impersonal style). On the basis of its findings, the corpus-based study argued for a more comprehensive characterization of discipline-specific registers through the use of corpus linguistics. However, the type of variation revealed in this illustrative study may in fact be more an argument for the analysis of social genres, such as research articles, in terms of their use of non-discipline-specific cognitive genres, such as narrative, rather than discipline-specific registers claiming particular linguistic features.

It now seems that the idea of particular varieties of English specific to certain activities or occupational groups (beyond what is referred to as *Restricted Repertoire English* – see Crombie and Rika-Heke, 1991) is not generally accepted, although a weaker form of the view still appears to be held by some writers. Despite this, studies and research still continue to be published which focus on aspects of grammar, syntax or stylistic features seen as significant in the written or spoken language of specialized fields or disciplines. Examples of texts from specific fields which are analysed in terms of specific linguistic features are: the use of the passive in astrophysics journal articles (Tarone *et al.*, 1981); the use of the present perfect tense in biology and biochemistry articles (Gunawardena, 1989); the use of conjuncts in business news stories and academic journal articles (Morrow, 1989); discourse functions of marked theme in scientific research articles (Gosden, 1992); indirect speech acts in résumés (Popken, 1993); lexico-grammatical features of geology textbooks (Love, 1993); reporting verbs in medical journal articles (Thomas and Hawes, 1994); directives in college laboratory sessions (Tapper, 1994); communication strategies in research articles (Sionis, 1995); lexical verb use in medical research articles (Williams, 1996); sentence types in email memos (Price, 1997); collocational frameworks in medical research papers (Luzon Marco, 2000); and tendencies in the register of email messages (Gimenez, 2000).

Thus, there still appears to be the assumption that language used in certain activities, occupations or texts for specific purposes will employ certain linguistic or stylistic features. Although none of these articles claims a whole register or variety of English specific to its particular activity or special purpose, the focus of such research is usually on the occurrence of a linguistic feature or set of features in texts which relate to a certain field of activity.

2.7 Genre as a means of analysis of ESP texts

Some researchers and writers working within the area of ESP use a social genre construct to provide a framework for analysing and teaching the types of written and spoken language said to be required in certain academic and professional settings (Hyland, 2002a, p. 115; Hyon, 1996, pp. 702–3). Thus, researchers sometimes use genre as a classification device to identify types of text which have a common purpose or goal within a certain field of activity. Examples of such genres that have been analysed for ESP purposes are: introductions to research articles (Swales, 1981, 1990, 2002, 2004); science dissertations (Dudley-Evans, 1986, 1989; Hopkins and Dudley-Evans, 1988); popularized medical texts (Nwogu, 1991); job applications, sales promotion letters and legal case studies (Bhatia, 1993); and grant proposals for European Union research grants (Connor and Mauranen, 1999). Examples of spoken genres that have been examined are: introductions to university lectures (Thompson, 1994); and lecture and poster sessions at conferences (Shalom, 1993). Genre has also been used as the basis for curriculum design and for programmes designed to provide language support for staff in a tertiary institution (Sengupta, Forey and Hamp-Lyons, 1999).

Among ESP researchers and theorists, Swales (1990) provides the most detailed proposal for a social genre construct, a construct he describes as 'a class of communicative events, the members of which share the same communicative purpose' (Swales, 1990, p. 58). Like Swales, Bhatia (1993, p. 43) sees communicative purpose as the main criterion for identifying different types of genre: 'of all of the contextualized factors associated with a conventionalized speech event, communicative purpose is the most privileged criterion for the identification of genres'.

In providing a working definition of genre, Swales (1990) includes the following defining features:

- A genre is a class of communicative events.
- The principal criterial feature that turns a collection of communicative events into a genre is some shared set of communicative purposes.
- Exemplars or instances of genres vary in their prototypicality.
- The rationale behind a genre establishes constraints on allowable contributions in terms of their content, position and form.
- A discourse community's nomenclature for genre is an important source of insight. (pp. 45–57)

In his original proposals for a social genre construct, Swales asserts that a communicative event which can be considered as belonging to a genre is 'one in which language plays a significant and indispensable role' (1990, p. 45), and that the prime determinant of membership of a genre is 'shared communicative purpose rather than similarities of form' (1990, p.

46). He proposed that this purpose will often be encapsulated in the naming of the genre. More recently, however, Askehave and Swales (2001) have cautioned that 'it would be prudent to abandon communicative purpose as an immediate or even a quick method for sorting discourse into generic categories' (p. 209). They say that, because of the complex and evolving nature of (social) genres, establishing genre categories on the basis of 'sets of communicative purposes' (p. 210) is possible, but that it involves extensive investigation of the operation of texts within contexts to establish different genre categories.

Swales proposes that genres exist within *discourse communities*, groups of people who have the following characteristics:

- A discourse community has a broadly agreed set of common public goals.
- A discourse community has mechanisms for communication among its members.
- A discourse community uses its participatory mechanisms primarily to provide information and feedback.
- A discourse community utilizes and hence possesses one or more genres in the communicative furtherance of its aims.
- In addition to owning genres, a discourse community has acquired some specific lexis.
- A discourse community has a threshold level of members with [the knowledge of] a suitable degree of relevant content and discoursal expertise. (1988, pp. 212–13; 1990, pp. 24–7)

Thus, according to Swales, a discourse community is a socio-rhetorical network which exists to achieve certain goals. To achieve these goals, it has certain commonly used and understood configurations of language, which may involve some specialized vocabulary. For example, air traffic controllers use certain established patterns of language to perform their occupational tasks. The communicative acts which are meaningful within this discourse community do not have the same currency among non-members, who are not required to perform the same occupational tasks and thereby communicate to achieve the same purposes.

Swales' (1990) proposal for discourse communities has been subsequently challenged in a number of areas (Borg, 2003). Issues that have been raised include: how large a discourse community might be; whether spoken language should also be a necessary defining element; the role of purpose as a defining element; and the degree of stability a discourse community ought to have. In another approach to the issue of disciplinary or occupational communities, Lave and Wenger (1991) have proposed the concept of *community of practice*. Wenger (1998) says that this involves belonging to a community through one or more of the modes of 'engagement, imagination and alignment' (p. 182) and participation (practice) within an 'historical and social context that gives structure and meaning to what we do' (p. 47). However, Wenger's (1998) more socially defined community of practice involves 'mutual engagement' and 'joint enterprise' (p. 78), requirements that separate the concept from the potentially more disparate *discourse community* that Swales originally proposed. Swales (1998, p. 204) distinguishes between the broader concept of a discourse community which may not be physically connected, and which communicates with itself through written communication, and *place discourse communities* which use both written and spoken communication.

According to Swales, genres differ in relation to:

- the complexity of rhetorical purpose – a recipe compared with a political speech;
- the degree to which they are prepared in advance of their communicative instantiation;
- the mode or medium through which they are expressed;
- the extent to which producers of prepared-text genres are conventionally expected to consider their anticipated audiences and readerships;
- the extent to which they exhibit universal or language-specific tendencies. (1990, pp. 61–7)

Swales claims that the exercise of genre skills in language production involves two types of knowledge: prior knowledge of the world, and knowledge of prior texts. Knowledge of the world comes from previous experiences of life and language experiences. These provide background knowledge patterns which Swales terms *content schemata* and likens to scripts (Schank and Abelson, 1977) and *scenarios* (Sanford and Garrod, 1981). On the other hand, knowledge of prior texts provides the formal patternings which are applied to content knowledge to create recognized genres. Swales uses the term *formal schemata* (Carrell, 1981, 1987) to describe these patterns. He argues that the recognition and production of genres in language involve the interaction between these two types of schemata, although he suggests that the exact nature of their interaction is not well understood. He refers to Carrell (1987) who suggests that understanding of rhetorical form (formal schema) may be more important when processing new or unfamiliar texts:

> Rhetorical form is a significant factor, more important than content; in the comprehension of the top-level episodic structure of a text, and in the comprehension of event sequences and temporal relationships among events. (p. 476)

However, in describing higher-level patterns of the organization of knowledge within genres, Swales' construct of *rhetorical moves* is largely described in terms of the stages of content itself, rather than any type of more abstract, textual patterning, such as formal schemata. This is evident in the move structure for introductions to published research articles and legal cases. The ESP approach does not attempt to fully accommodate the more general, rhetorical structures (such as the *formal schemata*) proposed by Carrell (1988). While acknowledging the roles of two types of schema, *content* and *formal*, Swales suggests that it may be difficult to maintain a distinction between the two when examining genre, in that 'the nature of genres is that they coalesce *what* is sayable with *when* and *how* it is sayable' (1990, p. 88). However, in failing to address the cognitive, rhetorical organizational dimension as an organizational influence in discourse, it appears that the ESP approach to genre, like the systemic functional approach, involves the attempt to match socially constructed patterns (used in the staging of content) with the linguistic systems of the language. Therefore, the ESP approach to genre is primarily a social genre construct although it acknowledges the existence of more general cognitive elements that are integral to the creation of discourse.

2.8 An ESP framework for genres

Below the genre level at which categorization is determined by the communicative purpose, the text-internal elements of content and linguistic encoding are analysed in relation to: (a) *rhetorical moves* and *steps*; and (b) linguistic structures which relate to these moves and steps. Dudley-Evans (1994) suggests that 'decisions about the classification of the moves are made on the basis of linguistic evidence, comprehension of the text and understanding of the expectations that both the general academic community and the particular discourse community have of the text' (p. 226). For example, Swales (1981) proposes a four-move structure for the introductory section of research articles, consisting of:

- Establishing the research field;
- Summarizing previous research;
- Preparing for present research;
- Introducing the present research.

Later Swales (1990, p. 141) revises this structural model, proposing a three-move *CARS* (create a research space) structure:

- Establishing a territory;
- Establishing a niche;
- Occupying the niche.

This structural pattern is then discussed at a micro-level in terms of the linguistic elements which may occur within the moves and steps framework. More recently, Swales (2002) discusses the potential further variations of the CARS model of move structures and in his 2004 book he proposes further possibilities for step structures within the three overall moves (pp. 230–2).

Bhatia describes moves as 'discriminative elements of generic structure ... [which depend] upon the communicative purpose(s) that it serves in the genre and that is why it varies from one genre to another' (1993, p. 32). In analysing legal cases, Bhatia (1993, pp. 135–6) offers a four-move structure consisting of:

- Identifying the case;
- Establishing the facts of the case;
- Arguing the case;
- Pronouncing judgement.

As well as examining legal cases at the level of moves, Bhatia also examines their linguistic properties in terms of sentence length, nominal character, complex prepositional phrases, and binominal and multinominal expressions (Bhatia, 1993, pp. 106–110).

Other studies that examine texts in terms of moves and steps include Crookes (1986); Dudley-Evans (1986, 1989, 1994); Hopkins and Dudley-Evans (1988); and Connor and Mauranen (1999).

2.9 ESP approaches to the analysis of texts: summary

ESP-related analysis of texts appears to involve two broad approaches:

- identification of a type (or types) of linguistic features which commonly occur within texts from certain fields of special-purpose activity;
- a genre-based approach involving the identification of a genre by investigating the operation of texts within a context in terms of 'sets of communicative purposes' (Askehave and Swales, 2001, p. 210). Such a genre is employed by a discourse community engaged in a common sphere of activity.

In both types of analysis, the focus is on certain types of language (linguistic features) proposed as characteristic of the language of certain fields of activity. In the case of the genre-based approach, attention is paid to lexical or syntactic elements that are commonly employed within certain functionally related sections of texts. Thus, although Swales does not accept the concept of subject-specific registers, he nevertheless claims that genre is 'a determinant of linguistic choices' (1990, p. 42).

ESP genre analysis has focused on a range of (social) genres from academic and professional domains, sometimes confining their analysis to one or more sections of texts belonging to these genres (such as the introduction sections of research articles). The organizational structuring proposed is a structuring of content (content schemata) and is usually relatively specific. This socially recognized staging of the content of a genre is identified in terms of moves and steps, which are discussed in relation to those linguistic features which are commonly employed for their realization. The higher-level structuring patterns of texts belonging to a genre category are not the type of more broadly applicable formal schemata which Carrell (1988) proposes. Although there is an acknowledgement of different types of schema, those who work within the ESP context generally do not attempt to describe a more universal, interdisciplinary rhetorical patterning. Rather, they propose schemata which are specific to texts within a particular field or subject area. Bhatia (1998), however, notes the need for approaches to the teaching and learning of academic discourses which are appropriate for university-level programmes concerned with interdisciplinary and multi-disciplinary approaches to knowledge. In comparing textbooks in different subjects (linguistics vs law), lectures in different disciplines (humanities and social sciences vs law lectures), and the genres of cases in business and law, Bhatia observes:

> We need the sophistication and subtleties of ESP but at the same time we need to master the power of generalizations across disciplinary boundaries ... One could see a movement away from the discipline-based ESP course design and methodology to a more discourse and genre-based cross-disciplinary approach, which will change the entire ESP paradigm by taking into account the dynamic aspects of disciplinary boundaries ... However, in order to deal with the complexity of generic patterns so commonly intertwined in academic discourse across disciplines, one needs a system of linguistic analysis which is powerful enough to account for the intricacies of academic genres across disciplines. (1998, pp. 26–7)

In a further expansion of his ideas about the types of knowledge that genres draw upon, Bhatia (2004) revisits his six proposed steps for analyzing genres and includes situational/contextual analysis, textual/intertextual and discursive perspectives, and ethnographic analysis (pp. 164–5).

2.10 The two pedagogic approaches to genre: discussion

In this chapter, two approaches to social genre – both of which have been influential in pedagogic contexts – were reviewed. In both cases, genre is seen primarily as a social construct, existing in order to achieve some kind of conventionalized purpose within a particular cultural context or discourse community. In both of the approaches attempts are made to relate the conventionally recognized, organizational stages of a social genre to actual linguistic features of exemplar texts, these features being seen as characteristic of the particular genre that the text belongs to. In the case of the systemic functional approach, the lexico-grammatical characteristics tend to be regarded as genre-defining. It is interesting, however, that Biber's extensive corpus-based study of texts does not support such an approach: '[g]enres are defined and distinguished on the basis of systematic non-linguistic criteria, and they are valid in those terms' (Biber, 1989, p. 39). Thus, for example, Biber (1988, 1989) proposes that genre categories (such as novels, newspaper articles and editorials, academic articles, public speeches, radio broadcasts, and everyday conversations) are 'defined primarily on the basis of external format, [these distinctions being] related to other differences in purpose and situation' (Biber, 1989, p. 6). Furthermore, Luke (1996), in discussing genre from a sociological perspective and drawing on Voloshinov's notion of *speech genres,* emphasizes that (social) genres are 'sites for the contestation of difference' (p. 318), which is not reflected in a 'finely grained synchronic analysis of texts' (p. 333).

The view that social genres cannot be identified in linguistic terms is also supported by Paltridge's (1993a, 1997) investigation of a single social genre, using the systemic functional approach to genre analysis. Paltridge found no systematic relationship between social purpose and lexico-grammatical characteristics. It may be, however, that there is a systematic relationship between genre and some aspects of language. What is likely, however, is that it is a relationship involving or mediated by cognitive genre rather than social genre. This will involve making a distinction along the lines proposed by Pilegaard and Frandsen:

> *text genres,* (e.g. novels, instructions, newspaper editorials, legal text or business letters); ... [and] ... *text types* ... (e.g. narrative, expository, descriptive, argumentative or instructional text types). (1996, p. 3)

Pilegaard and Frandsen suggest that *text genre* and *text type* may be distinguished in the following way:

> The criteria defining texts as text types will usually apply only to text parts (or text sequences ...) whereas the criteria defining text as *text genres* will commonly apply only to whole texts, i.e. except cases where one text genre is embedded within another genre. (p. 3)

They go on to define a *text type* on the basis of the following criteria:

1. *the cognitive operation* it reflects or represents (e.g. to describe or narrate);

2. *the linguistic means* it deploys to perform this operation (the structural criterion);
3. *the communicative function* the sender or receiver intends to realize (the functional criterion). (Pilegaard and Frandsen, 1996, pp. 3–4)

This distinction between text genre and text type is similar to that proposed between social genre and cognitive genre in Chapter 1.

To conclude, it is suggested that an adequate approach to discourse analysis, such as in terms of genre, must involve three elements:

- *the social motivation and socially constructed elements of genre*: this area of knowledge will almost certainly include the functionally related staging of the content (in terms of a schematic structure or moves and steps), an element considered central to the two pedagogic approaches to genre reviewed in this chapter. However, as the research of Swales (1998), in his detailed examination of a particular discourse community (systematic botanists) suggests, there needs to be a greater focus on issues of context in relation to the genre and the contextually driven elements of genre knowledge, knowledge that Bhatia (2004) suggests could be uncovered by ethnographic investigation. Chapter 6 following provides further discussion of this area and proposes a heuristic for expanding the scope of examination of these elements of genre knowledge by novice writers. In addition to the functional staging of content, this chapter also discusses the aspects of context, epistemology and metadiscourse in the proposal for a wider approach to social genre knowledge;
- *cognitive organizational structures*: the corpus research of Biber (1988, 1989) and the genre research of Paltridge (1993a, 1997) both question the idea of a deterministic link between social genre knowledge and linguistic features. Paltridge (2002) and Pilegaard and Frandsen (1996) see genres (social genres) and text types (cognitive genres) operating synergistically as part of discourse knowledge, and Paltridge suggests that both should be included in any discourse focus of an EAP course. The cognitive genre constructs proposed initially in Chapter 1 are further developed in detail in Chapters 4 and 5 following. In Chapter 4 a model for cognitive genres is proposed, drawing on Biber's categories of text types that occur in academic prose. However, rather than describing them in linguistic terms, they are proposed to be cognitive organizational structures employing procedural knowledge;
- *the actual linguistic realizations of the discourse*: this includes distinguishing between the socially driven elements of lexical choice (such as specialized technical lexis and linguistic features influenced by the epistemology and metadiscourse of the particular field in which the genre occurs), and the aspects of linguistic choice deriving from rhetorical purpose and their influence on coherence and cohesion.

Discourse production involves the representation of a language user's understanding of concrete features of the real world, or of abstractions. That representation may involve either speech or writing. Rosch (1978), when discussing human categorization of knowledge, observes that 'it should be emphasized that we are talking about the perceived world and not a metaphysical world without a knower' (p. 29). With reference to the ideas of Putnam (1981), Johnson (1987) observes that 'all knowledge requires structure and categorization. Specifically human knowledge requires categories of understanding that humans can make sense of in terms of their own mediated experience and can use for human purposes' (p. 206). It is suggested, therefore, that discourse creation is a process of representation. It involves the representation of cognitive categories in terms of the linguistic possibilities of a language (which will, of necessity, employ the organizational and categorizing systems of that language), usually to achieve a social purpose in socially prescribed ways (see Hyland, 2003, p. 166). It is concluded, therefore, that an adequate theory of discourse (and discourse categories, such as genres) takes into account the types of social, linguistic and cognitive knowledge that are involved in the representation process.

Chapter 3 reviews a range of cognitive approaches to the classification of knowledge, including schema theory, prototype theory and related constructs. The review will particularly focus on approaches to knowledge classification that relate to the structuring of extended written discourse, in order to establish the principles that ought to constrain any theoretical approaches to describing discourse in terms of cognitive genres.

Chapter 3: Constraints on a cognitive genre construct

3.0 Introduction

In Chapter 2, the review of two influential approaches to social genre used to categorize and analyse texts (for pedagogic purposes) reveals that both approaches tend to focus on the conventionally recognized staging of content, which is related to the actual linguistic features of exemplar texts. These two aspects are seen as characterizing the particular genre to which a text belongs although corpus and genre studies appear to question the validity of this approach. In neither of the two approaches to genre that were reviewed is there an attempt to acknowledge the additional existence of more general cognitive discourse structures that may in some way mediate between socially constructed, conscious patterns of textual organization and the linguistic systems that they employ. However, if a case for modelling such mediating structures is to be presented, it is firstly necessary to identify the aspects of cognitive theories of knowledge categorization and organization that ought to *constrain* any such model. To identify these constraints, the first part of this chapter reviews the principal features of theories and constructs proposed for the categorization and structuring of knowledge. This review includes:

- fundamental notions in cognitive approaches to categorization, including those of *prototype* and *hierarchy*;
- theories of underlying patterns employed in the structuring of knowledge in specific domains, including: *schema theory, scripts and goals, scenarios* and *frame theory*;
- theories of procedural or organizing structures that integrate knowledge from multiple domains, including *mental spaces* (Fauconnier, 1985); *image schemata* (Johnson, 1987); and *idealized cognitive models* (Lakoff, 1987).

At the end of the review of each theory, a summary section discusses implications (of the reviewed theory) for developing an approach to categorizing extended discourse. The second part of the chapter then provides further discussion of the significance of this range of concepts in terms of how they might constrain any approaches to discourse classification and organization.

3.1 Fundamental notions in cognitive approaches to categorization: prototype and hierarchy

This review begins by examining the two central concepts in categorization theory, the concepts of *prototype* and *hierarchy*. This review will consider the origins of these terms and also consider how they relate conceptually to any type of categorization, including the categorization of discourse.

Wittgenstein and 'family resemblances'

The ideas of the linguistic philosopher Ludwig Wittgenstein have been influential as a basis for categorization theory and related research, including the categorization of aspects of language. Wittgenstein proposes that a complete human understanding of words involves what he terms 'ostensive definition'. He proposes that a language user is not able to achieve an understanding of the ostensive definition of a word until 'the overall role of the word in the language is clear' (Wittgenstein, 1953/1963, Remark 30). He explains this by analogy: explaining to a learner of chess how the king piece functions involves the assumption that the learner 'has already played other (board) games, or has watched other people playing and understood – and similar things' (Remark 30). The suggestion seems to be that to develop an ostensive definition of a word requires a knowledge paradigm or setting into which the new word may be grafted. The new word, therefore, draws its meaning, in part, from the learner's previous understanding of the meaning setting to which the word most closely relates. This view has implications for the nature of categories and how they are formed. It also begins to question the idea of the bounded nature or separateness of categories, implying a degree of overlap in the way the mind builds up its knowledge of a category.

In questioning classical ideas of bounded categorization in relation to language, Wittgenstein (1953) develops the idea of *family resemblances*, an idea that he presents by analogy with board games:

> We see a complicated network of similarities overlapping and criss-crossing: sometimes overall similarities, sometimes similarities of detail. I can think of no better expression to characterise these similarities than family resemblances ... one might say the concept, 'game', is a concept with blurred edges. (Remark 71).

Wittgenstein acknowledges that adopting this position implies an open-endedness of meaning, an open-endedness that may be detectable even within a single sentence. However, whereas 'the sense of a sentence ... may ... leave this or that open ... the sentence must nevertheless have a definite sense' (Remark 99). Thus, there is a necessity for boundaries which are, nevertheless, 'indefinite' (Remark 99). This, at first sight, appears to contradict the reference to 'a definite sense'. In fact, however, the contradiction may be more apparent that real: a sentence may, in one context, convey the meaning required for interpretation in that context; in another context, however, what is conveyed by the same sentence may be different. In other words, there is an open-endedness in relation to sense which is generally resolved in relation to adequate contextualization. Thus, as Wittgenstein (1953/1963) observes, 'what we call "sentence" and "language" has not the formal unity that I imagined, but is the family of structures more or less related to one another' (Remark 108).

In reflecting on thought and its relationship to language, Wittgenstein proposes some kind of cognitive ordering of concepts before they are encoded as language:

> Thought is surrounded by a halo – Its essence, logic, presents an order, in fact the a priori order of the world: that is the order of possibilities, which must be common to both world and thought ... the order existing between the possibilities of proposition, word, truth, experience and so on. This order is a super-order between – so to speak – super concepts. (Remark 97)

In these very brief remarks, Wittgenstein raises issues and questions of considerable importance to later cognitive psychology and information processing. The extreme brevity of his remarks and, therefore, their own lack of full contextualization means that they remain open to a range of interpretation, and thus serve as little more than an illustration of his thesis. Nevertheless, Wittgenstein's discomfort with any concept of stable categories, unrelated to context, is clear.

Thus, Wittgenstein prefigures many of the ideas of modern cognitive psychology related to category. In particular, he:

- presents the concept of family resemblances in attempting to account for how categorization occurs in language (using as an example the analogy of the category of games) and proposes that categories should be seen as consisting of more typical and less typical members;
- proposes the idea of thought imposing its order on language, thus prefiguring the ideas of cognitive model and category effects that were later developed in cognitive psychology;
- points to the cognitive phenomenon of commonly shared concepts, taking as an example human perception and colour attribution.

Summary and implications for discourse categorization

Wittgenstein's ideas point to underlying processes of cognitive ordering involved in different types of human categorization, such as of activities and colours, and therefore, by logical extension, more complex concepts such as types of discourse. He argues that an understanding of the ostensive definition of words requires a range of experiences in which these words are contextualized. Similarly, it will be argued here that understanding what characterizes acceptable examples of a discourse category or genre requires a range of experiences in which texts are seen as being representative of the particular category. Just as Wittgenstein notes that meaning must, in a sense, be open-ended, being subject to revision in the light of experience, so it is argued here that categories used for the classification of discourse (such as genres) are open-ended, being subject to increasingly complex reformulations in the light of experience.

Rosch and 'prototype theory'

Wittgenstein 's idea of family resemblances was confirmed by the research of Rosch (1973, 1975) and Rosch and Mervis (1975). Their findings provide empirical evidence that, when categorizing certain types of objects, shapes and colours, the principle of family resemblance – central and peripheral category members – is fundamental to human perception and understanding. Knowledge of a category and ability to categorize appropriately appear to relate to knowledge of the central members or prototypes of the category. Since the research of Rosch and her colleagues, the 'family resemblances' idea of Wittgenstein has been termed *prototype theory*. The following paragraphs are brief summaries of some of the research that Rosch and her colleagues carried out, the findings of which support the family resemblance approach to human categorization.

Rosch (1973) performed colour experiments involving the Dani, a tribe in Irian Jaya in Indonesia, whose language had only two colour categories: *mili* (dark-cool, including black, green and blue) and *mola* (light-warm, including white, red and yellow). She demonstrated that, in learning a range of colour names, the Dani acquired focal colour terms (the presumed natural stereotypes) with greater ease than they did those relating to non-focal colours. Even when grouped in categories with focal colours as non-central members of a category grouping, focal colours were learned with greater ease. In addition, using two-dimensional figures which pilot research showed were not already classified into form classes by the Dani tribe, Rosch demonstrated the role of natural prototypes in form (shape) categories, thus providing a parallel study to that involving colour terms, but one that involved a different area of perception. The same hypothesis concerning the learning of a category was tested – that is, that the presumed natural prototype shapes were central members of the category, and a group of distortions were peripheral members. It was found that the natural prototypes were learned faster than the distortions, even when they (the prototypical shapes) were taught (to some subjects) as peripheral members of a grouping of shapes. On the basis of her research on perceptual categories with the Dani, Rosch (1973) concluded that prototype effects – more easily recognized central members and less easily recognized peripheral members – could be observed in the learning of the names of the members of the perceptual categories of colour and shape.

In a different series of experiments that involved native speakers of English, Rosch (1973) attempted to determine whether centrality and peripherality were also meaningful for those types of noun category that did not relate directly to perception. When asked to make selections as to the centrality or peripherality of a word, subjects' reaction times were much faster when the word was selected as a central member of a category than when it was a peripheral one. A second study in this series hypothesized that central or prototypical members of a category are learned before less typical, more peripheral members of the same category. Here, the experiment involved answering 96 true/false questions about the category membership of nouns. Both children and adults readily recognized the central members of a category, although children required more reaction time than adults. For the recognition of peripheral category members, children required more time and made more errors, whereas the proportion of errors adults made in relation to central and peripheral category membership was not significantly different. Adults, however, took longer to recognize peripheral category members than they did to recognize central members. In both cases, the recognition time required by adults was less than that required by children. Furthermore, the proportional difference between the times required for the two types of recognition was much less for adults.

Thus, Rosch was able to demonstrate prototype effects operating in a variety of types of noun category, including colour and shape perception categories. From her experiments with other semantic categories with adult and child subjects, it appears that categories are learned, and that prototypical members of a category are learned before peripheral ones. Similar findings emerged from a further series of nine experiments in which various aspects of the prototype-effect in the area of categorization were examined (Rosch, 1975). Most of these experiments involved the use of a 'prime' (a superordinate category name) which was then followed by a second noun, the aim being to examine the nature of cognitive representation of categories.

Three key findings emerged from these experiments:

- The internal structure of a category representation appears to affect the perception of subsequently represented stimuli when they are activated /primed by a category name. When activated, this internal representation appears to be more effective in facilitating the recognition of central members of the category than it does in the case of peripheral ones.
- The effect of category representation appears to be due to the abstract representation of the category's name, rather than to concrete physical features associated with the category.
- The meanings of superordinate category terms (for groups of nouns,

> e.g. 'vehicle' for car, truck, motor-cycle) are not specifically coded in terms of words or pictures. However, the fact that less time is needed to classify pictures suggests that pictures may be closer to the underlying meaning than are words.

As an extension of the experiments that identified prototype-effect within categories, Rosch and Mervis (1975) proceeded to investigate how the internal structure of categories arises. Anecdotal information and some indications from the previous study (Rosch, 1975) suggested that the identification of prototypes develops through learning. Rosch and Mervis, however, did not intend to provide a processing model for learning or developing knowledge of prototypes. Rather, their intention was to research 'one of the major structural principles which . . . may govern the formation of the prototype structure of semantic categories' (p. 574), that is, the principle of *family resemblances.* Here, the central basic hypothesis was that 'members of a category come to be viewed as prototypical of a category as a whole in proportion to which they bear a family resemblance to (have attributes which overlap those of) other members of the category' (p. 575).

Central to this hypothesis is the *cue validity model* proposed by Reed (1972). Rosch and Mervis (1975) define cue validity as a characteristic of a category which depends on its 'total frequency within [that] category and its proportional frequency in that category relative to contrasting categories' (p. 575). However, they retain the term family resemblance (rather than cue validity) in order to indicate that their concern is with providing a description of the structural principles of categories, rather than developing a processing model for categories. Three types of noun category were used in the study: *superordinate categories* (such as 'furniture' and 'vehicle'), *basic-level categories,* (such as 'car' and 'chair') and *artificial categories* formed from sets of letter strings. For each type of category, the two aspects of the family resemblance hypothesis were examined: 'that the most prototypical members of categories are those with most attributes in common with other members of the category', and that they 'are those with least attributes in common with other categories' (Rosch and Mervis, 1975, p. 576). In this study, family resemblance, defined in terms of discrete attributes, was shown to be a major factor in category formation, although family resemblance in this research was 'a descriptive, not a processing principle' (p. 600). The primary findings were as follows:

- Prototype effect was found to operate in certain categories, specifically colour and form perception and several other noun categories. In each case, the prototype effect contained central examples that were strongly identified as representing the category. The identification of peripheral examples was graded in relation to degree of representativeness.
- Activation of the cognitive representation of a category appears to

affect the recognition of individual items as members. The underlying representation facilitates more rapid recognition of central or prototypical members of a category rather than peripheral ones.
- Subjects' ratings of prototypicality and family resemblance attributes were significantly correlated. This supports the idea of graduated category membership or prototype-effect in relation, at least, to the categories examined.

These experiments on prototype-effect do not, in themselves, constitute an explanation of categorization. As Rosch (1978) herself notes:

- prototype ... is a convenient grammatical fiction; what is really referred to are judgements of degree of prototypicality;
- prototypes do not constitute any particular processing model for categories ... [but] ... processing models should not be inconsistent with the known facts about prototypes;
- prototypes do not constitute a theory of representation for categories ... the facts about prototypes can only constrain, but do not determine models of representation;
- although prototypes must be learned, they do not constitute any particular theory of language learning. (pp. 40–1)

Summary and implications for discourse categorization

The empirical studies of Rosch (1973, 1975) and Rosch and Mervis (1975) provide powerful evidence for the operation of a prototype effect within human cognition and categorization. However, prototype effect does not, in itself, provide a theory of categorization. Nor do the experiments to which reference has been made provide an explanation of prototype effect. They do, however, establish a basis for later research that seeks to (a) provide a theory of categorization, and/or (b) explain prototype effect (see the following section). If categorization involves making 'judgements of degrees of prototypicality' (Rosch, 1978, p. 40), this would suggest that the development of a complex language skill (such as exercising discourse competence relating to academic writing) would appear to require familiarity with the prototypes that occur within this type of discourse. In relation to discourse knowledge and discourse competence, it may suggest that identifying and becoming familiar with discourse prototypes (such as social genres and cognitive genres) may assist novice writers in developing the type of awareness that underpins their effective later exercise of such a competence.

Hierarchy in categorization

Brown (1958, 1965) suggests that there are three levels of categorization: superordinate, basic-level and subordinate. According to Brown, basic-level categorization may be the first level of categorization to be learned, 'the level of distinctive action' (e.g. 'flowers', 'dogs', 'cats'). He suggests that the next type of category to be learned is the superordinate category, involving 'achievements of the imagination' (e.g. 'plants' and 'animals'). The final type of category to be learned is, according to Brown, the subordinate (e.g. 'jonquil' and 'Siamese').

The first type of categorization to be acquired (basic-level) was judged by Brown to have the following converging properties:

- the level of distinctive action;
- the level learned earliest and at which things are named;
- the level at which the names are shortest and most frequently used;
- the natural level of categorization, as opposed to the level created by 'achievements of the imagination'. (1965, pp. 318–19)

In documenting the folk categories of plants and animals of the Tzeltal people living in the Chiapas region of Mexico, Berlin, Breedlove and Raven attempted to provide a basis for psychological research on basic-level categorization. They postulated that this level of categorization, which they referred to as *folk generic*, was psychologically basic because folk generic taxa:

- represent the most commonly referred to groupings of organisms in the natural environment;
- [are] the most salient psychologically; and
- [are] likely to be among the first taxa learned by the child. (1974, p. 27)

Stross (1969), in studying Tzeltal language acquisition, discovered that the bulk of the child's first-learned plant names are basic-level categories, categories which are in the middle of the taxonomic hierarchy of Brown (1958) of superordinate, basic-level and subordinate. Children then work up the hierarchy generalizing, and down the hierarchy specializing. This means that after learning basic-level, gestalt-related words such as 'chair' and 'potato', children learn more abstract, organizational categories within which to structure their basic-level knowledge, such as 'furniture' and 'vegetable'. Later, they learn to reduce their known basic-level categories to smaller subordinate units, or more specific examples of each category, such as 'kitchen chair', 'armchair', 'toilet chair', and 'Idaho', 'Red King', 'Black Kidney' potatoes.

Basic-level categorization depends upon experimental aspects of human psychology: gestalt perception, mental imagery, motor activities, social function and memory. Berlin (n.d. in Lakoff, 1987, p. 37) suggests that certain cultures, for example urban cultures, under-utilize certain human capacities used in basic-level categorization: for example, they under-use the capacity for gestalt perception. Thus, people in urban cultures may treat the category 'tree' as a basic-level one. Moreover, there may be sub-populations of specialists within a culture who, through training, achieve a more finely honed gestalt perception for a limited range of domains, for example horse breeds or types of cars. Berlin predicts, however, that there will be no culture in which all the levels of categorization differ fundamentally from those of other cultures. In most domains, the levels of categorization will be the same for all human beings because human beings share the same general capacities for gestalt perception, and holistic motor movement plays a major role in determining basic-level categorization.

Summary and implications for discourse categorization

Research on superordinate, basic-level and subordinate categorization suggests a sequence or order in developing knowledge of categories. This may also be related to stages in the development of a discourse competence – the ability to recognize and create examples of types of extended text. In the case of teaching academic writing, novice writers may benefit from an initial exposure to prototypical examples of cognitive genre, as a type of basic level discourse category. The basic level discourse unit of cognitive genre may then be analysed, and practised so that its constituent elements may be developed into knowledge that is more automatically employed (see Chafe, 1994, pp. 137–8) when the language user is involved in the creation of social genres.

3.2 Theories of underlying patterns employed in the organization of knowledge relating to specific domains

Schema theory

In his 1932 monograph entitled *Remembering*, Bartlett described a series of experiments in which students began by reading stories from unknown cultures. The students then retold the stories from memory to other subjects. The recipients of the stories then retold the same stories yet again from what they were able to recall. Bartlett (1932) reported systematic changes that took place during the retelling of the culturally unfamiliar stories. These were:

- *levelling/flattening* where story-specific details, such as proper names and unfamiliar cultural concepts, are lost;
- *sharpening* which involves the retention of a smaller number of details which receive more emphasis, or are sharpened;
- *rationalization* which involves (a) the compacting of passages that are made to conform to readers' expectations, and (b) the omission of unfamiliar cultural references, such as to ghosts and spirits.

Bartlett argued that readers, in attempting to make stories conform to their own cultural expectations, are engaged in 'effort after meaning'. He proposed that learning or assimilating new material requires some matching by the learner of the new material to his or her existing concepts or *schemata*: 'without some general setting or label, as we have repeatedly seen, no material can be assimilated' (p. 172). Bartlett proposes that remembering involves a 'process of construction' in which details recalled are matched to an existing schema, which is then used to fill out unrecalled details.

Rumelhart (1975) examined memory and recount of stories, the purpose of his research being to uncover the 'supra-sentential relationships' that are implied in ordinary discourse in order 'to infer the causal relationships between propositions' (p. 212). On the basis of his research, Rumelhart presents a tentative theory, involving two sets of rules in terms of a *story grammar*, to account for the internal structure of simple stories. These two sets of rules are: (a) a set of syntactical rules that generate the constituent structures of stories, and (b) a corresponding set of semantic interpretation rules which determine their semantic representation (p. 213).

Rumelhart's story grammar is an attempt, using a top-down form of analysis, to uncover the schematic patterns within what he terms 'the syntax and semantics' of simple stories, simple stories that are, he suggests, reducible to a series of summary propositions. This story grammar is applicable only to simple narratives, narratives that are generally chronologically sequenced. More complex, rhetorically organized discourse, such as that involving reported information or argument, would arguably require a considerably greater level of complexity in terms of what Rumelhart describes as syntactic rules and semantic relationships.

Rumelhart and Ortony (1977) present a summary of schema theory, aiming to describe the features common to their own earlier work and that of Bobrow and Norman (1975), Minsky (1975), Norman, Rumelhart and the LNR Research Group (1975), Rumelhart (1975), Schank and Abelson (1977) and Winograd (1975). First, schemata are defined as follows:

> [Schemata are] data structures for representing the generic concepts stored in memory. They exist for generalized concepts, underlying objects, situations, events, sequences of events, actions and sections of actions. (Rumelhart and Ortony, 1977, p. 101)

They say that schemata are said to have four essential characteristics. They:

- have variables that are associated with the context within which they operate: 'a schema for give would have three variables: a giver, a gift and a recipient' (p. 102);
- can be embedded within one another as in the case of the schema for FACE which involves embedded schemata ('subschemata'), such as for those for eye and mouth (pp. 106–7);
- can represent generic concepts at various levels of abstraction, such

as schemata for lexical items that refer to things, to action sequences or plots of stories (pp. 109–10);

- represent knowledge rather than definitions (pp. 100–11).

Thus, schemata represent the constituents and interrelations that are 'normally' to be found: 'schemata attempt to represent knowledge in the kind of flexible way which reflects human tolerance for vagueness, imprecision and quasi-inconsistencies' (Rumelhart and Ortony, 1977, pp. 110–11). They are postulated as having four functions:

- *comprehension*: involving making use of schemata that appear to give a sufficient account of the information (p. 120);
- *remembering*: involving making use of episodic memory, of 'those memories for particular events which we have directly or indirectly experienced' (p. 116);
- *inferencing*: involving assignment of values to variables on the basis of whole/part or part/whole perception. Thus, for example, a RESTAURANT schema contains sub-schemata such as WAITER, MENU, ORDERING, EATING, and PAYING; the RESTAURANT schema can activate the related sub-schemata (and their parts) for the purpose of making inferences.
- *action*: involving the engagement of schemata in the performance of actions. For example, juggling involves a TRANSFER schema which contains sub-schemata of TOSS, TRAJECTORY, APEX and CATCH.

Three main types of schema have been identified by theorists and researchers:

- *content schemata* which are configurations of knowledge or concepts specific to certain domains or contexts;
- *formal or rhetorical schemata* which account for patterns of organization of knowledge in language and the interrelationships between parts or sections of language;
- *abstract schemata* (introduced by Oller, 1995) which involve deductive reasoning.

Content schemata involve the representation of knowledge resulting from some kind of human perception. They are based on abductive judgements about facts or states of affairs in the real world, that is, they involve judgements relating to human (often sensory) perceptions: 'Abduction occurs at just the point where a particular fact ... is linked with a distinct representation' (Oller, 1995, p. 284).

Formal schemata involve inductive reasoning which links different events, details or states in terms of similar, shared characteristics: 'To connect such separate and individual, abductive inferences and to know them as pertaining to the same, logical object, induction is required' (p. 284). Thus, for example, in spite of physical differences, hotel lobbies will have formal similarities which remain relatively invariant and which enable observers to classify them as being members of the same group. These similarities, judged by induction, are dependent upon structures and arrangements abstracted to some degree from the particular facts of any given context (p. 286).

Abstract schemata involve a 'kind of inference identified as *deduction* [in which] reason works on the basis of an abstracted symbol which applies not only to the case in hand, but to all possible cases' (p. 285). According to Oller, these are the most general and, therefore, the most powerful of schematic constructs:

> For instance, if hotels are businesses that aim to make a profit, they must generally charge more for their services than those services cost the owners. Thus, deductive inferences give us a great deal of information about all possible hotels that could not be acquired by merely examining or auditing the records of however many individual cases. (Oller, 1995, p. 287)

In memory and language, the research of Meyer (1977) points to the role and operation of structural (formal) schemata as higher-level organizers of *recalled knowledge*. Meyer analysed a number of passages of prose in terms of the logical relationships within their content using Fillmore's (1968) case grammar. Based on her analysis, she identified ideas within the prose passages as belonging to different levels, such as ideas at an organizing or superordinate level in relation to other ideas within the same passages which stand in subordinate relationship to the upper-level ideas. Thus, 'a passage is viewed as being a complex proposition that can be decomposed into sub-propositions bearing certain relations to one another' (p. 181). Using the analysed passages, Meyer performed a number of experiments which involved subjects in listening to, or reading, prose passages. These subjects were then asked to (a) produce a free recall of the content of the passages immediately after listening or reading, and (b) attempt to recall the content again some time later. Over a range of experiments in which she controlled for types of content within passages, the findings showed that:

- in the case of free recall (a) subjects were more likely to recall higher-level (rather than lower level) subject matter immediately after encountering a passage, and (b) higher-level content was less likely to be forgotten over time than was lower level content;
- in the case of cued recall, higher-level content was more readily remembered, although some aspects of higher-level content (such as, for example, problem-solution relations) appeared to be recalled more readily than others.

In examining reading comprehension, Carrell (1988) further distinguishes between *formal schemata* and *content schemata* as constructs which organize knowledge within written texts:

> One type of schema, or background knowledge, a reader brings to a text is a *content schema*, which is knowledge relative to the content domain of the text. Another type is a *formal schema*, or knowledge relevant to the formal, rhetorical organizational structures of different types of texts. (Carrell, 1988, p. 461)

Previous research had indicated that texts with schemata based on familiar cultural material were more easily understood than texts with unfamiliar cultural content (Carrell, 1981; Johnson, 1981). Similarly, it had been shown that texts with familiar rhetorical organizations were more easily understood than texts whose rhetorical structure was unfamiliar. What was not known was (a) how different types of schema influenced understanding of written text, and (b) how different types of schema influenced one another. Carrell, therefore, investigated the influence of both types of schema (formal schemata and content schemata) in a series of reading comprehension experiments with students from two cultural backgrounds: students of Muslim background and students of Spanish Catholic background.

Carrell's research involved presenting two biographies of religious figures (one of a Catholic saint, and one of a Muslim religious figure) to the two above groups of subjects. The texts were historical narratives with a setting and two episodes. Two versions of each text were used, one in straightforward temporal order, and the other involving a mixing of events from the two episodes (but with markers of time and place added to facilitate comprehension).

Analysis of the subjects' understanding of all four texts indicated that familiar content, even when organized in an unfamiliar way, is more easily understood than unfamiliar content, even when that unfamiliar information is presented in a familiar rhetorical form. Analysis of recall of the higher-level ideas – the two episodes of each text – indicated that the form of the text was an important factor. Subjects were more likely to recall the main episode ideas from the rhetorically unadulterated (temporally organized) versions of each text. Thus, irrespective of rhetorical structure, familiar content appears to be more readily understood than unfamiliar content. However, high-level ideas are more likely to be recalled if they were originally presented in chronological order.

Summary and implications for discourse categorization

There are different approaches to schema theory, and these different approaches use different terminology for the constructs proposed. However, the following general principles emerge:

- schemata are generic knowledge patterns which are stored in our memory;
- there are different types of schemata which operate in relation to different types and levels of knowledge;
- higher-level schemata relate to more general knowledge, and lower-level schemata relate to more specific knowledge.

Before proposing any cognitive genre-exemplifying texts for pedagogic purposes (such as the teaching of academic writing skills), it will be necessary to discover the patterns, sequences and relationships that are typical of the cognitive genre in question. In most cases, these are likely to be more complex that those that Rumelhart (1975) proposed for simple narratives. However, the way in which Rumelhart approached the problem of specification may nevertheless provide a useful starting point.

If different types of schemata play a role in comprehension, memorization, inferencing and action as proposed by Rumelhart and Ortony (1977), they will also be called on in interpreting and creating texts and will, therefore, be relevant at all stages of text comprehension and production. However, so far as novice writers of whole texts belonging to a particular social genre are concerned, different types of schemata may need to be prioritized at different stages. Thus, content schemata may be particularly relevant where background information is processed, abstract schemata may play an important role in making decisions about the ordering of content, and formal (rhetorical) schemata may need to be prioritized during the text creation process. All three will, however, play a role in creating a new text or interpreting an unfamiliar one.

3.3 Other schematic constructs: scripts, plans, goals, frames and scenarios

The fundamental tenets of schema theory have been used as the basis for research and theoretical modelling in a number of different fields requiring constructs for the organization of knowledge within language. Within the context of linguistics, a schematic basis for the formal or rhetorical organization of ideas has been proposed within the *frame semantics* model (Fillmore 1976, 1977, 1985; Minsky, 1975). Within the context of artificial intelligence, the *script/plan model* performs a similar function (Schank and Abelson, 1977). In relation to textual content (as opposed to rhetorical ideas), the work of Sanford and Garrod (1981) on *scenarios* has been influential.

Schank and Abelson: aims, goals, plans and scripts

Much of the research on schemata relates to the processing and storing of knowledge – comprehending, inferencing and recall. Considerably less attention appears to have been paid to the use of schemata in knowledge representation, in, for example, creating spoken and written discourses. One exception is the work of Schank and Abelson (1977), which gives attention to the roles of schemata in both knowledge understanding and knowledge representation. Working in the area of artificial intelligence, they aimed to devise computer programs that would enable computers to 'understand and interact with the outside world' (p. 1).

Schank and Abelson distinguish between two types of knowledge which people employ to interpret and understand situations with which they are confronted: *general knowledge* and *specific knowledge*. According to them, specific knowledge, which is employed by a language user in the interpretation of the more detailed events of a situation, is organized in terms of *scripts*:

> A script is a structure that describes appropriate sequences of events in a particular context. A script is made up of slots and requirements about what can fill those slots. The structure is an interconnected whole, and what is in one slot affects what can be in another. Scripts handle stylized everyday situations. (1977, p. 41)

They claim that the purpose of scripts is economy in cognitive processing. A stylized or default version of a situation can be called up for the interpretation of a new situation, and points of difference which individualize the new situation may be identified.

Schank (1975) notes that scripts are associated with the definition of certain situational nouns, such as restaurant, football, game, birthday party, classroom and meeting. In this context, they consist of 'predetermined sequences of actions that define a situation' (p. 264). He observes that scripts are recognizable because, after they have been entered, objects that are part of the script may be referenced as if they had been mentioned before. He cites the following example:

> John went into a *restaurant*. When he looked at *the* menu, he complained to *the* waitress about *the* lack of choice. Later he told *the* chef that if he could not make much, at least he could make it right. (p. 264)

Thus, Schank proposes that a word, such as restaurant, calls up a script. On the basis of that script, roles and props are referenced (by the use of the definite article) as previously mentioned information. For relatively common scripts, such as riding a bicycle, much of the information in different people's scripts is the same.

In attempting to deal with the more complex processing demands involved in creating as well as understanding discourse, Schank and Abelson propose the concept of *plans* and *goals*. Whereas scripts deal with specific information, *plans* and *goals* deal with more general information.

A plan relates to an overall general goal and may be fulfilled by a number of more specific *delta-goals* (**D**-goals) or *instrumental goals* (**I**-goals).

According to Schank and Abelson, plans fulfil goals. For example, when we listen to a story we have certain expectations. These expectations will relate to events and to goals. In the case of goals, our expectations will be generated from our belief systems; in the case of events, our expectations will be derived from our expectations in relation to goals. For the monitoring and tracking of underlying goals in discourse, Schank and Abelson propose a 'goal monitor': 'an interrelated bundle of processes which recognizes when goals are triggered, interprets their nature, keeps track of their fate, and makes predictions about goal-related events' (p. 102). In dealing with a story, they suggest that the goal monitor should be able to deal with *goal origin, goal specification and substitution, goal suspension and goal embellishment.*

Schank and Abelson claim that 'such top-down predictions form the basis of our understanding' (p. 82). However, they also acknowledge that the process of discourse creation cannot be accommodated in this way. They see discourse creation (creating a plan) as involving 'stringing methods together in an optimal or admissible way to realise a goal. Plan creation is problem solving' (p. 73).

Summary and implications for discourse categorization

While the top-down goal–plan–script hierarchy of Schank and Abelson's approach relates to the inferential processes involved in reading and decoding text, it appears less able to account for the process of writing of discourse, in that it is a process which does not necessarily involve prediction and the matching of input to predictions. A writer may, for example, begin with (a) an existing set of data or ideas, with, in other words, the entire conceptual content of the discourse, or (b) a clear plan or idea of the direction of the discourse which s/he seeks to encode in as overt a way as possible. Thus, the writer may actually aim to minimize a reader's need to make extra-linguistic inferences. In this kind of creation process, the requirement is to create something that is not so much predictive or transactional as rhetorical or structural. Frequently, academic writing involves the organization of already known knowledge, the problem being how best to organize or present a set of ideas or data. Creating extended written discourse appears to involve a process that is primarily organizational or representational, rather than being predictive and inferential.

Sanford and Garrod: scenarios

Sanford and Garrod (1981) present a further schema-like construct – *scenarios* – in relation to the decoding and representation of written text. In particular, scenarios are related to a number of psychological aspects of the reading process including *primary and secondary processing, topicality, foregrounding and backgrounding, explicit and implicit reference.* Sanford and Garrod see text comprehension as involving a contract between the writer and the reader:

> A writer wishes to convey an idea to his readers. In essence, this means that he must establish in the mind of his reader a situational model which is the same as (or closely similar to) the one in his own mind. (p. 8)

They therefore propose the construction of the scenario to accommodate a number of aspects of this contractual relationship, and suggest that 'knowledge of settings and situations [can be thought of] as constituting the interpretative scenario behind a text' (p. 110).

Sanford and Garrod propose that a text serves to set up a search in long-term memory for a model of a recognizable episode or situation (the scenario) into which it will fit (p. 117). Scenarios may be simple and minimal (such as in relation to a concrete noun), or detailed, that detail relating to either (a) the information conveyed, or (b) the specifications or sequences of events expected in relation to an entity or setting. They may be activated by spatio-temporal setting or characterization, that is, the model that is built up of someone's personality. A characterization model is generally a representation of predispositions. Thus, for example, the decomposition of the meaning of a word may activate a possible domain of reference containing slots into which succeeding items within the same discourse may fit. Just as Schank and Abelson's (1977) scripts involve roles and props, scenarios contain *entities* and *role entities.* Thus, for example, a court-case scenario contains a judge, a jury and lawyers as entities. The role entities involved may be, for example, lawyers probing witnesses, or juries evaluating evidence and giving a verdict. In this respect, there is very little difference between scenarios, entities and role entities (Sanford and Garrod, 1981) and scripts, roles and props (Schank and Abelson, 1977). What *is* different, however, is the emphasis in the work of Sanford and Garrod on referencing and, hence, on the establishment of textual relationships.

This is supported by reading-time experiments which demonstrate that the activation of inappropriate scenarios (as, for example, in the case of a misleading title) will considerably increase reading processing time. Sanford and Garrod (1981) also carried out empirical tests measuring reading response times between pairs of sentences with stated antecedents and implied antecedents. Thus, they demonstrate that reading times for specifically identified entities are faster than for more general statements. They cite the example of:

> The tank came trundling around the bend.

The vehicle came trundling around the bend.

The research demonstrates that reading processing times of specific entities (basic-level categories), like 'the tank', are consistently faster than they are in the case of general items (superordinate categories) like 'the vehicle'. This was the basis for their proposal that pre-activated, context-driven inferencing is involved in cases where antecedents are implied. Based on these findings, they suggest that although 'understanding of general statements [such as that containing 'the vehicle'] may not go far beyond the explicit propositions of the sentence ... a specific statement [such as that containing 'the tank'] may well be more easily mapped into a scenario rich in default information, thus serving to facilitate later comprehension' (p. 120).

The scenario as a schematic construct is primarily concerned with textual referencing. It offers insights into topicalization at a macro-structural level through an integrated account of knowledge-types and referencing within extended discourse. The scenario-based modelling of Sanford and Garrod provides an account of the operation of implicit background knowledge (scenarios) as a necessary element in text processing. It also, however, provides an account of explicit, non-scenario-based knowledge, an account that involves a detailed explanation of the types of pronominal referencing that operate with both types of knowledge. Together, these types of modelling provide insights into text processing as well as into the procedural knowledge employed.

Summary and implications for discourse categorization

There are a number of pedagogical implications associated with the observations above (relating to scenario-based and non-scenario-based inferencing), especially in relation to the content of discourse-related instruction. First, it seems that basic-level category information and direct and/or concept-driven referencing should be used wherever possible in the early stages of familiarization with a discourse type such as a cognitive genre. What the research of Sanford and Garrod also suggests is that (a) the introduction of unfamiliar genres should be preceded by the presentation of information that will activate an appropriate scenario, and (b) the selection of titles of genre-exemplifying texts should be directly related to information provided in the presentation phase that precedes the introduction of the texts.

Frame theory

This section examines a further schema construct, that of *frames*. Two proposals for the construct of *frame* as a knowledge organizer for artificial intelligence will be examined: that of Winograd (1975, 1977) and that of Minsky (1975, 1985). Further approaches from linguistics that are then examined include the *frame semantics* of Fillmore (1977) and the approaches to frames (in language) of Van Dijk (1977) and Barsalou (1992).

In order to establish a basis for computer-based organization and representation of knowledge, Minsky (1975, 1985) proposes an integrated account of how the human mind organizes and represents knowledge in economical ways, ways which account for the use of a small number of cues to activate seemingly organized and ordered complex knowledge entities. In relation to a minimal 'story' example, Minsky puts forward the idea that perceptual experiences activate structures called *frames*, 'structures we have acquired in the course of a previous experience' (Minsky, 1985, p. 244). He defines a frame as 'a sort of skeleton, somewhat like an application form with many blanks or slots to be filled'.

> We'll call these blanks its *terminals*; we use them as connection points to which we can attach other kinds of information. For example, a frame that represents a 'chair' might have some terminals to represent a seat, a back, and legs, while a frame to represent a 'person' would have some terminals for a body and head and arms and legs. (1985, p. 245)

In an earlier explanation of the frame construct, Minsky (1975) argues:

> We can think of a frame as a network of modes and relations. The 'top levels' of a frame are fixed, and represent things that are always true about the supposed situation. The lower levels have many *terminals* – 'slots' that must be filled by specific instances or data. (p. 212)

Minsky suggests that frames are stored in the long-term memory with 'weakly bound *default assignments*' at every terminal (1975, p. 228). By default assignments, Minsky means what one usually assigns to the terminals of a remembered frame, such as a stereotypical realization of the frame in one's memory: 'The frame for a chair may involve four legs, a seat, a back and possibly arms for most people, as a conceptualisation of a stereotypical chair. These manifest themselves as often useful but sometimes counterproductive stereotypes' (p. 228).

Thus, Minsky suggests that default assignments of frames are the ways in which we represent our previous experience: 'We use them for reasoning, recognizing, generalizing, predicting what may happen next, and knowing what we ought to try when expectations aren't met' (Minsky, 1985, p. 245). Default assumptions fill our frames to represent what is typical. As soon as you hear a word like 'person', 'frog', or 'chair', you assume the details of a 'typical' person, frog, or chair (Minsky, 1985, p. 245).

In representing knowledge, Winograd (1977, p. 475) defines a frame as 'a collection of facts and procedures associated with a concept. It [a frame] does not correspond to a "single fact" as in a formal logic representation, but is a chunking of information around a single concept'.

Similar to Minsky's *default* assignments, is Winograd's proposal that each frame has a set of *important elements*, or *Imps*. These are the elements that contribute to the meaning of the frame. For example, in the frame for *giving*, Winograd proposes the following Imps:

> [T]he ACTOR doing the giving, the BENEFICIARY receiving it and the OBJECT being given are of primary importance. In [the frame for] *paying*, the OBJECT is further specified as being money, and the reason (which in general is an Imp for any act) is further specified as being some kind of debt. The frame for 'donate' would have a different further specification for its reason. (1977, p. 476)

An important element in frame representation, which accounts for the relationship between frames, is what Winograd terms 'hierarchies of generalization' (p. 485). For example, an ACT is a very general type of frame describing an action, whereas GIVE is a more specific type of ACT involving:

> an ACTOR: a person;
> a BENEFICIARY: a person;
> an OBJECT: a physical object.

PAY is a more specific type of GIVE, involving additionally:

> an OBJECT: money;
> a REASON: debt (summarized from Winograd, 1977, p. 475).

Thus, frames may be connected, with one being a more specific or more general example of another. Information is said to be organized hierarchically because of *inheritance of properties*. Thus, the *Imps* – important elements – which are true of any more general frame will be true of any more specific frame below it in the hierarchy of generalization:

> When we further specify a frame (that is, move down the generalization hierarchy) we also further specify the IMPs that go with it. This makes sense only if we think of each IMP as being another frame (which in turn fits into the hierarchy, and so on recursively). (Winograd, 1975, p. 200)

Fillmore proposes that there are three types of linguistic knowledge: knowledge about *grammar*, *lexis* and *frames*:

- [The grammar of a language is] 'the part of linguistic knowledge that can be represented by rules'.
- [The lexicon is] 'that part [of linguistic knowledge] that represents item-by-item knowledge'.
- 'The cognitive and interactional frames [are those aspects of linguistic knowledge] in terms of which the language-user interprets

> his environment, formulates his own messages, understands the messages of others, and accumulates or creates an internal model of this world.' (Fillmore, 1976, p. 23)

Two background principles which Fillmore (1976, p. 24) suggests are important for using and understanding language are:

- the meanings of words may, more than we are used to thinking, depend on contexted experiences; that is, the contexts within which we have experienced the objects, properties or feelings that provide the perceptual or experiential base of our knowledge of the meaning of a word (or phrase, or grammatical category) may be inseparable parts of those experiences;
- in order to perceive something or to attain a concept, what is at least sometimes necessary is to have in the memory a repertory of prototypes, the act of perception or conception being that of recognizing in what ways an object can be seen as an instance of one or another of these prototypes.

In describing a prototypical event, such as a commercial transaction, Fillmore (1977) proposes that there are two levels of conceptual framework: 'the one giving a general representation of all of the essential aspects of events of a particular category and the other giving the particular perspective on an event of the type dictated by a case frame' (p. 59). He labels the two levels of conceptualization *scenes* (the level of more general representation) and *case frames* (the linguistic choices associated with a scene, suggesting that individual words are learned within such meaningful contexts as scenes and frames, each word serving to foreground some part of the context). Furthermore, a single word may belong to more than one frame, even though the same history of experiences is responsible for each frame. He hypothesizes that the process of understanding a word requires recall of memories of experiences through which the labelling or describing function of the words has been used:

> A frame is a kind of outline future with not necessarily all of the details filled in ... Comprehension can be thought of as an active process during which the comprehender – to the degree that it interests him – seeks to fill in the details of the frames that have been introduced, whether by looking for the needed information in the rest of the text, by filling it in from his awareness of the current situation, or from his own system of beliefs, or by asking his interlocutor to say more. (1976, p. 29)

Fillmore suggests, rather than a checklist or 'list of conditions' approach to the categorization of knowledge, that categorization is based on a *prototype* or a *typical case* in one's experience. He believes that the research on colour categorization by Berlin and Kay (1969) and natural categories by Rosch (1973) both indicate that the way in which human beings categorize involves *experiential* rather than *formal* knowledge (Chafe, 1972). Fillmore says that 'formal knowledge is the kind of knowledge that can be expressed propositionally; experiential knowledge is the kind of knowledge that exists as memories of experiences' (1977, p. 57). Fillmore proposes that knowledge of prototypes or typical cases is *essentially experiential*:

> Prototype semantics can be thought of as a generalization of the view that a theory of language needs to distinguish between having a rule and using a rule. It may turn out to be much more useful to speak of the 'internalized' linguistic rules as being simple rules which cover prototypic cases. (p. 57)

Similar to Fillmore's proposal for propositionally based knowledge is Van Dijk's (1977, 1980) proposal for the construct of *macrostructures*, which he says are larger structures within discourse which organize micro-information into 'complex or hypercomplex information, such as discourse, conversation, action sequences' (1980, p. 12). He says that macrostructures serve an organizational and reductive function. They are essentially semantic: 'They define higher-level or global meaning derived from lower-level meanings ... macrostructures define the global coherence of a text' (p. 12).

Involved with the construct of the macrostructure is the idea of prominence or importance. The overall proposition of a macro-structure assumes a more important role in the global meaning of a text than its constituent information. In a sequence of such patterns, some sections may be more important to the global meaning than others. According to Van Dijk, macro-structures of discourse can be summarized in terms of *macro-propositions*. Macro-propositions are sometimes directly expressed by the discourse, usually occurring at the beginning of a text (such as the first sentence of a newspaper article). Thus, for example, the opening section of a narrative (the setting section) may be reducible to one or two summary propositions that express the central meaning.

Van Dijk says that *frames*, unlike macrostructures, organize our conventional knowledge of the world and 'enable us to perform such basic cognitive acts as perception, action and language comprehension. At some higher level the content of a frame is fixed, but its lower level terminal can be accommodated to the properties of information input' (Van Dijk, 1977, p. 19):

> We propose that frames define units or chunks of concepts which are not essentially, but *typically* related ... they usually denote certain normal courses of events or courses of actions involving several objects,

> persons, properties, relations, and facts. These kinds of denotata, or values, or frames will be called *episodes*. It is in this sense that frames are higher-level organizing principles. They unify concepts of various types and at various levels of representation under the constraint of typicality and normality. (Van Dijk, 1977, p. 21)

Later, Van Dijk (1980) distinguishes between: (a) frames which relate to 'complex conceptual structures only. Hence, prototypical knowledge about books, chairs, buildings, animals' (p. 233); and (b) scripts which relate to 'prototypical episodes, that is, sequences of events and actions, taking place in frames' (p. 234). Above these entities in the hierarchy, he places schemata, which he describes as:

> the most general in the prototypical organization of knowledge ... to denote the overall *structural* organization of complex conceptual units ... *schemata may have their origin in perceptual organization, along such categories as 'horizontal', 'vertical', 'surface', 'bottom', and 'top'.* [my emphasis] (p. 233)

Within Van Dijk's model, both macro-structures and frames organize complex semantic information.

> Frames, however, are conventional and general. Most members of a society or culture have approximately the same set of frames. Macro-structures do not have this character. Instead, they are ad hoc information, i.e., the particular global content of a particular discourse. (Van Dijk, 1977, p. 22)

Thus macro-structures are a device concerned with functioning to make a synopsis of a discourse in the memory of a language user. This gives the language user the basis for recall, although what is actually recalled will be a summary of the main elements of the particular discourse which has been processed. Frames or conventionalized units of knowledge will be included in a macro-structural summary of a particular discourse. If there is some loss through failure to remember the actual details of a discourse or through inaccuracies in a macro-structural summary, Van Dijk suggests that frame knowledge will then be used, and this may lead to some inaccuracies in recall as the details of a conventional frame may not all fit one particular situation. 'If such information [macro-structural] is no longer retrievable, it is supplied by the most probable components of the frames associated with the concepts of the relevant macro-structure proposition. Of course, this may lead to false recognition' (1977, p. 28).

Tannen (1993), while not concerned with categorizing different types of frame or schema, acknowledges that people have 'stored their prior experiences as "an organised mass" and ... see events and objects in the world and in relation to their prior experience' (pp. 20–1). Tannen says that this stored knowledge creates 'expectations about the world' (p. 21) at a number of levels. In a research project involving subjects viewing a short film and retelling the events of the film, Tannen shows that, from close examination of the retelling, frame knowledge 'can be seen in the surface linguistic form in the features of a narrative' and that 'close analysis of linguistic evidence can reveal the expectations or frames which create them' (1993, p. 53).

The idea of the use of stored multiple frames, which are used interactively for the complex interpretation of knowledge in a number of areas including written text, underpins the approach to framing of MacLachlan and Reid (1994), who say that identification of a literary genre:

> will depend on what frames are dominating one's reception of the text. Even minimal written forms such as graffiti, slogans or epitaphs cannot be comprehended unless they are framed in some way ... readers always need to 'place' it in relation to comparable text, in relation to surrounding information ... To read generically is to posit frames for interpreting the language used. (pp. 85–6)

In proposing yet a further account of a frame construct, Barsalou (1992) places a 'co-occurring set of attributes' at the core, and defines an attribute as follows:

> [An attribute is] a concept that describes an aspect of at least some category members. For example, *color* describes an aspect of *birds*, and *location* describes an aspect of *vacations*. ... A concept is only an attribute when viewed as describing some aspect of a category's members. (p. 330)

Thus, attributes combine to make a frame and they (i.e. attributes) are specified in terms of values which 'are subordinate concepts of an attribute' (p. 31) which inherit information from other attributes, so that they 'contain additional information not in their respective attributes, thereby making them more specific concepts' (p. 31). Thus, a frame for a car contains the attributes *fuel, engine, transmission* and *wheels.* Values for the fuel attribute could be *gasoline, diesel* or *gasohol.* Values for the engine attribute could be *four, six* or *eight* cylinders, and values for the transmission attribute could be *standard* or *automatic.* Barsalou suggests that the attributes within a frame may 'be associated with [their] own frame of more specific attributes'. Thus,

> in our recent work on real estate planning, the frame for *house* has an attribute for location, which in turn is a frame whose attributes include

> *convenience, utilities, zoning* and *security*. These secondary attributes often have frames as well. (1992, p. 33)

Barsalou also puts forward the idea of *attribute systematicity*, suggesting that frames contain certain core attributes that co-occur frequently whenever the frame is applied. As an example of attribute systematicity, the frame for *buy* will usually include the core attributes of *buyer, seller, merchandise* and *payment*. At the same time, he emphasizes that attribute systematicity is not necessarily rigid and that variation is possible as frames occur in different contexts.

Barsalou also puts forward the construct of *structural invariants* to describe relatively fixed conceptual relationships that occur between the attributes of one frame. An example is the *operates* relation between the attributes of *driver* and *engine*. Thus, *engine* in the *car* frame 'reflects people's conceptual understanding that the driver controls the engine's speed' (p. 35).

Frames not only provide a means of representing specific exemplars 'but also of representing specific information across exemplars' so that 'the prototype is simply the set of the most frequent values across attributes ... the prototypical bird is *small* in *size*, *brown* in *colour* and has a straight beak' (p. 47).

Frames are used in a variety of ways to determine category membership, which requires constraints:

- physical attributes, e.g. colour for a physical entity;
- possession of certain attribute values, e.g. human, female and adult count as evidence for species; sex and age as evidence for being a woman;
- possession of values beyond a fixed reference point can count as evidence for category membership, e.g. legal voters are 28 years or older.

Proposals for *frames* as cognitive constructs for organizing and storing knowledge are, in many ways, similar to approaches to the constructs of schemata and scenarios.

Summary and implications for discourse categorization

Originating from artificial intelligence and developed by linguists, most of the approaches propose frames as chunks of configured information that are based on experience rather than formally learned knowledge. They are stored in the long-term memory and can be readily applied to, or adapted to, appropriate situations. Some approaches to frames (e.g. Minsky, 1975; Van Dijk, 1980) suggest that at the upper level, the structure of a frame is fixed, whereas at the lower levels they may be realized in a number of ways. Associated with this is the notion of the hierarchical organization of knowledge which in frame theory is described in

Winograd's (1975) 'hierarchies of generalisation' (p. 485) with more general knowledge at a higher level and more detailed, specific lower-level knowledge, allowing for interrelationship and combination. In addition, several of the approaches suggest that frames operate as prototypes, and that the application of frame knowledge to situations involves judgements of prototypicality, with frames allowing for variation in the assignment of lower-level features or attributes to a frame, depending on the situation in which it is applied. Simpler frames, such as those of book and desk, combine to form larger frames, such as library.

Several of the approaches to frame theory distinguish between the operation of frame-based and non-frame-based knowledge in attempting to explain how frames are employed in extended discourse. Thus, Van Dijk (1977, 1980) proposes that frames function in conjunction with macrostructures (ad hoc summaries of non-frame-based knowledge), both of which may be organized at the highest level by schemata, which may themselves be gestalt-based (1980, pp. 233–4). However, none of the approaches to frame theory reviewed here is integrated into a more detailed proposal for a larger framework that accounts for interrelationships between different types of knowledge.

3.4 Theories relating to procedural knowledge

In the section that follows, theories that attempt to account for the operation of procedural knowledge – *knowledge that organizes knowledge* – are reviewed. Common to each is the idea that metaphor plays a pivotal role in connecting together and organizing a variety of types of knowledge from different domains, in order to create discourse that is a representation of complex thought and that is both coherent and cohesive. The theories that are reviewed are Fauconnier's (1985) *mental space* theory; Johnson's (1987) *image schemata*; and Lakoff's (1987) *idealized cognitive models.*

Fauconnier: mental space theory

Fauconnier's mental space theory (1985) seeks to develop a cognitive account for the coherent structuring of discourse, an approach which goes beyond a grammatical/syntactical description of language, and provides possible explanations for aspects of meaning, in particular, aspects of reference in language which are difficult to account for in other ways. Fauconnier (1985) sees mental spaces as types of interconnected containers of ideas, saying that they are 'constructs distinct from linguistic structures, but built up in any discourse according to guidelines provided by linguistic expressions' (p. 16). Although Fauconnier describes mental spaces as primarily a psychological construct, he proposes that they are manifested through their encodings in language, noting that 'linguistic expressions will typically establish new spaces, elements within them and relationships holding between the elements' (p. 17).

A key element in Fauconnier's theory is the device of *space builders*, a group of discourse markers, which may be linguistic devices derived from a number of syntagmatic/paradigmatic language categories, devices which play a boundary-marking role in discourse, providing essential knowledge for successful processing of textual meaning by a language user. A second key element in correctly interpreting discourse information within a mental space conceptual unit is Fauconnier's proposal for *types of equivalence* relating to the interpretation of linguistic material within a mental space construct. Central to the creation of a mental space is the role of metaphor in setting up many of the connections that are made between pieces of information.

Fauconnier refers to linguistic expressions which set up new spaces or refer back to earlier spaces, as 'space builders'. Space builders may be prepositional phrases (*in Len's picture, in John's mind, at the factory, from her point of view*), adverbs (*really, possibly, theoretically*), connectives (*if__, either___, or__*), underlying subject/verb combinations (*Max believes___, Mary hopes___*). Furthermore, a space builder, in setting up a new space, will always connect it with another space, its parent space, by the type of syntactic embedding or reference contained within the space builder itself.

The types of connections that operate between mental spaces are possible because of the use of metaphor, which Fauconnier terms *pragmatic functions* (Nunberg, 1978). Pragmatic functions can 'establish links between objects of a different nature for psychological, cultural or locally pragmatic reasons'. Fauconnier (p. 5) calls this type of connection the 'ID principle':

> The ID principle states that in a connected situation, a description of the trigger may suggest the target. An example of this is: 'Plato is on the top shelf'. This sentence can be taken to mean that the books by Plato are on the top shelf. (Fauconnier, 1985, p. 4-5)

In Fauconnier's account of categorization, noun phrases, rather than simply identifying people, things or concepts are seen as performing roles, or what Fauconnier calls *role functions*. Thus, 'definite descriptions are primarily role functions and secondarily the value taken by such roles (identifying). The domain of the role may include times, places, situations, contexts and much more' (1985, p. 40). Some examples of the role functions of noun phrases are:

- The president changes every seven years.
- Your car is always different.
- Your apartment keeps getting bigger and bigger. (1985, p. 39)

'The president', 'your car', and 'your apartment', therefore, do not have one fixed referent in reality. Thus Fauconnier, in describing noun phrases, says that they can have 'a fixed identity, but their other properties can change' (1985, p. 41). In explaining this, Fauconnier says that 'roles are also elements, but such that identity (i.e. role value) can change, while one particular property (e.g. president, car, apartment) is fixed; for such elements, identity is a variable property' (p. 41). The linguistic elements of a mental space may identify a role (as in the three examples above) or its role value.

Fauconnier suggests that ambiguity of interpretation of language may not necessarily be the result of a contrast between role and value interpretations, but rather may arise from contrasts between 'particular (one value) interpretations and general (all value) interpretations' (p. 51). What he calls *first order equivalence* reading is where the mental space within which language exists contains all of the relevant parameters necessary for the interpretation of the linguistic material contained within the space. As an example he offers the sentence: 'In 1929, the president was a baby'. In discussing the possible interpretations of this sentence, he proposes that an example of *first-order interpretation* is that in 1929, the person who was the president was a baby. He proposes that first-order interpretation can be employed to express a universal idea. In such a case, the proposition will not be attached to a tightly specifying space-builder. An example of this more universalist, less mental space-bound statement, would be: 'The president governs the country'. The *non-first-order* interpretation of the example sentence, and the more salient one, would be that the man who is currently the president was a baby in 1929. Fauconnier points out that this type of interpretation (non-first order) takes place using more than what he calls the *lexical* properties of the nouns or verbs involved. Non-first-order interpretation is essentially interconnectionist in that it does not simply rely on the roles and values of the elements within the mental space, but on their *interlinkage with, or reference to,* elements outside the space. It is also for this reason that non-first order is often the more salient method of interpretation.

Summary and implications for discourse categorization

Fauconnier's approach bears some similarities to the macro-structure/frame constructs of Van Dijk (1980) and the constructs of scenario/non-scenario-based information in discourse of Sanford and Garrod (1981). Essentially, what theorists are aiming to describe are the different types of knowledge that are represented within discourse and the different cognitive systems that are employed in structuring such different knowledge-types into coherent discourse. What these approaches seem to have in common is the idea that socially shared knowledge (often relating to the real world) is stored using schema or frame-type structures for ease of retrieval and use in discourse. However, the coherent representation of such knowledge in extended discourse itself is complex and employs a range of further cognitive structuring systems, systems that may involve more abstract or formal schematic constructs.

Johnson: image schemata

This section examines the construct of the *kinaesthetic image schema* proposed by Johnson (1987) as a fundamental device by which humans structure knowledge. First, the theory of knowledge on which Johnson bases his image schema construct is summarized. Secondly, the image schema itself and its *gestalt* nature is discussed. Thirdly, Johnson's ideas concerning the role of metaphor in the operation of this construct as a categorizing device are examined, along with evidence which Johnson claims points to the existence and operation of image-schemata. Finally, the image schema construct is discussed in relation to its possible structuring role in written discourse.

Based on the ideas of Putnam (1981), Johnson puts forward a theory of knowledge upon which he bases his proposal for the construct of image-schemata:

- Knowledge is shared by humans, and there is no absolute 'God's eye' knowledge.
- Knowledge is mediated by understanding. There is a shared community of understanding and, to be shared, understanding has to be expressed through language and some system of description.
- Shared understanding is not just a matter of concepts and propositions, but also involves image schemata which constitute form in our experience.
- Understandings develop from bodily experiences and interactions with our environment.
- What psychologists call 'basic-level' experience and conceptual organization is the level at which we react with our environment. It is the level characterized by gestalt perception of overall shape, by our capacities for motor movement in interaction with the object, and by our ability to form rich mental images of an object.
- Our conceptual system is plugged into our most relevant experiences at two levels:
  (a) the basic level – the level of interaction with the environment
  (b) the image schematic level – which gives a general form to our understanding. This is extended imaginatively by category formation and by metaphorical and metonymic projection.
- To interpret our experience, we need categories that are superordinate and subordinate to basic-level categories. (summarized from Johnson, 1987, pp. 206–9).

Johnson contends that semantics, in its concern with 'truth conditions', often ignores non-propositional structures, such as images, schematic patterns and metaphorical projections. He claims that these structures, although frequently ignored, are central in conveying meaning that relates to abstractions. Johnson refers to the proposals of Kant (1781/1998) for *transcendental schemata.* Kant suggested that there are empirical and abstract types of knowledge, as well as a third type of knowledge, which he called *transcendental schemata,* a type of knowledge which can mediate between the other two types. Drawing on Kant's ideas, Johnson describes *image schemata* as 'non-propositional structures of imagination' (1987, p. 19). This is a proposal for a type of schema that is different from that proposed by Rumelhart (1975) (i.e. schemata for knowledge structures) and that of Schank and Abelson (1977) (i.e. schemata for scripted activities).

According to Johnson's proposal (1987, p. 29), the construct of *image schemata* conforms to the following concepts:

- A schema consists of a small number of parts and relations, by virtue of which it can structure indefinitely many perceptions, images and events.
- The patterns [of image schemata] emerge as meaningful for us, chiefly at the level of our bodily movements through space, our manipulation of objects and our perceptual interactions.
- They operate at a level of organization that falls between abstract propositional structures on the one side, and particular concrete images on the other.

Johnson sees image schemata as gestalts, defining a gestalt structure as 'an organised, unified whole within our experience and understanding that manifests a repeatable pattern or structure' (p. 44), and claiming not only that image schemata fit the requirements of gestalt structures according to the above definition but also that 'all image schemata are characterizable as irreducible gestalts' (p. 44). Examples of image schemata are: the CONTAINER schema, the LINK schema, the CENTRE-PERIPHERY schema, the PATH schema, the UP-DOWN schema, the FRONT-BACK schema and the LINEAR ORDER schema. The first four of these are outlined here.

Johnson (pp. 21–2) contends that at an early age humans develop the CONTAINER schema gestalt from experiencing their bodies as containers and as things in containers (e.g. being in a room or a bed). The structural elements of the container schema are: interior, boundary, exterior. The classificatory idea of the CONTAINER schema is that everything is either inside or outside of the container.

According to Johnson (pp. 117–19), the LINK schema develops from the physical link of the umbilical between a child and its mother. During their development, children are often physically held by, or hold onto their parents to determine physical location. The use of the link to determine location can be both spatial and temporal. The structural elements are two items with a link connecting them. The classificatory idea of the link schema is: given two linked elements X and Y, X is linked to and dependent on Y, and conversely Y is linked to and dependent on X.

The CENTRE PERIPHERY schema, according to Johnson (pp. 124–5), develops from our bodies as the perceptual centres of the world through which we experience sensations, objects and relationships. The structural parts of this schema are an entity, a centre and a periphery. The classificatory idea is that the centre is most important and the periphery is less important. This schema almost always operates with other schemata, such as NEAR-FAR (for establishing a scale or degrees of importance).

The PATH schema (pp. 113–17) develops from the bodily experience of any kind of movement. The structural parts of this schema are the source (the starting point), the path (the course or direction) and the goal (the endpoint). The classificatory idea of this schema is accounting for anything that literally moves or figuratively progresses.

Johnson claims that schemata are the primary means by which we construct or constitute order, and that they are flexible enough for us to apply to any number of instantiations in varying contexts. He also claims that schemata for temporal and spatial orientation 'are so pervasive and so constitutive of our ordinary experience that they are taken for granted (and thus overlooked) in standard accounts of meaning and understanding' (1987, p. 31).

One of the central ideas of Johnson's theory is the metaphorical projection of a schema from the physical to the non-physical. He claims that the conventional view of metaphor in objectivist metaphysics involves the similarities conveyed by metaphor as '[existing] objectively in the world and [being] expressible in literal propositions' (p. 68), and he observes that Davidson (1978) and Searle (1979), while holding different views on the non-propositional aspect of metaphorical meaning, 'both share the recognition of a non-propositional operation of metaphorical projection' (p. 73). In developing this idea, he argues that metaphors play a 'constitutive' role in structuring human experience, illustrating this by examining the operation of the BALANCE schema where the concept of metaphorical balance is said to emerge out of an understanding of the preconceptual gestalt structure that begins with balancing as a bodily activity. An understanding of balance in visual perception involves metaphorically projecting the idea of weights and forces from a physical experience to a visual experience. Thus, Johnson argues, by metaphorical projection the BALANCE schema becomes the organizing concept for the relations that operate in a number of other domains. Examples to which he refers are: systemic balance, psychological balance, the balance of rational argument, legal and moral balance, and mathematical balance.

Johnson presents a number of arguments in support of the construct of image-schemata and their metaphorical projection. These include language phenomena relating to the operation of metaphor as well as empirical psychological studies. In natural language, Johnson argues, the systematic nature of metaphor, extensions of conventional metaphor and polysemy indicate the operation of image-schemata. As an example of systematic metaphor, referring to Lakoff and Johnson (1980, pp. 92–6), he cites metaphor related to argument, particularly the content of an argument, which usually relates to buildings or construction. Examples are: support, construct, form, shore up, stand or fall, buttress with solid arguments.

Another aspect of natural language which Johnson argues indicates the existence of image-schemata and their metaphorical operation is polysemy. He defines polysemy as 'the multiple, related meanings for terms' (1987, p. 107), claiming that it exists because of underlying schemata which structure a network of related meanings by metaphorical extension. As an example, he discusses the OUT schema which, he argues, can be applied prototypically to the spatial domain, but is also metaphorically projected into a wide variety of cognitive areas such as: selection (leave out), withdrawal (get out [of], back out, weasel out [of]), producing (put out), despatching (get out, send out), distributing (hand out, give out), emphasizing (bring out).

Perhaps more significantly, Johnson cites several studies which have demonstrated that the human mind performs operations involving image-schemata that are analogues of spatial operations. For example, a series of experiments by Brooks (1968) involved subjects being shown physical figures which were then removed. The subjects were then questioned on their memory of them, their responses indicating that the scanning operations performed were analogues of spatial operations. Anderson (1980) reports that subjects distinguished between simple, gestalt-based images and more detailed or rich images (which he calls 'mental pictures'). Furthermore, experiments conducted by Marmor and Zabeck (1976) demonstrated that congenitally blind subjects performed mental operations in ways similar to sighted subjects as a result of kinaesthetic experiences.

Summary and implications for discourse categorization

Image schemata, as conceptualized by Johnson, are simple irreducible gestalt-based patterns. Essentially what Johnson argues is that these patterns, which are learned early in life as basic-level knowledge, may later form the basis of more general or superordinate categorization. He proposes that image schemata organize knowledge in a wide variety of domains and, using the BALANCE schema as an example, he argues for instantiations of it in the visual, systemic and psychological domains, as well as in rational argument, moral and legal argument, and mathematics. This is similar to Van Dijk's (1980, p. 233) earlier proposal that a 'schema is perhaps the most general in the prototypical organization of knowledge' and that 'schemata may have their origin in perceptual organization, along such categories as "horizontal", "vertical", "surface", "bottom", and "top"'.

A number of studies have considered the construct of image-schemata as a categorizing principle for linguistic categories. These include Japanese cause markers (Matsumoto, 1997); German prepositions (Serra-Borneto, 1997) and spatial prepositions (Beitel, 1995). Johnson himself makes no specific claims for image-schemata as discourse-organizing constructs. However, Lakoff (1987) suggests that propositional information may be structured by image-schemata, and a study by Salies (1998) actually examines whole texts as instantiations of image-schemata.

If, in the identification of discourse categories such as cognitive genres, the construct of image-schemata were to be applied to the higher-level categorization of discourse, certain issues would have to be addressed. First it would be necessary to identify the connection between discourse type and the image-schema which would organize discourse of a certain type, such as narrative. Secondly, attention would need to be paid to how an image schema typically maps onto larger sections of discourse. Thirdly, the influence of image schemata on the selection of lower-level categorizing structures (such as semantic relations, syntax and lexis) would also need to be explored.

Lakoff: idealized cognitive models

This section will briefly examine key aspects of the approach to categorization proposed by Lakoff (1987), an approach which draws on many of the theories previously reviewed in this chapter. In particular, attention is drawn to two aspects of Lakoff's proposals concerning human categorization: his proposal for different types of prototypes (called *idealized cognitive models*) and, related to this, his *spatialization of form hypothesis*.

Lakoff supports the view that categories are cognitive concepts, and that the use of prototypes provides the basis for making a categorizing judgement. He argues that the type of prototype used for a particular category is related to the subject matter being categorized. Different types of category will employ different types of prototype, which he terms *idealized cognitive models* (hereafter ICM). Thus, 'our basic claim will be that prototype effects result from the nature of cognitive models, which can be viewed as theories of some subject matter' (Lakoff, 1987, p. 45). In his proposal, Lakoff incorporates aspects of frame semantics (Fillmore, 1985), metaphor and metonymy (Lakoff and Johnson, 1980), mental spaces (Fauconnier, 1985) and cognitive grammar (Langacker, 1987).

Central to Lakoff's ICM approach is the idea of conceptual embodiment: 'The idea [is] that the properties of certain categories are a consequence of the nature of human biological capacities and of the experiences of functioning in a physical and social environment' (p. 12). Lakoff proposes that basic-level and image-schematic concepts (Johnson, 1987) are directly understood in terms of physical experience, and that they form the basis for more complex human categorization: 'Given basic-level and image-schematic concepts, it is possible to build up complex cognitive models. . . . Image schemata provide the structures used in those models' (p. 282).

As a result of his theory of conceptual embodiment, Lakoff proposes that the kinds of image schemata that structure people's experience of space (e.g. CONTAINER, SOURCE-PATH-GOAL, LINK, PART-WHOLE, UP-DOWN) are also used to structure concepts in abstract domains. He terms this the *spatialization of form hypothesis*, and provides the following summary of this hypothesis:

- Categories (in general) are understood in terms of CONTAINER schemas.
- Hierarchical structure is understood in terms of PART-WHOLE schemas and UP-DOWN schemas.
- Relational structure is understood in terms of LINK schemas.
- Radial structure in categories is understood in terms of CENTER-PERIPHERY schemas.
- Foreground-background structure is understood in terms of FRONT-BACK schemas.
- Linear quantity scales are understood in terms of UP-DOWN schemas and LINEAR ORDER schemas. (p. 283)

Lakoff emphasizes the role of metaphor in employing an image-schema which relates to a physical domain as a means of structuring an abstract domain: 'image schemas (which structure space) are mapped into the corresponding abstract configurations (which structure concepts)' (p. 283). Five types of idealized cognitive models are proposed: *image-schematic*, *propositional*, *metaphoric*, *metonymic* and *symbolic*:

- *Image-schematic*: organization within a mental space is done by a schema, based on patternings derived from gestalt perceptions, such as the image-schemata proposed by Johnson (1987) for *higher level categorization* e.g. PART-WHOLE, CONTAINER, LINK, CENTER-PERIPHERY and SOURCE-PATH-GOAL (p. 284).
- *Propositional* (a mental space which is not organized by imaginative devices): 'A simple proposition consists of an ontology of elements (the "arguments") and a basic predicate that holds of these arguments' (p. 285) and semantic relations may hold between the elements in this type of schema.
- *Metaphoric:* 'a metaphoric mapping involves a source domain and a target domain: the source domain is assumed to be structured by a propositional or image-schematic model' (p. 288).
- *Metonymic*: 'a metonymic mapping occurs within a single conceptual

domain which is structured by an ICM. Given two elements A and B in the ICM, A may stand for B. If B is a category, and A is a member or subcategory of B, the result is a metonymic category structure, in which A is a metonymic prototype of B' (p. 288).

- *Symbolic*: when an ICM is used to structure or organize linguistic elements, such as grammatical categories, Lakoff calls this a symbolic ICM (p. 289).

Summary and implications for discourse categorization

The concept of idealized cognitive models (ICM) proposed by Lakoff is another example of an attempt to explain how categorization involving prototype occurs in relation to different types of knowledge. Lakoff assigns a significant, knowledge-organizing role to simple gestalts – described as image schemata by Johnson (1987) – in a certain type of category. He proposes that through metaphorical projection, image-schema structures (which relate in the first place to knowledge in the physical realm) are able to structure other, more abstract types of knowledge at a superordinate level – his 'spatialization of form hypothesis'. This idea was first proposed by Van Dijk (1980, p. 233) and again in a more developed form by Johnson (1987), both of whom suggest that it is simple gestalt knowledge that may operate as the highest-level, structuring element in many categories, not just in one type of category. In his ICM proposal, Lakoff focuses on specific knowledge types and proposes types of categorization that may relate to each knowledge type. He does not, however, provide an integrated approach which could be related directly to written discourse involving more than one knowledge type (e.g. content knowledge and linguistic knowledge).

3.5 Discussion: implications of categorization theories for discourse creation

So far in this chapter, a range of theories and constructs relating to the categorization and organization of knowledge have been reviewed. In this section, these are discussed under the following headings:

- a cognitive basis for the categorization and organization of knowledge;
- the role of prototypes in making categorizing judgements;
- approaches to types and levels of category;
- issues of complex categorization within discourse.

A cognitive basis for the categorization and organization of knowledge

The research of Bartlett (1932) and the ideas of Wittgenstein (1953/1963) raised important questions about the ways in which the human mind organizes and categorizes knowledge. In relation to the organization of knowledge, Bartlett (1932) proposed that knowledge is often organized by means of schemata which use existing concepts as a basis for processing new information. This idea has been developed by a number of theorists who have put forward a range of knowledge-organizing constructs, variously termed: schemata, frames, scripts or scenarios. In relation to categorization, Wittgenstein (1953) put forward a family resemblance view of categorization, which allows for central or prototypical members of a category as well as less typical or peripheral members of a category. This is supported by the empirical studies of Rosch (1973, 1975) and Rosch and Mervis (1975), which point to a prototype effect that operates when categorizing judgements are made in a number of fields. This idea is summarized by Fillmore (1976) who, in putting forward his theory of *frame semantics*, proposes that prototypes play a role in the organization of knowledge:

> [In] order to perceive something or to attain a concept, what is at least sometimes necessary is to have in memory a repertory of prototypes, the act of perception or conception being that of recognizing in what ways an object can be seen as an instance of one or another of these prototypes. (p. 24)

These approaches to knowledge organization and categorization raise specific issues in relation to the connection between language and referents. If categorization and organization of knowledge is based on already held concepts or prototypes – which, as Bartlett demonstrated, may be culturally influenced or determined – the representation of knowledge through word and referent relationships cannot be treated as fixed. Rather, it will be seen as being determined by cultural and contextual factors that vary according to the situation of language use.

Therefore, it is proposed here that categories of knowledge are cognitive constructs, which are based on a human view of the world; they are, therefore, essentially a human creation based on human perception and human reasoning about different types of knowledge.

The role of prototypes in making category judgements

Associating objects or phenomena with categories, in many areas of knowledge, appears to involve assigning a category in relation to a prototype. This involves more prototypical, central category members, and less prototypical, peripheral category members. Categorizing judgements thus involve 'judgments of degree of prototypicality' (Rosch, 1978, p. 40), which can be related to the family resemblance ideas of Wittgenstein (1953). This appears to be an underlying principle in all of the categorizing constructs which relate to frame or schema theory, where this principle is involved in:

- the assignment of values to the variables of a schema (Rumelhart and Ortony, 1977, p. 105), and
- the application of the whole schema to examples of a category (Bartlett, 1932).

Judgements of prototypicality also appear to be the categorizing principle in the other schema-like categorizing constructs which were reviewed, such as scripts (Schank and Abelson, 1977); scenarios (Sanford and Garrod, 1981); frames, (Fillmore, 1977; Van Dijk, 1977; Barsalou, 1992); and idealized cognitive models (Lakoff, 1987). Moreover, categorization based around a prototype (such as a central example schema, scenario or script) is proposed as the categorizing construct relating to both empirical knowledge, such as scripts (Schank and Abelson, 1977) and abstract knowledge, such as cognitive grammar categories (Langacker, 1987).

Approaches to types and levels of category

The idea of levels of category appears in much of the literature reviewed here (especially that which concerns more complex categorization involving categories that include more than a single type of item or concept). In most of the approaches, category levels relate to the degree of specificity of the knowledge represented. Categories which classify knowledge in a more general way are referred to as high-level categories, those dealing with more specific knowledge as low-level categories.

Brown's (1958, 1965) three-level category construct (superordinate, basic-level and subordinate) provides the basis for a variety of approaches to the investigation of the categorization of knowledge, such as the research of Rosch (1973, 1975) and Rosch and Mervis (1975), which related to the categorization of single objects or colours. It is also employed in theories accounting for complex categories which relate to connected or related data, such as objects, events, scenes or situations. For example, in schema theory, higher-level schemata are said to involve general types of knowledge, and lower-level schemata more specific types of knowledge (Rumelhart and Ortony, 1977 pp. 109–10). Oller (1995) proposes three levels of schemata – abstract, formal and content – in descending order of increased specificity. In script theory, scripts are envisaged as more specific than plans, which are in turn more specific than goals (Schank and Abelson, 1977). Similarly, in their approaches to frames the artificial intelligence theorists, Minsky (1975) and Winograd (1977), argue for a hierarchical organization of frames, from general to specific. Barsalou (1992) has argued that '[frames] for what were once primitive concepts produce complex concepts that are used to build more specific concepts' (p. 43). Thus, complex categorization is generally treated as involving a hierarchy of related knowledge types. In considering high-level categorization, Van Dijk (1980, p. 233) and Johnson (1987) argue that gestalts may provide a basis for upper-level or superordinate categorization.

Issues of complex categorization within discourse

In schema and frame theory, there are a number of approaches that attempt to address the issue of different knowledge types with different organizational structures, and the ways in which they intermesh with one another in order to represent complex knowledge through language (Schank and Abelson, 1977; Sanford and Garrod, 1981; Carrell, 1988; Oller, 1995). The systems of categorization relating to discourse need to take account of:

- the categorization involved in classifying the conceptual content of the discourse;
- the classificatory categories involved in the procedural knowledge for organizing the conceptual content in ways appropriate to the discourse community audience;
- the categories for the syntactic and grammatical systems of the language that encodes the discourse content.

To account for the first two of these systems within discourse organization, Carrell (1988) proposes constructs of formal and content schemata, and attempts to account for the relative influence of each type of schema. Her empirical studies revealed that culturally familiar content schemata appear to be more important than formal schemata in terms of assisting subjects in understanding the meaning of texts. However, her experiments also showed that rhetorically organized texts (employing formal schemata) were still better understood than those whose rhetorical organization had been disrupted and did not follow a formal schema pattern, regardless of whether the content was familiar or unfamiliar.

Also in respect of the content knowledge that is represented by discourse, another issue which arises is the distinction between:

- knowledge which is being specifically referred to in the discourse and;
- knowledge which is in the background, or to which reference is implied and not directly stated.

A number of theoretical approaches deal with this explicit/implicit focus distinction. The first reviewed was Sanford and Garrod's (1981) explicit and implicit focus reference. Rumelhart and Ortony (1977) refer to this as episodic (explicit) knowledge and generic (implicit) knowledge, and Van Dijk (1977) refers to explicit knowledge being able to be summarized by higher-level macro-structures and implicit or background knowledge as organized by frames. A further approach was Fauconnier's (1985) types of equivalence.

Implications for discourse categorization

As has been seen in the variety of approaches to the issue of categorization that have implications for creating discourse, the organization of language output is not a homogeneous activity to which a single type of categorization can be applied. Any representation of knowledge in coherent discourse involves intermeshing systems of categorization. In the approaches reviewed, the intermeshing systems of categorization employed will involve:

- the conceptual content of the discourse, both empirical and abstract, including knowledge which is explicitly and implicitly referred to in the discourse;
- the type of language use, such as spoken or written language, and how this influences the type of language which is used;
- abstract organizational or procedural knowledge, particularly in the case of extended, monologic discourse;
- the categorizing systems of the language itself.

The previous chapter extensively reviewed two approaches to genre and discourse classification which classified texts in terms of conventionalized approaches to the staging of content in terms of either a schematic structure or a system of moves and steps. These structures for the staging of content were, in turn, linked to lexico-grammatical features of the discourse. This is an approach which research appears to indicate is not sustainable (see Biber, 1989; Paltridge, 1993a, 1997). The review concluded that both approaches to genre failed to acknowledge a cognitive organizational element – such as the cognitive genre construct proposed in Chapter 1 – as playing a mediating, organizational role between the conventionalized staging of content and the lexico-grammar.

Taking into account the cognitive approaches to the categorization and principles related to the organization of knowledge reviewed in this chapter, Chapter 4 following presents a cognitive genre model and discusses the role of cognitive genre knowledge in the teaching of academic writing, and Chapter 5 proposes the use of cognitive genres as a basic unit of organization for syllabuses that teach academic writing to interdisciplinary classes preparing for university study.

Chapter 4: Operationalizing cognitive genres in academic writing

4.0 Introduction

Chapter 2 reviewed two approaches to social genre used to classify and deconstruct extended texts (mainly written) for pedagogic purposes. The review of these genre constructs focused on (a) the types of genre knowledge proposed for the categorization of texts, and (b) claims relating to systematic associations between higher-level genre knowledge and the features of language employed in exemplar texts. As a result of this review, it was concluded that discourse categorization, in terms of constructs such as genres, needs to be able to account for three overall areas of knowledge. These three areas are:

- the socially recognized elements of a genre, which may include aspects of communicative purpose and the related conscious organization of discourse;
- the cognitive structures or procedural knowledge by means of which extra-linguistic knowledge is organized and represented in discourse;
- the actual linguistic systems employed to represent socially motivated, cognitively organized genre knowledge.

In relation to the second proposed category of genre knowledge (cognitive structures), Chapter 3 examined and discussed theories and research relating to the nature of human categorization. This review included approaches to the types of, and interrelationships between, classificatory structures employed in the categorization of complex knowledge, such as discourse-classifying knowledge. Central to that review was the emergence of the following principles:

- categorization is carried out on a cognitive basis;
- categorizing judgements are often made on the basis of, and in relation to, prototypes or typical examples of a category;
- categorization of complex knowledge involves more than one categorizing system and is organized on a hierarchical basis with more general higher-level categories which, in turn, organize more detailed lower-level categories;
- categorization of discourse involves several categorizing systems that intermesh.

This chapter is concerned with the level of the underlying structuring of written discourse in terms of cognitive rather than social genres. (The issue of social genre knowledge and academic writing is addressed later, in Chapters 6 and 7.) It is proposed that the structures that operate in this area involve procedural knowledge, knowledge which, among native-speakers of a language, is not (generally fully) engaged at a conscious level when encoding extra-linguistic content into extended written discourse in an organized and principled way. The idea of less conscious elements involved in the creation of discourse accords with the proposal of Chafe (1994) for *peripheral* or *semi-active consciousness* (p. 29) and *discourse topics* (p. 120). This is also similar to what Sanford and Garrod (1981) propose in their constructs of *foregrounded* and *background* information (p. 135). Both approaches suggest that background or semi-active information may involve both content and procedural information. It is proposed that a systematic approach to the identification of such semi-consciously applied procedural knowledge is of value to those engaged in the teaching of writing, such as to young learners and second language learners. In both cases, an understanding of organizational patterns relating to procedural knowledge can assist in their development of a discourse competence in the target language.

The chapter is divided into three sections. The first section provides some general observations about the need for writing pedagogy to acknowledge the operation of cognitive genres within extended written discourse. These observations include a discussion of the diversity of approaches and terminologies used in relation to this issue, suggesting that many of these approaches share considerable areas of common ground. In the second section, there is a review of a number of taxonomies of cognitive genres that have been proposed for extended, written discourse. In the third section, a model for describing cognitive genres that occur within the context of extended academic discourse is proposed. An overview of classificatory levels of the cognitive genre model is provided, along with an outline of its relationships to social genre knowledge and language systems. Following this, two studies that have led to the development and refinement of the cognitive genre model are reported.

4.1 Some observations on the cognitive structuring of discourse

Discourse production involves the representation of a language user's understanding of concrete features of the real world, or of abstractions. That representation may involve either speech or writing. Rosch (1978), when discussing human categorization of knowledge, observes that 'it should be emphasised that we are talking about the perceived world and not a metaphysical world without a knower' (p. 29). With reference to the ideas of Putnam (1981), Johnson (1987) observes that 'all knowledge requires structure and categorization. Specifically human knowledge requires categories of understanding that humans can make sense of in terms of their own mediated experience and can use for human purposes' (p. 206). It is suggested, therefore, that discourse creation is a process of representation. It involves the representation of cognitive categories in terms of the linguistic possibilities of a language (which will, of necessity, employ the organizational and categorizing systems of that language), usually to achieve a social purpose in socially prescribed ways (see Hyland, 2003, p. 166).

Language users employ transactional competence in successfully interacting in everyday situations in the real world. However, the production of extended written discourse for an audience involves a real, hypothetical or imagined third party. It also generally involves, if it is to successfully communicate the writer's intended meanings (in the absence of paralinguistic cues and interactional feedback), organizational patterns, which may include a complex series of macro- and micro-level choices. In Chapter 3, reviews of approaches to the cognitive structuring of extended discourse, such as those proposed by Sanford and Garrod (1981) and Oller (1995), suggest that these choices may relate to the content of the discourse, the categorization involved in the linguistic system, and possibly procedural knowledge which mediates between the other two systems. The production of extended written discourse, such as that often required in academic contexts, must therefore involve something other than day-to-day transactional competence.

In approaching the issue of identifying cognitive organizational constructs in relation to the writing of extended text, the current literature in the fields of education and applied linguistics presents a multiplicity of approaches with a wide range of terminology despite the fact that there appears to be considerable common ground in the actual concepts proposed. Kroll (2003), in introducing an overview work relating to the field of second language writing and the range of issues and variables relevant to this field, expresses the view that there is no single theory of writing 'capable of explaining the role of and interaction among key variables' (p. 6). Nevertheless, the variations in approach along with a lack of a common terminology appear to have inhibited progress in the development of pedagogy for the teaching of writing, in particular a pedagogy which acknowledges and builds on common knowledge and understandings.

An example of diversity of description and terminology in relation to a similar construct can be seen in the area of accounting for the differences between the linguistic competencies that are required to transact orally and those that are required to write extended written text. In describing this, Bakhtin (1986, p. 87) makes a distinction between *primary speech genres* which 'correspond to typical situations of speech communication' such as greetings, military commands and requests for information, and the more complex *secondary genres* of writing which derive from speech genres. The same issue is addressed by Martin in discussing the construct of *mode* in systemic-functional linguistics: 'Texts can then be divided into those organised primarily with respect to activity sequences (iconic texts) and those organised along different lines (non-iconic texts)' (Martin, 1992, p. 517). Martin argues that certain types of non-iconic texts are *genre-structured*: 'Genre-structured texts are divided into those which review field-structured texts (e.g. movie reviews), and so are partially determined by their activity sequences, and theoretical texts which are not organised around a sequence of events in any respect, e.g. editorials' (p. 518).

In approaching the same issue, Kaplan (1987) says that 'spoken language is more likely to provide information relevant to immediate need', whereas 'written language is more likely to provide elaborated information, that very elaboration being likely to require sequencing, structure, and stance not characteristic of spoken language' (p. 15). He goes on to draw a distinction between *writing* and *composing*:

> Once sound-symbol correspondence is established, it is likely that an individual can acquire the ability to write, but there is some serious question whether an individual can acquire the ability to write *text* – to compose.... [It] seems that composing is more likely to be learned than acquired. (p. 16)

This issue (that is, the distinction between writing and composing) is also discussed by Bereiter and Scardamalia (1987). They present two models which distinguish between writing which involves simple *knowledge-telling* and more complex *knowledge-transforming* writing. Their model for knowledge-transforming writing identifies a *rhetorical-problem need*, which draws on what they refer to as *discourse knowledge* in order to create more complex types of written text. In making these distinctions, the approach of Bereiter and Scardamalia has much in common with those of both Kaplan (1987) and Martin (1992).

Another writer who also addresses the issue of discourse-organizing knowledge, especially for writing, is Miller (1984). She emphasizes the hierarchical nature of any representation of meaning through language and proposes that a hierarchy of several levels of meaning is involved, with different forms of communication emphasizing different levels. She suggests that extended, monologic discourse may involve a greater hierarchical complexity than dialogue in the representation of meaning:

> [Monologue] and dialogue pose different problems, for example, they probably operate with differing hierarchical structures. In dialogue, because the audience tends to be small and constraints managed through interactive coordination, personal intentions manifest them-

> selves more easily. Such interaction requires elaboration of the rule structure at the lower levels of the hierarchy, to guide turn-taking, implicature, and management of multiple intentions. In monologue, personal intentions must be accommodated to public exigencies – because the audience is larger, the opportunity for complex statement is greater, and constraints are less easily managed; more elaborate rule structures at the upper end of the hierarchy, at the level of whole discourse, are therefore necessary for both formulation and interpretation. (Miller, 1984, p. 162)

As discussed previously (in Chapters 2 and 3), one of the crucial issues in many of the theories proposed for classifying discourse (such as in terms of genres or text types) is the nature of the relationships between extra-linguistic knowledge and linguistic knowledge. Some have found it convenient to focus solely on linguistic knowledge around a social genre construct, thus avoiding many issues associated with joint models that combine linguistic, cognitive and social knowledge within a framework for rhetorical organization. However, since procedural, organizational knowledge involves human categorization, there can be no valid reasons for attempting to separate linguistic and non-linguistic categorizing knowledge in relation to rhetorical structuring.

In relation to the literature accounting for different approaches to cognitive genre, a number of central questions arise in respect of the competence required to produce extended written text, the types of knowledge that this requires, and the exercise of that knowledge:

- If the process of organizing extended written discourse is, as Kaplan suggests, *learned* rather than *acquired*, what type of knowledge needs to be learned to provide a basis for this type of procedural, discourse-organizing competence?
- If this discourse-organizing knowledge is to be learned, it firstly has to be identified, analysed and described to provide a basis for instruction and learning.
- What are the stages and types of classificatory systems which constitute procedural, discourse-organizing knowledge?

To propose answers to these questions, the next section of this chapter will review a number of approaches to identifying cognitive genres. First, in order to provide a framework with an empirical basis on which to consider the taxonomies of pedagogic approaches to cognitive genres, Biber's corpus-based research on text types (1988, 1989) is reviewed. The cognitive genres that are reviewed involve taxonomies that have been developed in order to teach writing to young first-language learners or to older EAL students who are learning English and mainly focusing on written discourse.

Corpus studies reveal that one (social) genre category of written texts can employ more than one *text type* (cognitive genre). Biber, in some of his earlier corpus research, puts forward a typology of text types (cognitive genres) with respect to a five-dimensional model of lexical and syntactic variation (Biber, 1988, 1989). The dimensions are:

- involved versus information production;
- narrative versus non-narrative concerns;
- explicit versus situation-dependent reference;
- overt expression of persuasion;
- abstract versus non-abstract style. (Biber, 1989, p. 10)

Within these five dimensions, Biber examines co-occurrence distributions of groups of linguistic features in 481 spoken and written texts of contemporary British English taken from the London Oslo Bergen and the London Lund Corpora. Biber's typology of texts is identified solely in terms of linguistic and stylistic features. He emphasizes that they are not socially recognized genres, which he sees as being 'defined and distinguished on the basis of systematic, non-linguistic criteria' (1989, p. 39). In avoiding social genre descriptions, Biber identifies his eight text types in terms of their rhetorical or communicative purpose:

- intimate, interpersonal interaction;
- informational interaction;
- scientific exposition;
- learned exposition;
- imaginative narrative;
- general narrative exposition;
- situated reportage;
- involved persuasion. (1989, pp. 20-2)

Biber (1989) proposes that academic prose texts employ four of the eight text types:

> *Scientific exposition* (type 3), which is extremely informational, elaborated in reference, and technical and abstract in style and content;
> *Learned exposition* (type 4), which is similar to scientific exposition except that it is markedly less abstract and technical in style; ...
> *General narrative exposition* (type 6), which is a very general text type which combines narrative forms with expository, informational elaboration ...
> Type 8: is labelled *involved persuasion*; these are texts that are primarily argumentative and persuasive in purpose and style. (Biber, 1989, p. 38)

Biber's corpus-based research provides a useful background against which to discuss pedagogic classifications of extended written texts which are cognitive in orientation, classifications that have been proposed to assist in the teaching of writing to both young learners and more advanced-level learners receiving instruction in academic writing.

4.2 Cognitive genres and young learners

To avoid, initially at least, the complexity involved in the synthesis of rhetorical patterns that appear in authentic texts, educators have often found it useful to identify cognitive genres (such as narration, description and exposition) discretely for pedagogic purposes. These have been used in the teaching of reading and writing to young learners (Crowhurst, 1990; Meyer, 1977; Richgels *et al.*, 1987; and Spiro and Taylor, 1987). Studies of isolated, single (cognitive) genres or *meta-genres* (Grabe, 2002; Grabe and Kaplan, 1996) in educational contexts have shown that students process and produce cognitive genres in different ways.

Two issues arise in respect of cognitive genre-based approaches to the teaching of reading and writing. The first is the difficulty of identifying whole reading texts (social genres) which conform to one single type of a cognitive genre category (Spiro and Taylor, 1987, p. 79). The second issue is that in studies of writing, researchers have found that young learners tend to mix cognitive genres (such as exposition, narration and description) in their responses when they are required to write texts employing one such genre. Thus, for example, Crowhurst (1990, pp. 206–10) found that younger writers tended to mix narration with persuasion when required to write a persuasive response to a task. She concluded that persuasion was a more difficult genre pattern, and that educators often gave little instruction in the construction of persuasive compositions.

Alternatively, it could be suggested that pure persuasion is a relatively rare written rhetorical pattern, and one which is not often encountered by young learners in their reading, whereas Biber's Type 6 text type (*general narrative exposition*) has probably been encountered by young learners more frequently, for example in school textbooks. Thus, their familiarity with this text type in their reading may, in turn, influence their responses to persuasive writing tasks. Crowhurst's (1990) identification of exposition simply as a genre which involves persuasion may be an oversimplification in relation to what persuasive writing involves in an academic setting, especially when considered in the light of Biber's three text-type categories of expository writing. In an attempt to address this issue when teaching writing, Martin (1984) distinguishes between *hortatory* writing (writing which 'persuades to') and *analytical exposition* (which 'persuades that') (1984, pp. 16–17). Martin suggests that hortatory persuasion usually involves the use of more personal language than does analytical exposition, which is more impersonal and makes greater use of nominalization.

The desire of educators of young learners to find authentic texts that conform to a single cognitive genre category is also reflected in the comment of the systemic functional genre theorists Knapp and Watkins (1994) who say 'science books that shift from explanation to narrative to instruction, with the grammar moving backwards and forwards between personal and impersonal voice, make heavy language demands on the reader' (p. 23). However, this phenomenon may simply be the normal synthesis of different types of cognitive genre in the creation of a complete text that realizes a social genre.

It is not the intention here to discount the value of isolating cognitive genres for pedagogic purposes, quite the contrary. It is important, however, to be aware that authentic, whole texts (exemplars of social genres) usually involve a combination of cognitive genres. Nevertheless, for pedagogic purposes, isolating specific cognitive genres can be helpful and can provide a useful basis for teaching so long as research that identifies the actual cognitive genre prototypes that are the building blocks of whole texts within a certain culture is taken into account.

Examples of some of the taxonomies of pedagogic (mainly cognitive) genres proposed as a basis for teaching writing to the young by educationalists in Australia include those of Macken, Kalantzis, Kress, Martin, Cope and Rothery (1989); Martin (1989); Derewianka (1990); Knapp and Watkins (1994); Butt, Fahey, Feez, Spinks and Yallop (2000) and Martin (2000). Derewianka (1990) proposes a taxonomy of genre categories for the teaching of writing in elementary schools. This includes: *recount, instruction, narrative, information report, explanation* and *argument.* Generally these appear to be cognitive genre categories although in her explanations and examples Derewianka appears to attempt to present them as if they were simple social genres (see Paltridge, 1996, p. 238). She identifies each of her genres through descriptions of different types of rhetorical purpose:

Recount: 'A recount is the unfolding of a sequence of events over time. [Its purpose is] to tell what happened' (pp. 14–15).

Instruction: '[Instructions] ... are concerned with procedures, which tell us how something is accomplished through a sequence of actions or steps. [Their purpose is] to tell someone how to do or make something' (p. 27).

Narrative: 'The basic purpose of a narrative is to entertain, i.e. to gain and hold the reader's interest in a story. But Narratives may also seek to teach or inform, to embody the writer's reflections on experience, and – perhaps most important – to nourish and extend the reader's imagination. The focus of the text is on a sequence of actions' (p. 40).

Information Reports: 'The function of an Information Report is to document, organise and store factual information on a topic' (p. 51).

Explanation: 'To give an account of how something works or reasons for some phenomenon' (p. 60).
Argument: 'To take a position on some issue and justify it' (p. 75).

As well as a detailed description of rhetorical purpose for each genre, Derewianka gives considerable attention to the staging and structuring of ideas. For example, for Recount genre, she specifies a text organization of *orientation* and *events*. Orientation is explained as providing background information in relation to who, what and where for the subsequent events of a recount. The events section explains what actually happens; this is usually organized chronologically. Derewianka also specifies the linguistic features which, she claims, usually occur in the Recount genre.

Derewianka's taxonomy of pedagogic genre types is one of many approaches that see teaching the writing skill to young learners as involving cognitive genre constructs. Generally such cognitive genres are proposed as discourse categories that are predicated on types of rhetorical or communicative purpose, and where the taxonomy is more elaborated, each has its own category-internal structure for the organization of ideas. The approach of Derewianka (1990) appears to go some way to bridging the gap between the conscious, social conventions of discourse and the semi-consciously applied language patterns through which these are realized. However, pedagogic applications of cognitive genre categories need to find some way of accommodating the relationship between authentic discourse and the pedagogic genre under consideration given the fact that extended, whole texts are usually a synthesis of several cognitive genres.

4.3 Cognitive genres and academic writing in university contexts

A number of studies have investigated the writing requirements of university assignment tasks and the expectations of university staff in respect of responses to such tasks. Research in this area has generally been carried out in three ways:

- surveys of undergraduates and the types of assignment tasks and writing which they have experienced (Kroll, 1979);
- surveys of university teaching staff (involving asking the types of tasks which they assign and their expectations of student responses to those assignments) (Braine, 1989; Bush, 1994; Pearson Casanave and Hubbard, 1992);
- surveys of actual university assignment tasks (involving, for example, gathering a sample of such tasks from a range of departments and faculties and analysing the actual requirements of the assignments) (Braine, 1989; Canseco and Byrd, 1989; Moore and Morton, 1999, 2005).

Using the third of these approaches, Moore and Morton (1999, 2005) examined the types of writing tasks required of university students at undergraduate and postgraduate level. They carried out a survey of 155 written assignment tasks from a wide variety of faculties and subject areas at two Australian universities. The purpose of their study was to investigate 'the authenticity of the Task 2 component of the IELTS [International English Language Testing System] writing test (academic module). Specifically, the study's aim was to find out the extent to which this component of the writing test corresponds to the writing requirements of university study' (Moore and Morton, 1999, p. 64). The possible tasks that may occur as Task 2 of the IELTS writing test (academic module) are:

- present the solution to a problem;
- present and justify an opinion;
- compare and contrast evidence, opinions and implications; or,
- evaluate and challenge ideas, evidence or an argument.

(IELTS Handbook, July 2001, p. 12)

Within their sample of writing tasks, Moore and Morton identified twelve categories of university writing task: *essay, review, literature review, experimental report, case study report, research report, research proposal, summary, exercise, short answer, written argument/case,* and *other.* Moore and Morton analysed each of the university writing task types in terms of:

- *genre,* by which they meant university assignment task type – 'the genre of a task was taken to be the name given to the required written product as outlined in the task rubric' (Moore and Morton, 1999, p. 72);
- *information sources* from which the information in the assignment was drawn (the writer's prior knowledge, primary reports of research and secondary sources) (p. 75);
- *rhetorical function,* a 'concept [that] can be modified to mean that which a task (or unit of a task) is instructing students to do' (p. 76), including '*evaluation, description, summarization, comparison, explanation, recommendation, hortation, prediction* and *instruction*' (p. 77);
- the object of the enquiry, *phenomenal* or *metaphenomenal*: 'The phenomenal category was used for those tasks which directed students primarily to consider such "real world" entities as events, actions, processes, situations, practices etc. The metaphenomenal category, in contrast, was applied to tasks concerned mainly with the abstract entities of ideas, theories, methods, laws etc.' (p. 79).

Moore and Morton found that, in terms of the types of task (what they termed genres), essays (58%) were the most common, followed by case study reports (10%) and exercises (8%). All the other types of task were relatively rare in their frequency of occurrence. In terms of information sources, almost all of the assignment tasks involved gathering information of some kind, requiring the use of secondary sources (in 55% of assignment tasks), primary sources (in 18% of assignment tasks) or a combination of secondary and primary sources (in 21% of assignment tasks).

In terms of the percentages of tasks which employed the different rhetorical functions, Moore and Morton found the following frequencies of occurrence in their sample: evaluation (in 76% of assignment tasks); description (49%); summarization and comparison (both 35%); explanation (28%); recommendation (23%). Lower percentages were found for hortation (5%), prediction (5%) and instruction (3%). For the objects of enquiry of the surveyed tasks, 61% were phenomenal, and 39% were metaphenomenal. (Tasks with a metaphenomenal object of enquiry were distributed across a wide range of subject areas, but occurred more frequently in humanities subjects.)

Although Moore and Morton analyse the sample of assignment tasks in terms of (social) genres and cognitive genres (rhetorical functions), the study takes a unitary view of academic writing by analysing all the assignments from the different disciplines as a single sample. (This is because the IELTS writing test is predicated on a similar unitary view of academic writing.) In the study, social genres are simply identified in terms of the names of assignment tasks of the sample (e.g. essay, review, literature review, experimental report) regardless of the discipline in which the assignment task occurred. For example, they define essay, the most frequently occurring genre in the sample, as 'a task with a variety of features and specifications. In its prototypical form, an essay is a task requiring the presentation of an argument in response to a given proposition or question' (p. 74). Despite acknowledging that this single (social) genre can be realized in a number of ways, the study does not attempt to identify the different requirements and specifications of essays in different disciplines. On the other hand, Askehave and Swales (2001, p. 207) propose that (social) genres can be identified on the basis of 'sets of communicative purposes' (p. 210), but caution that this involves extensive investigation of the operation of texts within *contexts* [my emphasis] to establish different genre categories.

Johns (1997) emphasizes the difficulty of identifying a (social) genre in an academic context through nomenclature, saying that '[s]ome genres, particularly in pedagogical contexts, are loosely, and almost casually named' (p. 23). This variation in the types of writing requirement of university assignments (assignments using a common nomenclature) also emerges from a number of studies of university writing tasks (see Braine, 1989, p. 10; Canseco and Byrd, 1989, p. 312; Johns and Swales, 2002, p. 14). A study by Samraj (2004), which examined the genre of the *research paper* in two different disciplines, also confirms this. She says that 'research papers can have multiply layered communicative purposes, which may vary in different disciplinary courses, resulting in texts characterized by different discoursal features' (p. 5).

As Moore and Morton themselves indicate, *essay* appears to be a blanket term. As an example of a social genre, essay is difficult to describe as a type of discourse with a conventionally recognized structure and features. In fact the types of rhetorical purpose (which Moore and Morton term *rhetorical functions*) associated with a particular essay task, such as prompts or instructions that specify requirements of the task, are often central to understanding the types of discourse required in the assignment response. This may, for example, involve argument.

At the level of cognitive genre, Moore and Morton employ the construct of rhetorical functions to analyse the university writing tasks, defining rhetorical functions as '[that] which a task (or unit of a task) is instructing students to do' (Moore and Morton, 1999, p. 76). They divide rhetorical functions into two broad categories: *epistemic* and *deontic*, a distinction based on an approach to the modality of clauses. They note that 'an epistemic clause ... has the status of a proposition; it asserts whether something is true, partly true, false etc.' whereas '[A] deontic clause ... has the character of an action ... whether something is going to be done' (p. 76). Within the epistemic and deontic categories, other sets of rhetorical function categories are grouped:

- *epistemic*: comparison, description, explanation, evaluation, prediction, summarization;
- *deontic*: hortation, instruction, recommendation.

It is difficult, however, to see how the rhetorical function of, for example, *comparison* can be assigned solely to epistemic knowledge. While some academic writing tasks might require the comparison of graphic data about real world entities, others might, for example, involve a comparison of the arguments for and against a solution to a problem. Similarly, evaluation or even summarization could relate to deontic argument as much as to epistemic phenomena. Furthermore, there appears to be a degree of overlap in the categories of rhetorical functions that they employ. If the intention is that each different rhetorical function instantiates a different discoursal structure, it is difficult to see how this could be established in the case of *recommendation*, *hortation* and *evaluation* (which do not appear to have any necessary distinguishing features). Thus, the rhetorical categories employed to analyse the tasks do not appear to have a rationale that is sufficiently clear. They are based loosely on the rhetorical function construct of Trimble (1985, pp. 69–113), but using Trimble's definition of rhetorical function rather than his categories. A theory of cognitive genre which has the capacity to classify the rhetorical requirements of the rubrics of academic writing tasks (by means of a smaller number of prototypical categories) would have been useful. It would also help to overcome the problems associated with the terminology used in analysing and classifying the rhetorical functions involved in assignment tasks (or assignment task rubrics).

As in the case of social genres, Moore and Morton's categories of rhetorical function (cognitive genres) are also described in terms of their frequency of occurrence over the whole sample of the 155 assignment tasks, again underlining the unitary approach that the study takes to academic writing. The assignment tasks are not, however, analysed in terms of the frequency with which rhetorical functions cluster or combine within one type of task or genre (e.g. research reports or reviews), although Moore and Morton actually observe that 'assignments were generally found to prescribe more than a single rhetorical function' (p. 87). A more detailed picture of the range of requirements associated with writing tasks would involve identifying which rhetorical functions tend to co-occur or cluster within the types of assignment tasks (genres) examined, such as essay tasks assigned in different disciplines.

4.4 Towards a cognitive genre construct for academic writing

In proposing a taxonomy of text types (cognitive genres) for use in designing curricula for tertiary level writing courses for EAL students (writing courses which use a genre-based approach), Quinn (1993) observes:

> The problem with this approach – a genre-based approach to teaching writing – is that in real life, academic texts [social genres] are more diverse and complex than the existing limited (or finite) range of models would suggest. There is more variety in the range of possible academic text types than any prescriptive, genre-based approach can predict. (p. 33)

This appears to confirm the view of Biber (1988, 1989) (based on corpus studies) and that of Pilegaard and Frandsen (1996), that authentic whole texts (which are examples of what are referred to here as social genres and by Pilegaard and Frandsen as text genres) can be a synthesis of different text types (cognitive genres). On the basis of a needs analysis for his writing course, Quinn presents a taxonomy of text types 'based on family resemblances or similarities and differences within each family' (1993, p. 35). He offers the following 'family resemblance' groups of text types as a basis for instruction in English for Academic Purposes (EAP) courses (pp. 34-5).

Table 4.1: Summary of Quinn's taxonomy of text types for EAP courses

Reports			
Technical/Scientific classification (scientific reports)	Describing a graph or a table of numbers (numerical reports)	Describing a proposal or proposition (ideas, reports, or action reports in the past and future e.g. describing a political or business strategy)	
Explanations			
Description of a process (how)	Description of cause and effect (why)	Description of historical cause and effect (when/where)	Descriptions of hypothetical cause and effect (historical speculations or hypothetical explanations)
Discussions			
Compare and contrast objects e.g. consumer reports	Compare and contrast proposals (possible future actions) or propositions (hypotheses and ideas) e.g. discussions of the best site for the 3rd runway in Sydney	Compare and contrast hypotheses about historical causation and effect e.g. theoretical astronomy discussions about possible origins of the solar system	
Recounts			
Personal topics with human participants	Abstract topics with non-human participants	Formal academic recounts	

(Quinn, 1993, pp. 34-5)

Quinn's view is that authentic texts are 'blends, hybrids or mixtures of numerous [cognitive] genres' (p. 33). In order to develop the framework for an English for Academic Purposes curriculum, Quinn (1993) examined a range of authentic texts and isolated what he saw as the 'elementary genres [cognitive genres] which go to make up these more complex, authentic text types [social genres]' (p. 34). He said that his main criteria for identifying the four main genres were '*purpose* and *staging*' (p. 35), and that 'the main criteria for assessing family differences [within each genre] were textual choices made concerning modality, modulation, tense, theme-rheme organization, voice, agency and lexis' (p. 35). Quinn suggests that his proposal for genre is a heuristic concept, but one which enables teachers and course planners to identify the (cognitive) genres in texts 'which learners are most likely to encounter' (p. 45).

As mentioned previously, Biber (1989, p. 39), on the basis of corpus research, proposes that academic prose texts relate to four of the eight text types that he proposes. Although there appears to be some similarity between these and Quinn's pedagogic taxonomy of text types (see Table 4.2 following), the two taxonomies actually differ considerably in their conceptualization and purpose. Biber's taxonomy is corpus-based and

Table 4.2: Comparison of Biber's and Quinn's text types for academic prose

Biber's Text Types (Academic Prose)	Quinn's Text Types
Type 3: *Learned Scientific Exposition* 'focus on highly abstract and technical information ... they are, therefore, concerned with entities being acted on (the patients) [rather] than any active agents. They further depend on the frequent use of conjuncts to specify the logical relations among propositions' (Biber, 1989, p. 29).	*Explanation* Descriptions of a process, cause and effect (when? where? why?), historical and hypothetical cause and effect (Quinn, 1993, p. 34).
Type 4 *Learned Exposition* 'Type 4 texts tend to be less technical in content ... show a preference for a more active style' (Biber, 1989, p. 29)	*Report* Describing a scientific or technical classification, a graph, table of numbers, proposal or proposition (ideas, reports, or action reports in the past and future e.g. describing political or business strategy) (Quinn, 1993, p. 34).
Type 6: *General Narrative Exposition* 'They are primarily informational and expository but often use narration to convey information ... the narrative portions in these texts are not imaginary or for entertainment; they are rather an integral part of the expository information being conveyed' (Biber, 1989, p. 31)	*Recounts* personal and academic recounts with human participants, formal academic recounts (Quinn, 1993, p. 35)
Type 8: *Involved Persuasion* 'the texts in Type 8 are primarily distinguished by their persuasive and argumentative emphases ... this orientation is typically combined with an involved, often interactive, style, which aids the persuasive force of the text by developing a sense of solidarity with the listener or reader. In other cases though, these texts can be overtly persuasive while having a marked informational focus' (Biber, 1989, p. 38)	*Discussion* compare and contrast objects, proposals, propositions, hypotheses and historical causation and effect (Quinn, 1993, p. 35)

descriptive. Quinn's taxonomy is based on a needs analysis and is prescriptive, having been designed for pedagogical purposes.

Quinn identifies four text types (referred to here as cognitive genres): *Explanation, Report, Recount* and *Discussion.* The four are predicated on types of rhetorical purpose, and are not the same as context-specific, social genres, such as a newspaper editorial or a book review. Like Pilegaard and Frandsen (1996), Quinn suggests that these text types are likely to occur in combination rather than singly in the realization of a whole text (social genre). In terms of their overall communicative or rhetorical purposes, Quinn's text types (based on needs analyses) resemble the four types (or prototypes) of academic prose texts described by Biber in relation to a corpus-based study.

Summary

A variety of approaches to the analysis of written text in terms of what is referred to here as cognitive genre have been reviewed. These approaches all aim to describe the structuring of extended written texts for the purpose of teaching writing. In relation to this review the key findings are:

- whole authentic texts, examples of social genres, may be realized by different cognitive genres or a synthesis of different cognitive genres;
- cognitive genre, rather than social genre, often appears to be the preferred unit of discourse that is used as a basis for instruction in writing for young or novice writers;
- whatever cognitive genre construct is used as a basis for instruction, there is a need to reflect the reality of how cognitive genres interact in relation to social genres in authentic discourse.

In the section that follows, the cognitive genre construct is proposed as an organizing structure in extended written texts of academic prose. Rhetorical purpose is taken as a basis for identifying four different cognitive genres. Drawing on Biber's corpus-based findings, and Quinn's needs-based analysis, the four classifiers – Report, Explanation, Recount, Discussion – are employed as the types of rhetorical purpose underlying the cognitive genres which are proposed.

4.5 A model for cognitive genres in academic discourse

It is suggested here that the discourse competence to create a whole, extended written text (such as an academic article – see Figure 4.1 following) may draw on three areas of knowledge, each of which employs prototypes as a basis for categorization:

- social genre;
- cognitive genre(s);
- linguistic systems.

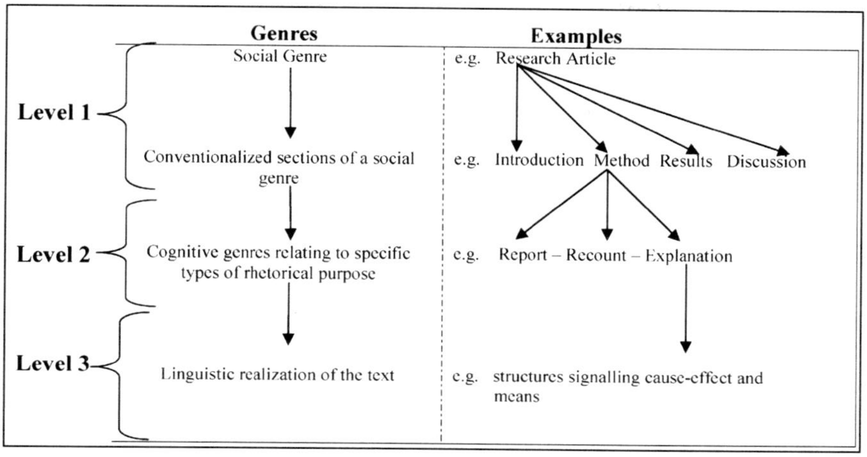

Figure 4.1: The relationship between social genres and cognitive genres

At the first level of classification, Askehave and Swales (2001, p. 207) suggest that social genres may be identified by investigating the operation of sets of communicative purpose within social contexts. According to loose Swales (1990, p. 8), such (social) genres exist within a discourse community, that is, 'within socio-rhetorical networks that form in order to work towards sets of common goals'. However, the model that follows does not relate to socially recognized genres (such as academic articles or book reviews), or recognized text segments (such as abstracts of, or introductions to, research articles), but to cognitive genre structures of the second classificatory level which, singly or in combination, may be used to organize the realization in language of such texts. (Chapter 6 addresses the issue of social genre knowledge, and Chapter 7 discusses how social and cognitive genre knowledge can be related in the context of a writing course.)

In relation to the categorization of extended, written discourse at the level of cognitive genre, involving procedural or organizational knowledge, it is proposed that:

- certain types of rhetorical purpose aiming to represent a type of information instantiate a small number of prototypical discourse patterns (cognitive genres) which are, in effect, a type of highly complex category;

- as complex categories, cognitive genres may be described in terms of different systems of intermeshing procedural (organizing) knowledge, which relate hierarchically (higher-level general and more specific lower-level structures);
- this procedural knowledge is fundamental to a cognitive genre, and this has a considerable influence on linguistic choice.

The model proposed, and the study that is reported thereafter, focus on four cognitive genres that occur in English academic prose: *Report, Explanation, Discussion* and *Recount.* The rhetorical purpose of each is based on the four pedagogic text types of Quinn (1993) and the four corpus-based text types that Biber (1989, p. 39) identifies as relating to academic prose. However, their use in the model involves a reinterpretation of Biber's and Quinn's text type constructs to include extra-linguistic as well as linguistic information. Thus, cognitive genres are psychologically driven, discourse-organizing patterns, and can be described at a number of levels. They are not usually whole texts but are used, usually in combination, to create texts in socially driven ways. On the other hand, social genres, which are realized by whole texts, are socially prescribed and accepted constructs.

The internal structure of cognitive genres

This section provides an overview of the proposed model for cognitive genres that occur in academic prose. The constituent structures of the model are presented, explained and summarized in Table 4.3 following.

It is argued here that social genre influences linguistic choice indirectly and that its influence is mediated by cognitive genre patterns. Thus, in an extended, academic prose text, the immediate type of rhetorical purpose of a single section or segment of the text (such as reporting, explaining, recounting or discussing) engages a hierarchical, cognitive genre structure for that section or segment of text.

Based on the idea that categories are formed in relation to intentionality and purpose, and drawing on the two existing taxonomies of text types (Biber 1989; Quinn 1993 – see the previous Table 4.2), the types of rhetorical purpose of the four proposed cognitive genres are:

- the presentation of data or information that is essentially non-sequential (termed Report);
- the presentation of information with the orientation on means (termed Explanation);
- a focus on the organization of data in relation to (possible) outcomes/conclusions/choices (termed Discussion);
- presentation of data or information that is essentially sequential or chronological (termed Recount).

Drawing on the idea from categorization theory that units of complex knowledge are hierarchically organized (higher-level general to more specific lower-level structures), the cognitive model employs the following, top-down, cognitive systems of classification:

- gestalts called image schemata (Johnson, 1987);
- discourse patterns (Hoey, 1983, 1994, 2001);
- cognitive processes (Crombie, 1987);
- interpropositional relations (Crombie, 1985).

Table 4.3 following summarizes the initially proposed model for the four cognitive genres relating rhetorical purpose to the systems of classification. (This model was later refined by incorporating information from a corpus study described in the next section.)

At the upper levels of the model, the rhetorical purpose of a particular cognitive genre will engage a higher-order, image schema gestalt (see Johnson, 1987). The function of this overarching pattern is to structure the content knowledge that is represented within the particular segment of text (a segment of text that realizes a cognitive genre). The notion that

Table 4.3: Proposed cognitive genre model

Cognitive genre	Rhetorical Purpose	Image Schemata	Discourse patterns	Cognitive Processes	Interpropositional Relations
Report	Presentation of information that is essentially non-sequential	WHOLE-PART; UP-DOWN	General-Particular (Preview-Details)	Associative	Amplification; Bonding
Explanation	Presentation of information with a focus on means by which something is achieved	SOURCE, PATH, GOAL; LINK	General-Particular (Preview-Details)	Logico-deductive; Tempero-contigual	Means-Purpose; Means-Result
Discussion	Focus on the organization of data in relation to possible outcomes, onclusions or choices.	CONTAINER; LINK	General-Particular (Generalization-Examples); Matching Relations; Problem-Solution	Logico-deductive	Simple Contrast; Contrastive Alternation; Bonding; Reason-Result; Grounds-Conclusion; Concession-Contra-expectation
Recount	Presentation of data that is essentially chronological.	SOURCE, PATH, GOAL	Problem-Solution	Tempero-contigual	Chronological Sequence

gestalts operate at this most general, overall level of category (and discourse) organization has been proposed by Van Dijk (1980, p. 233) and loose expressed in terms of a theory by Lakoff (1987, p. 283) in his 'spatialization of form' hypothesis. Thus, gestalts (image schemata) in the cognitive genre model relate to the most general, overall organization of ideas, but not to the actual arrangement of written discourse.

While the cognitive genre model proposes that gestalts (image schemata) refer to the overall organization of concepts or ideas, they lead to the engagement of non-genre-specific discourse patterns for overall organization of the actual written text (e.g. General-Particular, Problem-Solution), which have typical patterns of co-occurrence (see Hoey, 1983). Discourse patterns are reflected in the functional arrangement of paragraphs and sentences.

General rhetorical purpose, gestalt structure and discourse patterns have implications for the selection and combination of lower-order, more specific cognitive organizing categories, sometimes referred to by cognitive linguists as *discourse relations* (see Knott, Sanders and Oberlander, 2001). A number of taxonomies of these relations have been proposed, including *interpropositional relations* (Crombie, 1985), *rhetorical structure theory* (Mann and Thompson, 1988), *coherence relations* (Knott, 1996; Knott and Sanders, 1998), and aspects of metadiscourse theory referred to as *transition markers* Hyland (2005). The cognitive genre model draws on Crombie's interpropositional relations (1985) to account for lower-level, more specific discourse relations. Crombie's approach is employed in the model because it is based on binary relationships between propositions. As a result, it has the capacity to account for both semantic and pragmatic aspects of lower-level discourse relations. In this way it allows that the meaning of a particular signaller of a relation may depend on its context. For example, the word 'and' is generally considered to be additive (adding extra information), as in the sentence:

> *She speaks German at an advanced level and can also communicate in basic Japanese.*

However, in the following cases, 'and' is clearly performing different relational roles:

> *Do that again and I will call the police!* (Condition Consequence)
> *His spending exceeded the limit of his credit card and he was charged a penalty fee.* (Reason Result)

Thus the higher-level categories of the model of rhetorical purpose, gestalt structure and discourse patterns lead to the selection from a specific set of lower-order cognitive categories termed discourse processes, such as *causation, matching* and *spatio-temporal correspondence* (Crombie

1987) and *interpropositional relations* (e.g. Reason-Result, Chronological Sequence). Because these organizing categories involve related propositions, they have a direct effect on linguistic organization and linguistic selection (See Appendix 1 for a summary of Crombie's interpropositional relations).

4.6 Study 1: A corpus investigation of the use of cognitive genres in academic texts

A corpus study was carried out to identify and analyse, where possible, at least one instance of each of the four cognitive genres from a sample of academic texts in order to provide an empirical basis for the proposed model and a baseline against which to measure the written responses of a second study.

A sample of 20 academic journal articles or book chapters, selected from a population of 99, was analysed for occurrences of each of the four cognitive genres (see Appendix 2 for the method of selection of the population and the sample of texts). From 16 articles (of the 20 articles of the sample), multiple instances of all four cognitive genres were found, and from four articles, multiple instances of at least three of the four cognitive genres were found. A corpus was then developed by analysing, in detail, one instance of each of the cognitive genres that appeared in each article or book chapter of the sample. The corpus consisted of 70 analysed part texts. Table 4.4, following, indicates the actual numbers of each of the cognitive genres that were analysed.

Table 4.4: Cognitive genre corpus

Cognitive Genres	Total analysed
Discussion	19
Report	18
Recount	17
Explanation	16

All of the text segments were rater analysed (by the writer) in order to determine how the three different types of organizational knowledge for each of the four cognitive genres were represented. Table 4.5 following shows the revised cognitive genre model based on the findings from the text analysis of the corpus study.

Table 4.5: The cognitive genre model incorporating the corpus findings

Rhetorical Types	Rhetorical Purposes	Image Schemata	Discourse Patterns	Cognitive Processes (calculations include Bonding [Coupling])	Interpropositional Relations (Bonding [Coupling] removed): only relations with 10% or more included
Report	Presentation of information that is essentially non-sequential	WHOLE-PART, UP-DOWN	General-Particular (Preview-Details)	Tempero-contigual (59%) Associative (26%) Logico-deductive (15%)	Amplification (approx. 18%); Reason-Result and Grounds-Conclusion combined (approx. 17%); Simple Contrast and Comparative Similarity combined (approx. 15%); Concession-Contra-expectation (approx. 10%); Condition-Consequence (approx. 10%)
Explanation	Presentation of information with a focus on means by which something is achieved	SOURCE, PATH, GOAL, LINK	General-Particular (Preview-Details)	Tempero-contigual (60%); Associative and Logico-deductive (20% each)	Means-Purpose and Means-Result combined (approx. 29%); Amplification (approx. 17%); Concession-Contra-expectation (approx. 12.5%)
Discussion	Focus on the organization of data in relation to possible outcomes, conclusions or choices	CONTAINER	General-Particular (Generalisation-Examples), Matching Relations	Tempero-contigual (46%); Associative (27%); Logico-Deductive (26%)	Grounds-Conclusion and Reason-Result combined (26%); Means-Purpose and Means-Result combined (approx. 22%); Concession-Contra-expectation (approx. 19%)
Recount	Presentation of data that is essentially chronological	SOURCE, PATH, GOAL	Problem-Solution	Tempero-Contigual (60%); Associative and Logico-Deductive (20% each)	Means-Purpose and Means-Result combined (approx. 19%); Amplification (approx. 17%); Chronological Sequence (approx. 15.5%); Grounds-Conclusion and Reason-Result combined (approx. 14.5%)

4.7 Study 2: Use of the features of the cognitive genres by three groups of writers

To investigate the use of the four cognitive genres by three groups of writers, a second study involving the collection and analysis of responses to four writing tasks was carried out. This study had three aims:

- Aim 1 was to determine the extent to which the organizational features present in the samples of writing conform to those identified in the proposed prototype models of the four cognitive genres that are the focus of enquiry;
- Aim 2 was to determine whether, and to what extent, the organizational features identified in the models differ in the case of texts written by more experienced and less experienced native-speaker writers of English;
- Aim 3 was to determine whether, and to what extent, the organizational features used by inexperienced writers differ in the case of native and non-native speakers of English.

The four writing tasks of the study each had a primary rhetorical purpose related to one of the four cognitive genres. The four tasks involved:

- reporting data from a numerical table (Report);
- explaining a flow-chart diagram conveying information about the means by which something is achieved (Explanation);
- discussing both sides of an issue (Discussion);
- recounting a sequence of events (Recount).

The responses to the tasks are analysed for their overall prototypicality (or closeness to the cognitive genre) in terms of the organizational features proposed for the relevant cognitive genre model.

The sample

After obtaining the necessary ethical consents, four samples of convenience (comprising the groups listed in Table 4.6 following) were used in conducting the study. The total numbers of responses in each task sample were as follows:

- Tasks 1 and 4 samples had totals of 75 responses each;
- Task 3 sample had a total of 72 responses;
- Task 2 sample had a total of 69 responses.

Each task sample was stratified, with equal numbers of responses being gathered and analysed from three different groups of writers. The three groups were:

- native-speaker teachers of English (all graduates);
- native-speaker students (including students in the final year of secondary school or students in their first or second year at university);

- non-native-speaker students, all in the initial stages of a first-year university writing course.

Table 4.6: The sample

Groups		Tasks	Number of Responses
1.	Native-speaker university students taking a second-year English course	Task 1	18
		Task 3	24
2.	Native-speaker university students taking a first-year English course	Task 4	12
3.	University ESOL* teachers	Task 3	10
		Task 4	10
4.	University ESOL teachers	Task 2	13
5.	Polytechnic ESOL tutors	Task 1	12
6.	Private language school ESOL teachers	Task 3	18
7.	Teacher group taking a postgraduate applied linguistics course	Task 2	10
		Task 4	4
8.	University ESOL teachers' group	Task 1	13
9.	Native-speaker university students taking a second-year applied linguistics course	Task 1	7
10.	Native-speaker secondary school students in their final year	Task 2	11
		Task 4	15
11.	University teachers of a foundation studies course	Task 4	11
12.	Non-native-speaker university students taking a first-year writing course (six different tutorial groups during one week)	Tasks 1, 2, 3, 4	137
13.	Native-speaker university students taking a first-year university linguistics course	Task 2	9
14.	Native-speaker university students taking a first-year university English grammar course	Task 2	3

* ESOL refers to 'English for speakers of other languages'

This stratification was to allow for a comparison of the features of the writing of the three groups – Aims 2 and 3 of the study.

Because the writing responses were gathered from a number of small groups at different times and in different places, a standard set of instructions for the supervisor (see Appendix 3) was used on each occasion so that the conditions under which the sample was gathered were as uniform as possible for each group.

Analysis of the responses

Each script was identified only by a number. A word-processed transcription was made of each handwritten script in order that the respondents' handwriting and other aspects of the physical appearance of the script, such as crossings-out and corrections, would not distract or influence the analysis. (In the transcription, no attempt was made to change features of the actual text, such as lack of paragraphing or defective spelling, grammar or syntax.) The text for each response was pasted into a four-column table, and the analysis was hand-written on the transcribed response. (An example of an analysed script from one of the four samples is provided in Appendix 4.)

The cognitive genre model in Table 4.5 provided a baseline against which each of the scripts was analysed. Prototypicality scores, such as 1 Highly Prototypical; 2 Moderately Prototypical; 3 Less Prototypical; 4 Not Prototypical, were assigned to each response in relation to three organizational features of the cognitive genre model (image schema, discourse pattern and interpropositional relations), and the three were aggregated to give an overall prototypicality score for each script. (Cognitive processes, which relate to the general categories of interpropositional relations, were not awarded a separate score as it was felt that this aspect of discourse organization was accounted for in the interpropositional relation analysis.)

Judgements about the prototypicality of the use of gestalt (image schema) structures and discourse patterns were made on the basis of the amount of text structured by and the completeness of those patterns. The analysis of the interpropositional relations was performed by marking in and counting all the relations that appeared on the script. The counted occurrences were compared with the percentage occurrences of the interpropositional relations in the cognitive genre model (Table 4.5).

The analysis was performed by the writer as the researcher but, on request, samples of the interpropositional relation analysis were checked personally by Winifred Crombie (Crombie 1985, 1987), and re-analysis on the basis of her feedback was performed.

The findings: Aim 1

Aim 1 is to determine the extent to which the organizational features present in the samples of writing conform to those identified in the proposed prototype models of the four cognitive genres that are the focus of enquiry.

The prediction that, given the rhetorical purpose of a particular cognitive genre, written discourse that seeks to fulfil that purpose will employ the organizational features of that cognitive genre model, appears to be confirmed. The findings indicate the operation of a prototype effect

Table 4.7: Total overall prototypicality ratings for each sample

Overall Prototypicality Descriptors	1 Highly Prototypical		2 Moderately Prototypical		3 Less Prototypical		4 Not Prototypical	
	Number of responses	Percentage of sample	Number of responses	Percentage of sample	Number of responses	Percentage of sample	Number of responses	Percentage of sample
Report (sample of 75)	4	5.5%	20	26.5%	28	37.5%	23	30.5%
Explanation (sample of 69)	9	13.0%	27	39.0%	19	27.5%	14	20.5%
Discussion (sample of 72)	19	26.5%	5	7.0%	17	23.5%	31	43.0%
Recount (sample of 75)	27	36.0%	13	17.5%	13	17.5%	22	29.0%

(Rosch 1975). That is, the responses can be classified on a continuum – from being more typical (displaying close adherence to the features of the model) to less typical (displaying less frequent use of features of the model). This operation of a prototype effect in relation to the use of cognitive genre procedural knowledge in the organization of written discourse appeared consistently throughout the four different samples. The prototypicality ratings for the four samples (showing the prototype effect) are summarized in Table 4.7 following.

Whether or not the closer adherence of a response to the hypothesized prototype and its features (such as in the responses that were assigned Descriptor 1 – highly prototypical) provides evidence of greater experience in writing was the focus of the second and third parts of the study.

The findings: Aim 2

Aim 2 was to determine whether, and to what extent, the organizational features identified in the model differ in the case of texts written by more experienced and less experienced native-speaker writers of English.

In all four samples, the experienced writer group (native-speaker teachers) produced responses that were closer to the prototype (cognitive genre) model than those of the less experienced (native-speaker students) group. The difference between the responses of the two groups to the four tasks is shown in Table 4.8 following (indicating the overall prototypicality ratings assigned to the responses).

Table 4.8: Comparison of the overall prototypicality ratings of teachers and native-speaker students

Overall Prototypicality Descriptors		1 Highly Prototypical		2 Moderately Prototypical		3 Less Prototypical		4 Not Prototypical	
		Number of responses	Percentage of sample	Number of responses	Percentage of sample	Number of responses	Percentage of sample	Number of responses	Percentage of sample
Report	Teachers (25)	4	16.0%	13	52.0%	8	32.0%		
	Students (25)			5	20.0%	10	40.0%	10	40.0%
Explanation	Teachers (23)	6	26.0%	14	61.0%	2	9.0%	1	4.0%
	Students (23)	3	13.0%	12	52.0%	6	26.0%	2	9.0%
Discussion	Teachers (24)	12	50.0%	4	16.5%	8	33.5%		
	Students (24)	7	29.0%	1	4.5%	9	37.5%	7	29.0%
Recount	Teachers (25)	16	64.0%	6	24.0%	3	12.0%		
	Students (25)	11	44.0%	7	28.0%	7	28.0%		

The findings: Aim 3

Aim 3 was to determine whether, and to what extent, the organizational features used by inexperienced writers differ in the case of native and non-native speakers of English.

The findings from the analyses of the three types of organizational knowledge and their combined overall prototypicality ratings indicate that, in all four samples, the native-speaker student groups produced responses that were closer to the prototype (cognitive genre) model than those of the non-native-speaker student groups. In the case of Report, the degree of adherence to the prototype model by the two groups was closer than for the other three cognitive genres. A possible reason for the closer degree of adherence to the Report prototype by the non-native-speaker group could be the fact that almost all members of the group had taken the IELTS test as a means of entry to the university. Their preparation for the first writing task of the test may have influenced their response to the Report task. The overall prototypicality ratings showing the difference between the responses of the two groups are indicated in Table 4.9 following.

Table 4.9: Comparison of prototypicality ratings of native-speaker (NS) students and non-native-speaker (NNS) students

Overall Prototypicality Descriptors		1 Highly Prototypical		2 Moderately Prototypical		3 Less Prototypical		4 Not Prototypical	
		Number of responses	Percentage of sample	Number of responses	Percentage of sample	Number of responses	Percentage of sample	Number of responses	Percentage of sample
Report	25 NS students			5	20.0%	10	40.0%	10	40.0%
	25 NNS students			2	8.0%	10	40.0%	13	52.0%
Explanation	23 NS students	3	13.0%	12	52.0%	6	26.0%	2	9.0%
	23 NNS students			1	4.0%	11	48.0%	11	48.0%
Discussion	24 NS students	7	29.0%	1	4.5%	9	37.5%	7	29.0%
	24 NNS students							24	100.0%
Recount	25 NS students	11	44.0%	7	28.0%	7	28.0%		
	25 NNS students					3	15.0%	22	88.0%

4.8 Conclusion

This chapter began by reviewing the approaches of a number of theorists to the structured nature of extended written discourse, structures that appear to relate to cognitive theories of the organization of knowledge. Using the benchmark of Biber's corpus investigations of extended written discourse, the chapter then reviewed a range of approaches to the classification of discourse for pedagogic purposes, noting that the taxonomies put forward relate to cognitive rather than social genres. This review also revealed that existing pedagogic approaches to discourse classification use a wide range of terminologies, often overlapping in terms of their objects of enquiry. The result of this is that there has been no consistent or common approach to pedagogy.

In the third part of the chapter, a model was proposed to identify the cognitive genres that are commonly employed in written academic discourse. In relation to the model, two studies were reported – a corpus study of published academic texts, and a survey and analysis of writing tasks from three different samples of writers. The findings from the corpus study appear to indicate that cognitive, organizational structures (related to rhetorical purpose and the nature of the knowledge being represented) appear to be employed in consistent ways in the writing of certain types of academic prose in English. In the second study, the samples of responses to each of the four tasks indicated patterns consistent with the proposed cognitive genre model in the overall structuring of ideas, the organization of larger sections of text, and the choice of interpropositional relations. Furthermore, the idea that the features of each cognitive genre constitute an actual prototype appears to be supported by the probability that mastery of these cognitive patterns relates to experience and levels of proficiency in writing. Evidence for this is provided by the fact that different levels of prototypicality in relation to the tasks were indicated in the responses of the three sample groups. Generally, experienced writers produced responses that were closer to the prototype than inexperienced writers, and inexperienced native-speaker writers produced more prototypical responses than inexperienced non-native-speaker writers.

However, it must be acknowledged that findings from the second study are indicative rather than conclusive in that the subjects who completed each of the four tasks were from samples of convenience and not randomly selected from a larger population, and that the analysis of the writing samples was largely performed by the writer as the researcher. A further limitation of the study was that, for logistical reasons, each cognitive genre was investigated by collecting and examining responses to only one task.

Yet, if (as the findings of the second study appear to suggest) knowledge of and ability to use cognitive genres relate to the level of discourse proficiency of writers, consideration then needs to be given to how this type of knowledge can be incorporated into the syllabus, materials and pedagogy of writing instruction, and the stage of learning at which novice writers should be introduced to this type of knowledge.

In relation to the teaching of writing to pre-university (general EAP) writers, Chapter 5 considers cognitive genres in relation to language learning theory and curriculum design, and exemplifies a syllabus unit designed around a particular cognitive genre – that of Report. Later, Chapter 7 considers the incorporation of both cognitive genre and social genre knowledge in the context of a writing course for postgraduate dissertation writers.

Chapter 5: Relating cognitive genres to the teaching and learning of writing[1]

5.0 Introduction

In Chapter 4, a model was proposed as a way of operationalizing the cognitive genres that occur in academic prose. The aim of this chapter is to relate the proposed cognitive genre model to language teaching and learning, and in particular to the development of discourse competence in academic writing. In the first part of the chapter, the cognitive genre construct is discussed in relation to the dual processing theory of language learning and language use, along with its capacity to extend the cognitive and metacognitive resources of novice writers. Following this section, principles that ought to constrain the design of general English for Academic Purposes (hereafter EAP) writing courses, such as at pre-university or foundation level, are discussed. Translating the cognitive genre model into a general EAP writing course syllabus is then considered and finally a syllabus unit based on one of the cognitive genres (Report) is presented as an exemplar for such a writing syllabus.

5.1 Cognitive genres and language learning theory

The focus of the previous chapters has not been centrally concerned with the operational processes involved in acquiring and using procedural knowledge to create academic discourse. However, the cognitive genres proposed here may play a role in these processes and could, therefore, be considered in relation to language acquisition models such as, for example, the dual-processing model proposed by Widdowson (1989), who argues that:

> [Communicative competence] is not a matter of knowing rules for the composition of sentences and being able to employ such rules to assemble expressions from scratch as and when occasion requires. It is much more a matter of knowing a stock of partially pre-assembled patterns, formulaic frameworks, and a kit of rules, so to speak, and

[1] Much of this chapter is reprinted from the *Journal of English for Academic Purposes*, Volume 4, Ian Bruce, 'Syllabus design for general EAP courses: a cognitive approach', pp. 239-56, © 2005, with permission from Elsevier.

> being able to apply the rules to make whatever adjustments are necessary according to contextual demands. Communicative competence in this view is essentially a matter of adaptation, and rules are not generative, but regulative and subservient. (Widdowson, 1989, p. 135)

Widdowson suggests that much of what a native speaker knows of his/her language is in the form of adaptable lexical chunks. He notes that this can be related to the proposal by Pawley and Syder (1983, p. 192) that a native speaker of English draws on several hundred thousand of what they refer to as 'lexicalised sentence stems'. For the second aspect of the dual-processing model, Widdowson suggests that the rules of grammar are applied to fit lexical chunks into certain contexts.

Skehan (1996) reviews a range of cognitive approaches to language learning, approaches that he suggests also appear to support the dual-processing model that Widdowson (1989) proposes. In dealing with the issue of whether learning takes place consciously or unconsciously, he notes that there appears to be accumulating evidence (see a review in Carr and Curren, 1994) that explicit learning of structured material is generally superior to implicit learning, suggesting that awareness of the learning itself and of what is to be learned confers advantages. In reviewing the issue of how second-language learners actually learn language, Skehan (1996) draws attention to studies that indicate that this involves both the induction of underlying abstract rules and the learning of exemplars, citing the studies of Matthews, Buss, Stanley, Blanchard-Fields, Cho and Druhan (1989) and Carr and Curren (1994), which point to both structured learning and exemplar-based learning operating synergistically.

In considering the issue of how knowledge of language is fluently applied in situations of actual use, Skehan (1996) says that:

> [Instance-based] approaches (Logan, 1988; Robinson and Ha, 1993) regard fluency as performance which is based not on rules which are applied more quickly nor on rules which are more efficiently organized, but on contextually-coded exemplars which function as units. Such units (which may be significantly longer than a word) are the product of previous rule applications that are now stored in exemplar form, and so require far less processing capacity because they are retrieved and used as wholes. On this view, learning is the result of instance creation, and performance (and the ensuing fluency) the result of instance use. (p. 44)

If the learning of structured material is advantageous in second language acquisition, as the studies of Matthews *et al.* (1989) and Carr and Curren (1994) appear to suggest, it would seem that the types of knowledge included in the cognitive genre model may provide the basis for generalizable discourse frameworks that can be employed in pedagogic contexts. Such an approach would appear to be consistent with the dual-processing model of language acquisition and use.

In relation to stored exemplar-based knowledge, it is proposed here that the discoursal structures of cognitive genres could be learned and retrieved in relation to their respective types of general rhetorical purpose. Thus, for example, the discussion cognitive genre, which has the rhetorical purpose of organizing knowledge in relation to possible outcomes, conclusions or choices, could inform the planning of courses and the creation and selection of course materials relating to discursive argument. The cognitive detail from the studies reported in Chapter 4 seem to indicate that, in prototypical examples of this type of discourse, overall arguments and elements of arguments are grouped contrastively, the actual organization of the written text employs a Generalization-Example structure and, at a more specific level, the discourse is frequently organized by the interpropositional relations relating to contrast and causation. In relation to the induction of underlying abstract rules, the range of structures for realizing the predominant interpropositional relations within the discussion cognitive genre could provide the focus for the linguistic content – grammar, syntax, and the means of achieving cohesion within discourse.

Furthermore, Devine (1993), in considering the role of *metacognition* in the area of second language writing, suggests that there is a need to:

> [expand the knowledge base to] provide explicit information about the role of metacognition in second language writing. First, since the ability to monitor any task depends in large part on the extent and appropriateness of the knowledge base, L2 writing researchers might direct more attention to that knowledge base. (Devine, 1993, p. 118)

The cognitive genre model proposed here may contribute to the type of metacognitive knowledge that Devine refers to as *procedural* (Paris, Lipson and Wixon, 1983, in Devine, 1993) and which she defines as 'knowledge about how strategies can be employed' (p. 106). Similarly, Wenden (2001) includes in her description of the types of metacognitive knowledge employed by second language users a category called *task knowledge*, in which category she includes 'knowing about a task's demands' which 'includes knowing what knowledge and skills are required to do a particular task; how to go about doing it; its anticipated level of difficulty; and awareness of the learning plan that is the outcome of their analysis of the task's demands' (p. 46).

The need for novice writers to be aware of procedural and task knowledge also appears to be supported by Hinkel (2002) who, on the basis of an extensive corpus investigation of the writing of non-native-speaker university students, concludes that such writers need a greater conscious awareness of the 'essential features of academic discourse and text' (pp. 261–2), and should be provided with opportunities for writing practice in the use of such features. A similar view is expressed by Reid (2001) who, in advocating a genre-based approach for the teaching of academic writing, says that for non-native-speaker students 'the need [for these types of knowledge] is critical because they often have little or no acquaintance with such functions and forms by which writers fulfill the linguistic and rhetorical expectations of the academic audience' (p. 153).

Two approaches to implementing this type of metacognitive approach in the teaching of writing are those proposed by Flowerdew (1993) and Badger and White (2000). Flowerdew (1993, p. 309) suggests a range of activities encouraging student analysis of (social) genres in order to develop a conscious awareness of and proficiency in the use of genre knowledge in their writing output. Badger and White (2000) put forward what they term a *process genre approach*. This involves the use of genre knowledge as the basis for writing instruction, such knowledge being presented by means of 'a demonstration by a teacher or other skilled writer, possibly accompanied by a commentary attempting to explain the mental processes that underlie the exercise of the skill' (pp. 159–60).

Thus, in terms of one recent approach to language learning and processing-related cognition (the dual-processing model), cognitive genre knowledge may provide a basis for deconstructing and reconstructing exemplar texts to uncover, acquire and practise procedural knowledge in relation to academic writing and, thereby, contribute to the kind of metacognitive knowledge base that Devine (1993) suggests is necessary to advance the teaching of second-language writing.

5.2 Principles of curriculum design for general EAP courses

This section discusses issues relating to the design of courses whose purpose is to prepare students to meet the requirements of academic writing, such as in pre-sessional or foundation courses. Pre-sessional EAP writing courses, such as senior secondary school and foundation studies courses, cannot meet learner needs in terms of a single discipline-specific focus. For example, they cannot just focus on the texts and practices of business, or humanities, or science – unless of course it is known that all the students within the group will be studying in only one of those areas. In relation to their language development and the performance of certain types of tasks, students at this level need to be gaining generic, procedural knowledge rather than topic-connected, discipline-specific knowledge. Specifically it is proposed that such courses need to have what Widdowson (1983) refers to as a *wide-angle* focus and need to be concerned with developing the types of general procedural knowledge he refers to as *capacity*, which relates closely to the notion of discourse competence introduced in Chapter 1. This section proposes the cognitive genre construct as the basic unit around which general EAP writing courses may be designed. The next section outlines possible ways in which the cognitive genre model can provide the basis for a general EAP course syllabus and the final section of the chapter provides an example syllabus unit.

In categorizing so-called English for Specific Purposes (ESP) courses, Widdowson (1983) differentiates between *narrow-angle* and *wide-angle* courses, depending on the degree of specificity of the aims of the course: 'By aims I mean the purposes to which learning will be put after the end of the course' (Widdowson, 1983, p. 7). *Narrow-angle* courses are essentially a training exercise to 'provide learners with a restricted competence to enable them to cope with clearly defined tasks' (p. 6). The specific types of language usages required to fulfil the tasks become the aims of the course. On the other hand, a *wide-angle* course is closer to general-purpose English courses, which 'seek to provide learners with a general capacity to enable them to cope with undefined eventualities in the future' (p. 6). Furthermore, in describing the underlying types of knowledge and skills that are the focus of ESP courses, Widdowson (1983) also makes a distinction between what he calls *competence* and *capacity*. He defines competence as 'the speaker's knowledge of the language system ... his knowledge also of social rules which determine the appropriate use of linguistic forms' (p. 7). *Capacity*, on the other hand, is defined as 'the ability to create meanings by exploiting the potential inherent in the language for continual modification in response to change' (p. 8). Widdowson suggests that narrow-angle courses that require a restricted repertoire of language are essentially a training exercise in developing a competence in the use of formulaic language to perform specific purposes. An example of this could be English for air traffic controllers. In contrast, wide-angle courses give far more attention to developing a capacity to exploit the social and linguistic aspects of language competence in ways that cannot be specifically identified in the aims:

> The purposes in ESP are arranged along a scale of specificity with training at one end and education at the other. As one moves along the scale in the direction of education, one has to account increasingly for the development of capacity, and at the same time, one has to take into consideration the pedagogic problem of establishing objectives which are projections of final aims. At the training end of the scale, objectives and aims will converge into close correspondence and will seek to impart restricted competence. At the education end of the scale will cluster courses of English for academic purposes which require the development of communicative capacity and which will call for pedagogic decisions in the formulation of objectives. At this end of the scale, ESP shades in GPE. (Widdowson, 1983, pp. 10–11)

Essentially, Widdowson is proposing that there are different aspects to be considered in syllabus and course design. Under *competence,* he groups the linguistic system, as well as the social rules for its appropriate use; under *capacity* he places the procedural knowledge required to exploit the competence elements effectively in a constantly varying range of contexts calibrated to constantly changing communicative purposes and uses:

> With wide-angle course design, the need to account for the procedural aspect of learning and use is more self-evident. Here, the intention is obviously not to get students to internalize the topical realizations, but to use them for learning. It is the process of relating these particular realizations to *more general schematic structure* [my emphasis] which is the central concern and the process must ... involve procedural activity. (Widdowson, 1983, p. 90)

A further issue that confronts designers of any language course is the level or unit of language around which they are to be constructed. For example, many syllabuses are organized around grammatical items, 'based on the premise that learners acquire one grammatical item at a time and that they should demonstrate their mastery of one thing before moving on to the next' (Nunan, 1998, p. 101). Wilkins terms this kind of syllabus a *synthetic syllabus,* where 'the different parts of the language are taught separately and step-by-step so that acquisition is a process of gradual accumulation of the parts until the whole structure of the language has been built up' (1976, p. 2). In modifying Wilkins' (1976) definition of synthetic syllabuses, Widdowson points out that the synthetic approach not only characterizes 'the nature of the content of syllabuses and courses that focus on teaching the structures of a language in a linear fashion, but also syllabuses concerned with the realizations of meaning which are usually claimed to characterize the notional/functional syllabuses' (1990, p. 136). Therefore the synthetic syllabus, be it structural or notional/ functional, would appear to assume that language learning is a systematic and cumulative process. However, as Nunan points out:

> [Learners] do not learn one thing perfectly, one item at a time ... the rate of growth is determined by a complex interplay of factors related to speech processing constraints (Pienemann and Johnston, 1987), pedagogical interventions (Pica 1985), acquisitional processes (Johnston 1987) and the influence of the discoursal environment in which the items occur. (Nunan, 1998, p. 102)

A further problem with the synthetic syllabus approach is also the complexity of language itself, complexity in terms of the multiplicity of inter-related systems that are engaged in any situation of authentic language use. Among other elements, these systems may include those that are described in terms of pragmatics, semantics, phonology or orthography, morphology, syntax and discourse analysis. Underlining this idea of language as a complex and multi-faceted whole, Widdowson says:

> To identify something as a component is to recognize the operational complex as a whole in which it functions as a part. If analysis isolates elements from this complex, then it must deny them the functional features which alone can give them their component status. (1983, p. 84)

In order to overcome the atomistic nature and artificiality of the *synthetic syllabus*, Widdowson (1990) turns to Wilkins' (1976, p. 2) proposal for another type of syllabus which he terms an *analytic syllabus*, which 'presents language as synthesised units to be analysed in the process of learning' (p. 134). Thus:

> An analytic syllabus, on the other hand, would not be bottom-up but top-down. That is to say, it would present language in the form of larger textual units and set tasks of different kinds which would direct the learners' attention to specific features, formal or functional, of the language they were exposed to. Analysis would then be induced by means of controlled procedural work. (Widdowson, 1990, p. 136)

Rather than follow the conventional linear, synthetic approach to language course design, Widdowson proposes that designers 'look for ways of defining the aims of our students in communicative terms by devising a means of analysis which preserves the essential discourse features of language use' (1983, p. 90), this being essential to the development of syllabus and course materials that aim to develop the discourse competence of students in relation to academic writing. This need to retain language components as functioning features of a larger system, and to avoid atomistic approaches to language teaching, has been the rationale for the various *genre-based* approaches to language course design and teaching (see Paltridge, 2001, 2002).

However, the crucial issue, and (as discussed in earlier chapters) one that gives rise to much confusion, is whether it is a social genre or cognitive genre construct that should provide the basic unit of a genre-based syllabus, such as a syllabus designed for an academic writing course. The answer relates to the level of the writers and the context of the course. If the course is pre-sessional and interdisciplinary, and the discourse competence level of the writers is relatively low, it is proposed that cognitive genres should be the central focus and should provide the basis for syllabus units of such a course. On the other hand, if the class is homogeneous – containing writers all studying in one discipline – the discoursal focus of the course may involve both social and cognitive genres of the particular field or subject area of the writers. Similarly, higher-level, interdisciplinary writing classes also need to focus on both social and cognitive genre knowledge. (Chapter 6 following discusses approaches to analysing social genres, and Chapter 7 provides an approach to incorporating cognitive and social genre knowledge within a higher-level writing course.) It is proposed here that, in courses at either of the two levels discussed, the issue is one of central focus rather than a mutually exclusive choice of cognitive or social genre. Cognitive genres are usually embedded as small stretches of text within social genres and, therefore, can be extracted and studied in relation to a larger text even with relatively low-level writing classes. Thus, learning context and writer need are really the determinants of the choice of genre focus in a particular writing course. However, it is proposed here that the first step in the development of a discourse competence by lower-level writers involves mastering the types of procedural knowledge that cognitive genres entail.

While adopting an analytic, top-down approach to syllabus design based on social genres may ensure that the contextual and discoursal elements of language are included, such as in the *text-based* approach to syllabus design of Burns and Joyce (1997) and Feez (1998), it is still possible that the outcome of such an approach for lower-level learners may be *narrow-angle* competence-building (in terms of language usage for situation-specific outcomes and purposes). For example, Burns and Joyce (1997, pp. 77–9), in approaching the issue of social genre-based syllabus design for courses involving speaking skills, use a top-down approach that may be implemented without overtly incorporating a procedural, capacity-building element. If the syllabus or course is a narrow-angle one, such an approach to course design may be entirely appropriate. However, if the course seeks to develop a more general 'capacity', one that is not situation-specific or discipline-specific, such as, for example, a general EAP writing course (e.g. a pre-sessional or foundation course), a wide-angle approach is required, that is, an approach that includes a cognitive capacity-building element. This also suggests that there needs to be a reconciliation of 'the opposing principles of synthesis and analysis' (Widdowson, 1990, p. 136). As an example of this reconciliation, Widdowson (pp. 136–7) points to Crombie's (1985) *relational* approach to syllabus design. This approach, which includes macro-patterning as well as semantic relational structuring, involves a combination of top-down and bottom-up focus (something that would appear to be necessary if a cognitive loop is to be an inbuilt feature of syllabus design).

Thus, in a wide-angle academic writing course, the focus is on developing what Widdowson (1983) terms 'capacity' rather than 'competence', and specifically 'capacity' in relation to processing and creating extended written discourse. This inevitably involves the use of procedural knowledge in the case of academic writing. Furthermore, if such a course is to be discourse-based (with units constructed around whole texts), it needs to focus on a genre construct that is not socially recognized and discipline-specific. In support of the development of this type of interdisciplinary course, Bhatia (1998) notes that 'to master the power of generalisations across disciplinary boundaries ... one needs a system of linguistic analysis which is powerful enough to account for the intricacies of academic genres across disciplines' (Bhatia, 1998, pp. 26–7). Similarly Widdowson, in proposing the wide-angle, capacity-developing nature of EAP courses, says:

> The challenge for a wide-angle approach to ESP, then, is to ensure that topics that have no direct bearing on aims are selected and presented in such a way that, despite their lack of specificity, they will activate the capacity for language use and learning. (Widdowson, 1983, p. 91)

All of this suggests that interdisciplinary courses (such as general EAP courses) need a discourse-focused approach to syllabus and course design that relates to cognitive genres, one that combines top-down and bottom-up approaches in order to develop capacity as well as competence (encouraging learners to reapply procedural knowledge about discourse in varying situations and forms).

5.3 Relating cognitive genres to a syllabus design

This section provides a discussion of ways in which the cognitive genre model proposed in Chapter 4 may provide the basis for the organization of a general EAP syllabus and particularly an EAP syllabus that has a central focus on the teaching of academic writing. In this section, the different elements of the model are considered in terms of their roles within such a writing syllabus. However, any discussion of a writing syllabus cannot be considered in isolation and will be related to approaches to language learning/acquisition theory, materials development and pedagogy. The first section of this chapter has discussed the cognitive genre construct in relation to a theory of language learning and language use, and within this section there is also some consideration of the implications of such a genre-based syllabus for the areas of materials development and pedagogy; however, consideration of these two areas will be only in terms of brief illustrative examples.

Using the cognitive genre model presented in Chapter 4, Table 4.5, this section will discuss a top-down approach to syllabus design involving the processes and types of knowledge relating to:

- rhetorical purpose;
- gestalt structuring;
- discourse patterns;
- interpropositional relations.

Thus, cognitive genres provide the extended language entity around which the units of a general EAP writing course may be organized. For example, a particular cognitive genre from the model and its constituent elements provide a framework for the specification of the types of discoursal knowledge to be located within a single syllabus unit. In realizing such a syllabus, authentic textual segments (input texts) may be used as examples of cognitive genres for the purpose of examining and deconstructing the types of abstract, procedural knowledge of the model. (In the next section there is an example of an input text for a general EAP syllabus unit based around the report cognitive genre – see Table 5.3 following). The different constituent levels of knowledge of the cognitive genre model enable a top-down approach to be employed in examining and deconstructing the input text. By using this approach, Widdowson's idea of considering language elements as parts of a 'functioning whole' (1983, p. 84) is not violated, and the overall approach also accords with Skehan's (1996) idea of cycles of analysis and synthesis within a modified task-based syllabus.

Overall syllabus objectives: rhetorical purpose

It is proposed that the four types of rhetorical purpose of the cognitive genre model can be employed to provide the basis for outlining the overall syllabus objective of each unit of a general EAP writing course. Under the overall syllabus aim for each unit will be subsuming aims related to gestalt structure, discourse pattern and interpropositional relations (in terms of the linguistic features that realize the relations). It is suggested that a general EAP writing syllabus may reasonably include more than one unit based around each cognitive genre. Each syllabus unit realization of a particular cognitive genre could recycle the higher-level, more general organizational elements (gestalt structure and discourse patterns), but include a different linguistic focus, based on one or more of the interpropositional relations that are salient to the particular cognitive genre. It would be unrealistic, for example, to introduce too many different items of grammar and syntax (related to various interpropositional relations) within a single syllabus unit. Table 5.1, following, outlines a possible ten-unit general EAP course based on the cognitive genre model in which each cognitive genre provides the basis for two or three units within the course.

Gestalt structure aim

Each syllabus unit will include an aim to focus on the gestalt structure (of the cognitive genre) as the higher-level, ideas-structuring pattern within the discourse. Like the overall aim, the gestalt aim can be expressed as a performative such as in relation to recount:

Table 5.1: Proposal for a general EAP writing syllabus

Cognitive genre: rhetorical purpose	Possible unit aims for a general EAP writing syllabus
Recount: the presentation of data or information that is essentially sequential or chronological	Unit 1 Students will be able to write a 200-word chronological recount of events from a timeline and other source information. Unit 2 Students will be able to write a 200-word chronological recount of events from a graph that displays sequential information.
Report: the presentation of data or information that is essentially non-sequential	Unit 3 Students will be able to write a 250-word report describing non-sequential data from a data table. Unit 4 Students will be able to write a 250-word report describing non-sequential data from a line graph or bar graph. Unit 5 Students will be able to write a 250-word report describing non-sequential data from a pie graph or pictograph.
Explanation: the presentation of information with the orientation on means	Unit 6 Students will be able to write a 250-word explanation of the stages of a simple manufacturing process. Unit 7 Students will be able to write a 250-word explanation of an abstract process from a flow chart.
Discussion: a focus on the organization of data in relation to (possible) outcomes/conclusions/choices	Unit 8 Students will be able to write a 300-word contrastive evaluation of the solution to an environmental world problem. Unit 9 Students will be able to write a 300-word discussion of arguments for and against a response to a social problem. Unit 10 Students will be able to write a 300-word critical evaluation of a selected text.

Students will use a SOURCE PATH GOAL schematic structure for structuring the information content of a recount.

Gestalt structure does not refer to the organization of paragraphs and sentences (which relates to the next level of the model, that of discourse patterns), but rather to the overall organization of the content ideas of a text. For example, in a recount, the SOURCE or starting point of the SOURCE PATH GOAL schema may be realized by the introductory paragraph, or it may be realized by only the first sentence of the introductory paragraph. Activities relating to the gestalt aim could involve first examining the gestalt structure of a model text, and then planning the ideas organization for new tasks that require the writing of similar texts.

Thus, an aim to examine the general ideas organization in terms of the gestalt structure leads to a preliminary reading of of an input text for both comprehension and for understanding of the structuring of the content. This is the first step in deconstructing the input text. Understanding the schematic structure provides novice writers with a basis for the structuring of content ideas when writing similar kinds of texts, and thus is the first step in developing a framework for planning their own future writing of the target cognitive genre.

Discourse patterns

Following the gestalt aim, each unit will have a discourse aim, relating to the organization of the content in relation to paragraphs and sentences. Although the written discourse will be a representation of the content that is generally structured by the gestalt pattern, its physical appearance on the page in terms of sections and paragraphs may or may not mirror the parts of the gestalt. The discoursal aim, therefore, focuses on the organization of the actual written discourse. Again the aim can be expressed as a performative, such as in relation to the discussion cognitive genre:

Students will incorporate a 'Generalization Example' discourse pattern in writing the report.
Students will have practice in writing topic sentences and developing paragraphs appropriate to this discourse pattern and the type of content involved.

The discourse pattern aim would lead to the examination of the organization of the paragraph structure of the input text exemplifying the particular cognitive genre. Specifically, it may lead to a focus on the types of information in the introductory paragraph and its relationship with the following paragraphs. It may also involve examination of the signallers of larger sections within the discourse, such as words or phrases that introduce a contrasting viewpoint, or a move to a summary of viewpoints that are represented in the text. Again, like gestalt structure, deconstructing discourse patterns in model texts helps to provide a focus on the types of general procedural knowledge that novice writers need to acquire to be able to plan and carry out their own writing of similar types of texts.

Interpropositional relations

At the lower level of the syllabus, aims relating to interpropositional relations will lead to an examination of salient markers of cohesion and coherence in terms of their linguistic encodings. As proposed earlier, one general EAP syllabus unit would ideally have a linguistic focus on no more than two points of linguistic knowledge, and variant syllabus units based on the same cognitive genre will have different interpropositional (and linguistics) aims. In relation to report cognitive genres, the linguistic aims from the sample syllabus unit in the following section (see Table 5.2 following) are:

Amplification:
Students will have practice in using:
1. *restrictive relative clauses (adjectival);*
2. *object noun clauses.*

Simple Contrast:
Students will have practice in using syntactic and lexical markers of contrast.

When dealing with each of the linguistic features that encode the interpropositional relations, examples can be extracted from the model text of the syllabus unit and practised in tasks that have a discoursal focus. In realizing this type of syllabus, it is important that the linguistic focus (deriving from interpropositional relations) is connected to the deconstruction and reconstruction of texts of the same cognitive genre.

5.4 A general EAP syllabus unit based on the report cognitive genre

This section provides the outline of a possible syllabus unit based on report cognitive genre with a summary of the aims and content of the unit shown in Table 5.2 following. In the cognitive genre model, report has the aim of : 'the presentation of information that is essentially non-sequential'. Typically this type of writing accompanies the presentation of numerical data, such as in the 'results' section of a research-reporting article or in a chapter of a dissertation that reports quantitative research findings. Often this type of writing accompanies a visual representation of the data, such as in a graph, table or pictograph. As outlined in the previous section, the objectives of the unit are expressed in terms of an overall objective (which is essentially the rhetorical purpose of the cognitive genre) along with schematic, discoursal, interpropositional and lexical objectives.

Table 5.2: Sample general EAP syllabus unit

Aims	
Overall	Students will be able to write a 200-word report describing non-sequential data from a line graph, bar graph, pie graph or table.
Schematic	students will use a WHOLE-PART schematic structure for whole reports and an UP-DOWN schema for the body section of information reports.
Discoursal	Students will incorporate a Preview Details discourse pattern in writing the report. Students will have practice in writing topic sentences and developing paragraphs appropriate to this discourse pattern and the type of content data involved.
InterpropositionalRelations	Amplification: Students will have practice in using: 1. restrictive relative clauses (adjectival); 2. object noun clauses. Simple Contrast: Students will have practice in using syntactic and lexical markers of contrast.
Lexical	Students will review vocabulary related to statistics, data description and commentary.

(Bruce, 2005, p. 250)

As stated in the previous section, the cognitive model first provides the basis for the selection of authentic texts (usually segments of texts) that have a common core of features that are not necessarily centred around any disciplinary topic, features that can be deconstructed and analysed. Such deconstruction and analysis of the discourse features can initially be modelled to learner-writers. Following that, given the procedural knowledge, learner writers then perform their own discourse analysis on existing texts and undertake new text-writing tasks.

At the pre-writing stage, once the rhetorical aim and the type of target information of the text has been identified, awareness of the gestalt structure provides a learner-writer with a heuristic in the form of a general framework within which to plan the ideas structure of a text. In conformity with the pedagogic approach of not internalizing topic-specific realizations but applying them to learning (Widdowson, 1983, p. 90), the learner, after being introduced to the gestalt patterning, then practises content-planning of similar data reports in relation to other graphs, tables or pictographs that are used to convey information. Once the ideas organization has been identified, it is related to a textual plan based on the *Preview-Details* discourse pattern. These plans are then employed at a later text-construction stage.

Table 5.3 following presents an analysed part-text that could possibly serve as an input text for the syllabus unit (described in Table 5.2 previously). Following this proposed input text is a commentary on the analysis including suggestions as to how the analysed information could be included within the proposed syllabus unit.

Gestalt structure

The example text in Table 5.3 is a fairly prototypical example of the report cognitive genre. The text is concerned with presenting data that is non-sequential from an accompanying table and largely mirrors the gestalt structure, discourse pattern and interpropositional relations of the model.

In terms of the overall organization of ideas (pre-writing), the report cognitive genre model proposes that non-sequential data will be structured by a WHOLE-PART gestalt structure. This draws on the *image schema* (gestalt) concept of Johnson (1987) as a high-level organizer of knowledge. The conceptual idea of the WHOLE-PART gestalt is that the parts of something properly configured can make a whole (based on Lakoff, 1987, p. 273). In the case of the sample text in Table 5.3, the WHOLE section of the gestalt structure is a description of the survey, its purpose and its parameters. The PART section involves describing, in detail, the various findings from the survey.

In examining a corpus of parts of academic texts that used the report, it was found (see Chapter 4, Table 4.5) that where the content data of the PART section is quantifiable (as is the case of the data of the sample text in Table 5.3), an UP-DOWN gestalt is also used to organize hierarchically the data of the PART section. (UP-DOWN indicates a progression from big to small, more significant to less significant.) For example in the sample text of Table 5.3, the PART consists of:

- the largest group of graduates – those up to the age of 29;
- the next largest group – graduates over the age of 30;
- a smaller group – international students who are graduates.

Discourse pattern

The WHOLE-PART gestalt relates to the overall organization of the conceptual content of the report. When actually realized as written discourse, this gives rise to what Hoey (1983) refers to as a *General Particular* discourse pattern, and in particular the *Preview Details* variation of *General Particular* in which:

> [t]he detail member of the relation supplies information about the Preview member that would otherwise typically be placed as postmodi-

Table 5.3: Report cognitive genre – sample text

Gestalt Structure	*Discourse Pattern*		*Interpropositional Relations*
Whole	*Preview*	The average age of New Zealand university graduates is	
		increasing, indicating that greater numbers of older	
		students are enrolling while their younger counterparts	
		may be taking longer to complete their degrees.	
		This is one of a number of significant developments	
		revealed in the latest survey of university graduate des-	Amplification
		tinations carried out by the New Zealand Vice-	
		Chancellors' Committee. All 23,821 individuals (13,007	
		females, 10,814 males) who became eligible to graduate	
		from this country's seven universities during 1998 were	Amplification
		sent the survey questionnaire and 10,149 (42.6%)	
		responded. The survey findings are contained in a report	
		– *University Graduate Destinations 1999* – which was pub-	Amplification
		lished in December. An executive summary to the report	
		states that the average age of respondents is 29, an	Amplification
		increase of a year on the previous survey.	
	Details	Further, the average age of respondents with Bachelor/	Simple Contrast
Part		Bachelor with Honours degrees is 26, as opposed to 25 for	
Up		the previous survey. This is particularly significant as this	
		first-degree group constitutes 68.6% of the total survey	Reason Result
		population. The view that university graduates appear to	(inverted)
		be taking longer to complete their first degree is sug-	Amplification
		gested by a report table which shows that 65.1% of	Grounds
		Bachelor/Bachelor with Honours graduates are in the 18	Conclusion
		to 24-year age group, a decline on the previous survey	(inverted)
		where the equivalent proportion was 73.0%. There is a	
		corresponding increase in the proportion of these	Simple Contrast
		graduates in the 25 to 29 age band, which at 18.3%	
		represents a 5.9% increase on the previous survey.	
		The trend to life-long learning shows up in the report	
		in the number of graduates who are aged 40 years or	Amplification
		older. In the previous survey this group constituted 11.7%	Simple Contrast
		of all graduates but that proportion has now increased to	
		13.8%. The report details that graduates aged between 30	Amplification
		and 40 make up 16.6% of the population for the most	
		recent survey whereas the equivalent proportion from the	Simple Contrast
		previous survey was 15.1%. Of all respondents to the	Amplification
		survey, 55.8% are in full-time employment (1998, 58.2%)	Simple Contrast
		while 29.3% are undertaking further full-time study	
		(1998, 26.6%). It is important to note in this context that	Amplification
		many respondents report more than one destination, for	
		instance part-time employment and part-time study.	
		Those who report seeking full-time employment are not	
		necessarily unemployed as such. They could be working	Simple Contrast
		full-time in an interim position while seeking a position	
		more appropriate to their qualification.	
		Other significant findings in the report include a	
		decline in the number of International graduates (those	Amplification
		who require a permit to study in New Zealand). In 1997	
		these graduates totalled 1411 but in 1998 there were 1335	Simple Contrast
Down		International graduates from New Zealand universities	

(The New Zealand Vice-Chancellors' Committee Newsletter, 2000, p. 4) fication to the appropriate noun or as adjunct to the clause. (Hoey, 1983, p. 138)

This refers to the linguistic encoding of the relationship between the overall information of the introduction and more specific, detailed information in the body of the text. If the overall idea of the opening paragraph and the principal idea of any one of the details paragraphs were to be summarized in one sentence, the detail information would be likely to be encoded in terms of a paratactic or hypotactic structure, e.g.

In 1999, the New Zealand Universities' Vice-Chancellors' Committee carried out a survey of graduates that year which showed: (This showed:)

- *65% of Bachelors or Bachelors with Honours graduates are ...*
- *the percentages of older graduates has ...*
- *the number of international students graduating was . . .*

Interpropositional relations

The text segment analysed in Table 5.3 is typical of the report cognitive genre to the extent that it includes examples of Amplification, Simple Contrast, Reason-Result, and Grounds-Conclusion.

At the lower levels of textual organization, the interpropositional relations of the cognitive genre model provide the syllabus designer with focus areas for examining the internal cohesion (and, thereby, coherence) of the text. A range of language elements that realize the salient interpropositional relations are isolated and practised in relation to the sample unit of discourse, and in preparation for the writing of language texts. Table 5.4 following provides a description of the salient interpropositional relations that occur in the Table 3 report sample text.

Examples of each of the structures that relate to the salient interpropositional relations will be identified within the model text, analysed and practised.

Because the report cognitive genre draws on a range of interpropositional relations, it is possible to sequence more than one unit constructed around a report, with each unit focusing on one particular relation and a range of syntactical and lexical realizations of the particular relation.

Once the exemplar text of the particular cognitive genre has been deconstructed, analysed and its constituent parts practised, the final phase of the syllabus unit involves the creation of new examples of the same cognitive genre, using the procedural knowledge of the model that has been practised. Initially this could involve guided, joint constructions of new texts with a degree of assistance from the teacher leading to independent, individual text constructions that provide further opportunities for employing the procedural and linguistic knowledge that has been the particular focus of the syllabus unit.

Table 5.4: Examples of interpropositional relations from the sample text

Interpropositional Relation*	Description*	Examples/Linguistic features from the sample text (Table 5.3)
Amplification: term specification	One member of the relation amplifies the information in the other by providing a specific term as a substitute for a general one.	This is one of a number of significant developments revealed in the latest survey of university graduate destinations. (*restrictive and reduced relative clauses*)
predicate specification	One member of the relation amplifies the other by specifying the content of the semantic predicate. Direct or indirect reporting may be involved.	The report details that graduates aged between 30 and 40 make up 16.6% of the population for the most recent survey. (*noun clauses as the object of a sentence, reporting verbs and other types of reporting structures*)
Simple Contrast	This is a relation involving the comparison of two things, events or abstraction in terms of some particular in respect of which they are different.	Further, the average age of the respondents with Bachelor/Bachelor with Honours degrees is 26, as opposed to 25 for the previous survey. (*grammatical and lexical markers of contrast*)
Reason-Result	Here, the reason member (which very often follows the result member in English) gives a reason *why* a particular effect came or will come about.	This is particularly significant as this first-degree group constitutes 68.9% of the total survey population. (*markers of reason*)
Grounds Conclusion	Here, a deduction is drawn on the basis of some observation.	The view that university graduates appear to be taking longer to complete their first degree is suggested by a report which shows that 65.1% of Bachelor/Bachelor with Honours graduates are in the 18 to 24 age group. (*verbs signalling deductions*)

*Crombie, 1985, pp. 21, 26)

5.5 Conclusion

A writing syllabus that is based on the cognitive genre model meets many of the requirements of wide-angle, general EAP courses. It is top-down, not discipline-specific and focuses on the realizations of common types of rhetorical purpose and the related organizational structures of written discourse in order to provide the foundations for the future development of the learner's discourse competence in discipline-specific literacies (Lea and Street, 1998). The top-down character of the model provides for cycles of synthesis and analysis by means of a mediated task-based approach in which the schematic and linguistic elements of discourse are identified by analysis, practised and reconstituted. In relation to the selection of language for such courses, this type of syllabus provides a basis for the selection of authentic model texts and targeted linguistic selection including lexis, grammar and syntax that are realizations of local interpropositional relations. The syllabus is not linguistically driven, but provides a framework for detailed linguistic analysis and practice within a discoursal setting.

In the context of an article (that compares the discourse patterns employed in two different academic disciplines – plant biology and highway engineering – in relation to the writing of Masters dissertations in each of the two fields), Dudley-Evans (1993) claims that 'an approach to the teaching of academic writing that implies that there are common patterns of organisation that will always apply in all disciplines is, in my opinion, dangerously misleading' (p. 147). This claim is made on the grounds that 'the differences in the *social* [my emphasis] roles of writing in the two departments can be seen in the organisational patterns of the key section of the dissertation, that is, the discussion section' (1993, p. 146). Dudley-Evans' comments about whether the focus of writing instruction should be discipline-specific or general-purpose summarize a debate which has been ongoing among those who are concerned with the teaching of academic writing to non-native-speaker learners (Ferris, 2001, pp. 298, 300; Hyland, 2002b). Although it is certainly true that what are referred to here as social genres cannot provide a basis for a *common core* approach to the teaching of academic writing, the argument here is that what are referred to as *cognitive genres* can do so because cognitive genres draw on non-discipline-specific procedural knowledge. Furthermore, those social genres that occur in discipline-specific academic writing (such as essays, case studies, research articles and dissertations) are amenable to examination in terms of (a) the selection and use of cognitive genres, and (b) the effect of the selection of cognitive genres on the higher-level organizational elements of gestalt organization and discourse patterns, as well as on cognitive processes, semantic relations and, by extension, linguistic selection.

Leki (2000) emphasizes that future research related to second-language literacy needs to explore further the social context of writing, and she speculates that 'the next decade will bring about greater attention to the multiplicity and complexity of literacy acquisition, at least partly through more detailed, "thicker" descriptions of individual acquirers within specific contexts' (p. 108). As part of the 'multiplicity' and 'complexity' of context-specific social genres that have to be acquired and mastered, examination of social genres in terms of their selection and use of combinations of cognitive genres could provide a fruitful area of research that may help to uncover a little more of that complexity.

In Chapter 6 following, the concept of social genre (first introduced in Chapter 1) is revisited and expanded by presenting and considering the constituent knowledge areas that give rise to social genres, and considering ways in which novice writers may investigate these knowledge areas. The following chapter, Chapter 7, provides a discussion of integrating cognitive and social genre elements within the context of a unit of a postgraduate-level writing course.

Chapter 6: The scope of social genre knowledge

6.0 Introduction

In Chapter 1, a dual approach to the classification of texts was proposed involving the two related but different constructs of social genres and cognitive genres. The principal focus of previous chapters up to this point has been on cognitive genres as text-organizing structures that mediate between conventionalized social genres and the actual systems of language. However, in this chapter we now turn to consideration of social genres as classifiers of whole texts or conventionally recognized sections of texts, and how they inter-relate with cognitive genres. This chapter has two aims: the first is to discuss the types of knowledge used in the construction of social genres, and the second is to consider the social genre/cognitive genre relationship, particularly in terms of its application to the teaching of academic writing. The chapter is divided into two parts to realize these aims. The first part undertakes a discussion of a proposed approach to examining social genres and the types of knowledge that they draw upon. Part of this discussion involves suggestions of ways in which novice writers can deconstruct the social genres of their field of study. The second part of the chapter considers the inter-relationship of social and cognitive genre knowledge within the areas of: the creation of discourse, developing a discourse competence in learner writers, materials design, and pedagogy and assessment.

6.1 Towards a construct for social genres

In Chapter 1, drawing on the concept of *text genre* of Pilegaard and Frandsen (1996), *social* genres were defined as 'socially recognized constructs according to which whole texts are classified in terms of their overall social purpose'. Along with this definition, examples of social genres provided were: personal letters, novels and academic articles. The term social genre, as used here, refers to a text as an outcome or product as well as the *social actions* (Devitt, 2004; Miller, 1984) that surround the creation of the text. (Genre as social actions is the view of genre theorists working in the North American, 'New Rhetoric' tradition.) In the approach employed here, the forces that give rise to a genre as a disciplinary practice are considered along with their actual textual manifestations.

In Chapter 3, two pedagogic approaches to social genres were examined – the approach of the genre theorists influenced by systemic functional linguistics, and that of the English for Specific Purposes (ESP) movement. As a result of this review, it was concluded that both approaches to social genre involve relating the conventionally recognized, organizational stages of the content of a text to actual linguistic features of exemplar texts – this combination of content staging and linguistic features being seen as characterizing the particular genre to which the text belongs. In the case of the approach influenced by systemic-functional linguistics, the lexico-grammatical characteristics tend to be regarded as genre-defining, while in the ESP approach, genre is seen as a 'determinant of lexical choice' (Swales, 1990, pp. 41–2). However, the discussion of this issue in Chapter 2 points out that the research of Biber (1988, 1989) and Paltridge (1993a, 1997, 2002) suggests that social genres cannot be simply defined in terms of patterns for the staging of content (such as schematic structure or moves and steps) linked to linguistic features. On the basis of extensive corpus-based research, Biber (1989) emphasizes that (social) genres cannot be described in linguistic terms but are 'defined and distinguished on the basis of systematic, non-linguistic criteria' (p. 39). Paltridge (2002, pp. 74–6) provides a very clear illustration of this issue with his illustrative analyses of the genre of letters to the editor.

Despite a considerable volume of research that has examined social genres in terms of the frameworks proposed by these two approaches, a number of writers and theorists now appear to support the view that an adequate description of a social genre involves more than just a 'finely grained synchronic analysis of texts' (Luke, 1996, p. 333). Reflecting this developing view, Swales (1998), in contrast with his earlier (1990) textual approach, adopts a more ethnographic approach to examining social genres produced within one particular institution. As a further development in this trend of broadening the conceptual base of genre (both social and cognitive), Bhatia (2004) has presented a dual approach to genre knowledge and genre research involving a *textual perspective* and an *ethnographic perspective* (p. 163).

Thus, from the reviews presented in earlier chapters (particularly in Chapter 2) and subsequent studies by theorists investigating social genres, it seems that social genres cannot simply be conceptualized in terms of a simple schematic framework for the regular staging of the content within a category of texts (linked to linguistic features), although this knowledge may well provide part of the picture. Rather, drawing on theories and research relating to a number of aspects of discoursal knowledge, it is proposed here that a grounded understanding of the nature and operation of a social genre (such as a category of written texts in an academic setting) involves knowledge of:

- context – involving specialist knowledge of a field and its means of communication (Widdowson, 2004);
- epistemology – 'disciplinary assumptions about the nature of knowledge' (Lea and Street, 1998, p. 162);
- stance – involving issues of addressivity and audience, such as Hyland (2005) describes in terms of the use of *metadiscourse*;
- content schemata – the recognized staging of content in texts, such as *schematic structure* (Hasan, 1989) or systems of *moves* and *steps* (Swales, 1990);
- the use of cognitive genres to realize localized rhetorical purposes within extended texts in relation to a particular move, step or stage of schematic structure.

This chapter aims to provide a detailed discussion of knowledge that relates to social genres in terms of the five areas indicated by the bullet points above: context, epistemology, stance, content schemata and cognitive genres. The underlying idea here is that, in relation to pedagogy, developing understandings of and frameworks for genre knowledge (both social and cognitive genre knowledge) is useful in two areas of activity:

- it provides a heuristic for the analysis of further texts (of the same genre) within a discipline;
- it provides the means for writers to create their own texts within the same discipline, which requires a synthesis of socially constructed, cognitive and linguistic knowledge.

Thus, each of the following subsections that focuses on the different aspects of social genre knowledge consists of two parts. The first part is a description of a particular aspect of (social genre) knowledge. This knowledge description is then followed by a small set of enquiry questions that are offered to assist novice writers in unpacking the particular aspect of genre knowledge in texts from the field in which they are engaged. The overall aim of different sets of enquiry questions (for each of the areas of knowledge) is to encourage novice writers to become discourse analysts in their own field by developing heuristic processes and frameworks to analyse the discourses of their subject areas. The enquiry questions require student writers to examine the discourse of their field from both an ethnographic and a textual perspective (Bhatia, 2004, p. 163). The ethnographic focus requires the novice writers to engage with experienced writers (of their field) and with textual tasks that involve the gathering and analysing of texts from their field. Both types of activity are important for developing understandings of the different types of knowledge needed to construct their own texts competently. Chapter 7 following revisits these enquiry questions within the context of a course unit that focuses on a part-genre, providing further discussion about the types of activities a novice writer can undertake to analyse and understand the genres of his/her particular discipline.

6.2 Social genres and context

In the two approaches to social genre reviewed in Chapter 2, it is the regularized, purposive use of a certain type of text within a certain context that is a fundamental characteristic of the operation of a (social) genre. Eggins and Martin (1997), in describing the approach to genre influenced by systemic functional linguistics, say that 'different genres are different ways of using language to achieve different culturally established tasks' (p. 236). In relation to the ESP approach, Swales asserts that the prime determinant for locating texts within a genre category is 'shared communicative purpose' (1990, p. 46). However, Swales later modifies his views on the role of communicative purpose to suggest that the identification of a genre is achieved by investigating the operation of texts within a context in terms of 'sets of communicative purposes' (Askehave and Swales, 2001, p. 210). Both approaches then attempt to establish stronger or weaker claims of deterministic connections between the context-specific staging of content and linguistic features.

In the approach taken here, it is accepted that the use of conventionalized textual forms to achieve certain types of communication within a discipline (social genres) is indeed influenced by a range of text-external factors that relate to context, but that the influence of these factors on linguistic choice (with the exception of technical or discipline-specific vocabulary) is mediated and not deterministic in the way suggested by these two approaches to social genre. In relation to creating social genres, context here is taken to be an overarching idea, which includes: knowledge of a discipline (and its lexis), its epistemology, schematic structure (for staging of content in texts), and the use of cognitive genres.

In a recent review of what is actually meant by context, Widdowson (2004) proposes that, in relation to creating discourse, context may usefully be defined as a 'schematic construct' involving both 'intralinguistic and extralinguistic factors', and that establishing a context is 'a discourse process engaged in by the participants themselves in the online achievement of pragmatic meaning' (p. 54). Widdowson proposes that 'there is no understanding of texts as a semantic process, separate from, and prior to, a pragmatic evaluation, which brings context into play' (2004, p. 35). Similarly, when relating context and (social) genre, Bhatia (2004) states that '[l]inguistic forms do carry specific generic values, but the only way one can assign the right generic value to any linguistic feature of the genre is by reference to text-external factors' (p. 119). Thus, in relation to categories of whole academic texts that belong to a particular social genre category, achieving what Widdowson calls a pragmatic evaluation would appear to draw upon both specialist knowledge of the field to which the text relates (the extralinguistic factors) and specialist knowledge of the forms of communication and the particular lexis of a field (the intralinguistic factors).

Thus, it is suggested that novice writers who are in the process of acquiring an insider understanding of a genre of their discipline should first consider the contextual features which endow the genre with specialist meanings for members of the particular discipline. They need to consider the features of the genre that make it coded in relation to the specific types of knowledge and forms of communication of their field.

For novice writers, some possible enquiry questions to interrogate the context of disciplinary genre may include:

1. *What is the main or overall reason why expert readers who work in the subject area would want to read this type of text?*
2. *What (if any) are the types of specialized knowledge necessary to fully understand the content information of the text?*
3. *What specialist vocabulary is necessary for processing and understanding this text?*

In developing discipline-specific answers to Question 1, novice writers could examine texts from their field (that relate to a particular genre) and form some hypotheses about reader purpose. They could then test their hypotheses by surveying academics or professionals who both read and contribute to the literature of the field. In relation to commonly named genres, such as research articles, students in the same class, after having investigated texts from their respective disciplines, could then compare their findings.

In responding to Questions 2 and 3, novice writers could evaluate the extent and influence of discipline-specific lexis in shaping the texts of the genres of their field. To achieve this, students can analyse their sample of texts for discipline-specific types of knowledge and lexical items.

6.3 Social genres and epistemology

An important aspect of contextual knowledge that influences the nature and form of written and spoken genres is epistemological viewpoint – reflected in how experts working in a particular field view, use and report knowledge. This is supported by those working in the *academic literacies movement* (see Lea and Street, 1998, 1999; Jones, Turner and Street, 1999; Stierer, 2000), who hold that a significant aspect of disciplinary differences in academic writing can be accounted for in terms of differences of epistemology. For example, Lea and Street (1998) suggest that 'what makes a piece of writing appropriate [within a particular discipline] has more to do with issues of epistemology than with surface features of form ... [and] underlying, often disciplinary assumptions about the nature of knowledge affect the meaning given to the terms *structure* and *argument*' (p. 162). This is also supported by Hyland (2000), who accounts for interdisciplinary differences in academic writing in terms of epistemological view and the role of the disciplinary community and its practices, including: '[discipline] community-recognised ways of adopting a position and expressing stance ... As a result, the rhetorical conventions of each text will reflect something of the epistemological and social assumptions of the author's disciplinary culture' (p. 11).

However, at this point it must be stated that understanding the epistemology of a particular discipline cannot be achieved exclusively as an atomized learning task in a writing class. To understand the epistemological viewpoints of academics working in a particular subject area – how they view knowledge – a necessary co-condition is to have an understanding of how they *create* knowledge. The research or knowledge-creating paradigms employed within a discipline (including the approaches, styles and methods of research – see Cohen, Manion and Morrison, 2000) clearly shape its research activities and give rise to the epistemological viewpoints that emerge in the writing of the discipline. Understanding the consequences of this knowledge-creating paradigm cannot, therefore, occur in a vacuum. It seems that a crucial aspect of the problems faced by apprentice student writers in the academy is that information about knowledge-creating within their particular fields is to some extent withheld until students reach postgraduate level. At this level they are more likely to encounter primary reports of research in their field and to undertake research methods courses and carry out research projects themselves. On the other hand, undergraduates tend to encounter research in secondary reports, such as in textbooks, and are less likely to be required to perform research themselves. As a result of this delayed exposure to the knowledge-creating paradigms of their fields, apprentice writers (both native- and non-native-speakers) are 'feeling their way' or following their instincts in the early years of their academic writing until the full picture of their chosen discipline or field emerges later in their studies. Therefore, tasks that relate to the epistemology of a particular field need to examine knowledge creating and how it is carried out in the field and subsequently how it influences knowledge reporting.

An illustration of the influence of epistemology that may be meaningful to more advanced postgraduate writers is provided by Berkenkotter and Hucken (1995) in relation to a trend in reporting biology research. They suggest that central to the focus on professional reading and presenting research findings in biology journals is the need to satisfy the search for interesting new information, especially in relation to topics or areas of enquiry that are closely related to scientists' own research interests. They see biologists as being engaged essentially in positivist research, gathering facts and, on the basis of these facts, making inferences. The literature of biology is mostly presented in the form of 'the four-part experimental article comprising of Introduction, Materials and Methods, Results, and Discussion sections, each of which serves to codify scientific activity into a coherent narrative of inductive discovery' (1995, p. 46). However, Berkenkotter and Hucken propose that articles in biology journals have, over time, modified their genre conventions to emphasize the news or newness aspect of the content of an article. To achieve this, they say that the articles that they examined spanning a 25-year period showed evidence of the gradual use of longer and more informative titles. Also, abstracts have become longer and more informative, and introductions contain more detailed summaries of the final results of the research. There is evidence of more use of informative subheadings to guide the reader to the 'newsworthy' parts of the article, and greater use of visual aids such as graphs, line drawings, schematic diagrams and photographs. Methods sections have become smaller and less prominent, in some cases being relocated to the end of the article in smaller type. They suggest that in the field of biology:

> The scientific journal article is gradually taking on text features that are analogous to those of news reports, and in so doing is conforming more to the actual reading practices of working scientists. In an increasingly competitive world where they are deluged with information, scientists must read quickly and efficiently. A top-down layout of important information facilitates a selective reading process. (Berkenkotter and Hucken, 1995, p. 39)

If epistemology is considered to be a major influence on the creation of discourse within specific academic disciplines, the task, therefore, for the novice writer is to gain a clear understanding of the (epistemological) viewpoints that underpin and influence the writing of their field. It seems that for many students, developing an understanding of this type of knowledge (particularly in terms of its influence on writing) has to be done over time during the beginner writer's engagement with their particular discipline, since this type of information is not always overtly taught. For example, when the methodologies of knowledge-creating are taught (such as in research methods courses), it is often the case that no direct links are made between such methodologies and the forms of knowledge-reporting of the particular field.

Thus, enquiry questions for novice writers seeking to uncover the epistemologies of the social genres of their particular discipline could include:

1. *How is new knowledge created in this subject area?*
2. *How do experts in this subject area view and use knowledge?*

3. *How is new knowledge reported in this subject area?*
4. *What makes a piece of writing of this type (of a certain disciplinary genre) appropriate?*

Knowing the answers to Questions 1 and 2 is central to the issue of novice writers gaining an understanding of the discourse of their particular subject area. To answer these questions, students need to begin to understand (even in a rudimentary way) the research or knowledge-creating paradigms of their field, and the underlying assumptions of those paradigms. They need to be able to identify the research methods that are most commonly used in their field, and to consider the assumptions underlying such methods and how those assumptions influence the communication of knowledge. To answer these questions, students could examine recent issues of the research-reporting journals of their field, and identify the research methods employed. They then need to consider the ontological and epistemological assumptions that underpin these methods.

Finding answers to Questions 3 and 4 involves considering how the particular aspects of knowledge creating and knowledge use (that they uncover when researching Questions 1 and 2) are mirrored in the written discourse of their field.

6.4 Social genres and writer stance

The overall context and epistemological viewpoint of a particular field, in turn, both exert an influence on the *stance* or *standpoint* that a writer adopts in communicating with his/her readers. Bakhtin (1986), in describing his notions of addressing a hearer through spoken language, states that 'from the very beginning, the utterance is constructed while taking into account possible responsive reactions' (p. 94). Bakhtin proposes that writing, like speaking, is also *dialogic* – a dialogue between the writer and the reader and that writing is constructed with the expectations and knowledge of the reader in mind. Like Bakhtin, Hyland (2005) also emphasizes that writing is dialogic 'because it [writing] presupposes and responds to an active audience, and because it makes links to other texts' (p. 88). Thus, in academic written genres created within specific disciplines, this awareness of a particular expert reader audience (involving the writer's and readers' shared knowledge of the activities and extant literature of the field) causes the writer to take into account a range of disciplinary contextual factors in order to create an acceptable realization of a genre. These contextual factors will involve the already mentioned areas of disciplinary content knowledge and epistemological viewpoint.

In the establishment of the appropriateness of the stance of a writer,

Hyland (2005) ascribes an important role to a category of linguistic features that he terms *metadiscourse.* He defines metadiscourse as 'the means by which propositional content is made coherent, intelligible and persuasive to a particular audience' (p. 39). Hyland presents a model for interpersonal metadiscourse features involving *interactive* and *interactional* resources (see Table 6.1 following).

Table 6.1: Hyland's interpersonal model of metadiscourse[1]

Category	Function	Examples
Interactive	*Help guide the reader through the text*	*Resources*
Transitions	express relations between main clauses	in addition; but; thus; and
Frame markers	refer to discourse acts, sequences or stages	finally; to conclude; my purpose is
Endophoric markers	refer to information in other parts of the text	noted above; see Fig; in Section 2
Evidentials	refer to information from other texts	according to X; Z states ...
Code glosses	elaborate propositional meanings	namely; e.g.; such as; in other words
Interactional	*Involve the reader in the text*	*Resources*
Hedges	withhold commitment and open dialogue	might; perhaps; possible; about
Boosters	emphasize certainty or close dialogue	in fact; definitely; it is clear that
Attitude markers	express writer's attitude to proposition	unfortunately; I agree; surprisingly
Self-mentions	explicit reference to author(s)	I; we; my; me; our
Engagement markers	explicitly build relationship with reader	Consider; note; you can see

(Hyland, 2005, p. 49)

Hyland 's model provides a useful approach to systematizing the linguistic resources employed by writers in establishing their stance in respect of their subject-matter and their engagement with their audience. However, in relating Hyland's metadiscourse model to the genre framework presented here (of cognitive/social genres), it is proposed that a focus on the linguistic devices in Hyland's model referred to as 'transitions' are more appropriately placed within the cognitive genre category if one also uses the cognitive genre model to analyse texts. In this way, transition markers are more comprehensively accounted for by Crombie's (1985) interpropositional relations, which, as Crombie herself says, involve both semantic and pragmatic considerations. It is important to note that in academic discourse such so-called 'transitions' cannot always be reduced to lists of grammatical signallers, since many discourse signallers, such as those of reason, means, purpose and chronology, are effected lexically (such as by the use of verbs, particles, nouns or nominal groups) or simply through the juxtaposition of propositional content to achieve certain meaning relationships.

Enquiry questions seeking to examine writers' stance in a particular disciplinary social genre could be:

1. *What parts of the text specifically guide or speak directly to the reader?*

[1] Page 49, Hyland, K. (2005). *Metadiscourse.* London: Continuum. Table reproduced by kind permission of Continuum International Publishing Group.

2. *What are the features of language that show the writer's attitude towards the text and its content?*
3. *What are the features of the language of the text that are trying to influence or persuade the reader in some way?*
4. *What features of language in the text are regularly used to connect ideas?*

Analysing the metadiscoursal elements of a genre involves also applying the enquiry questions to a set of texts from a particular genre. If a class of novice writers has a common sample of texts, their findings could lead to a particular focus on salient categories of metadiscourse markers from Hyland's model, for example *hedges* and *boosters*, if they are particularly in evidence in the commonly examined sample of texts. Another approach would be to present and exemplify the categories of Hyland's model first and then get novice writers (from different disciplines) to examine a particular genre from their own discipline for frequently occurring metadiscoursal features. The class could then undertake some discussion of the differences in the ways that different disciplines address their audience through their different use of metadiscoursal language.

6.5 Social genres and the staging of content

As already discussed in this chapter, it is regularities in common communicative forms used to achieve a particular communicative purpose (or set of communicative purposes) that are seen as central to defining social genres, such as for pedagogic purposes (Hyon, 1996). In particular, regularities in the staging of the content in certain types of texts were regarded as central to defining genres in the two approaches reviewed in Chapter 2. There, the review included the approaches to genre influenced by systemic functional linguistics and the approach of the English for Specific Purposes movement. In both approaches, attempts are made to relate the conventionally recognized, organizational stages of the content of a social genre to actual linguistic features of exemplar texts. The systemic functional approach to content staging is in terms of a schematic structure, and the ESP approach is in terms of moves and steps. Research that offers patterns for academic texts tends to largely follow the ESP approach to genre. Aspects of academic articles that report research have been quite intensively analysed, for example: Introductions (Gledhill, 2000; Samraj, 2002; Swales, 1990, 1998; Thompson, 1994), Results sections (Brett 1994; Williams 1999) and Discussion sections (Hopkins and Dudley-Evans, 1988; Jacoby, Leech and Holte, 1995; Peng, 1987; Swales and Feak, 1994). Other academic or professional genres that have been analysed in terms of a move and step structure include: science dissertations (Dudley-Evans, 1986, 1989; Hopkins and Dudley-Evans, 1988); popularized medical texts (Nwogu, 1991); job application, sales promotion letters and legal case studies (Bhatia, 1993); and grant proposals for European Union research grants (Connor and Mauranen, 1999).

Thus in approaching the teaching of a disciplinary genre or part genre (such as the Discussion section in research articles), the issue remains of how to employ a schematic or move and step structure (if one has been offered). In relation to learner writers, the key issue is that whenever this type of schema is presented, it should be able to provide a heuristic for the analysis of further texts (of the same genre) within a discipline, but a heuristic that should contain sufficiently general higher-level organizing structures to allow for a range of inter-textual differences within a single genre (see Paltridge, 1993a, 1997). While it is useful to provide learners with a content schema for a particular genre that relates to their learning, it is important to ask learner-writers to use it critically to examine a sample of texts, perhaps using some variation of the research questions offered below:

1. *What patterns of content staging have already been proposed for this category of texts? OR: What pattern appears to be used to organize the content of the texts?*
2. *To what extent does this pattern apply to the content of your sample of texts?*
3. *Which of your texts vary from the pattern, and in what ways?*
4. *Where variation from the pattern occurs, what are the possible 'local' reasons for this in the variant texts?*

The questions related to content staging could be applied to a sample of texts belonging to a particular genre category. However, when considering content staging for the purpose of student analyses of texts, it may be more useful to focus on higher-level, more general content structures (such as moves), rather than more specific content schemata (such as steps), since with an increased specificity of focus will come greater variation of organizational choices and, thus, greater difficulty in establishing generalizable patterns. Furthermore, if the focus is on a part-genre that relates to a relatively homogeneous purpose (for example Methods and Results sections in research articles), it may actually be more useful to examine the organizational structure of the text in terms of the use of a predominant cognitive genre than to focus on lower-level content schemata. Thus, it is important to separate the idea of content schemata from ideas of general rhetorical structure as the latter may be more usefully considered in relation to the use of cognitive genres; this issue is discussed in the following section.

6.6 Social genres and cognitive genres

In Chapter 1, it was stated that whole texts realizing different social genres (such as scientific reports) typically combine and frame a range of cognitive genres. However, some whole texts, such as for example instruction manuals, may be associated with a single cognitive genre by virtue of the fact that they have a single rhetorical purpose. (Cognitive genres, as stated previously, are stretches of text that realize a single rhetorical purpose.) In Chapter 4, a model for cognitive genres was proposed as a way of describing prototypical discourse patterns that result from types of rhetorical purpose that commonly occur in academic prose. Because the type of classification used here is described in terms of a *prototype effect* (see Rosch, 1978), actual textual realizations of the model may be graded on a continuum from examples that are highly prototypical (that show all of the characteristics of the model) to examples that are moderately or only slightly prototypical, displaying the use of fewer features of the model.

Much has been discussed and proposed in previous chapters relating to the internal structure and types of knowledge employed by cognitive genres, therefore there is no intention to revisit those issues here. (The last section of Chapter 5 provides an extensive discussion of the teaching of cognitive genre knowledge within the context of writing instruction.) At this point, however, the issue is considering the use of cognitive genres within larger social genres – usually whole texts. In larger, complex whole texts, such as research reports or dissertations, it can be helpful to examine parts of texts or conventionalized sections of texts in terms of their use of one or more cognitive genres. For example, students can examine a range of Methods sections in research reports in their field. This can provide a basis for examining organization of content, coherence and cohesion, and linguistic features of sections of texts that conventionally draw on certain types of cognitive genres.

Research questions relating to uncovering and examining cognitive genre knowledge within a particular social genre could be:

1. *What sections of the text aim to communicate a certain type of knowledge (e.g. describing data, describing a process, presenting contrastive arguments)?*
2. *How is the communication of this type of knowledge organized?*
3. *What types of language characterize the writing of this section of the text?*

6.7 Summary of social genre knowledge

As has been mentioned in earlier chapters, Biber (1989), on the basis of his findings from extensive corpus-based research, proposes that genres (social genres) 'are defined and distinguished on the basis of systematic non-linguistic criteria, and they are valid in those terms' (Biber, 1989, p. 39). Therefore, the approach outlined in this chapter has involved describing social genre knowledge in terms of the 'non-linguistic criteria' of context, epistemology, stance, schematic structure and use of cognitive genres (see the summary in Table 6.2 following). The suggested questions for learners in relation to each of these knowledge areas provide a heuristic to deconstruct social genre knowledge in a particular context.

Table 6.2: Framework for analysing social genres

	Types of knowledge	Research questions relating to
Overall context	Specialized subject knowledge relating to concepts and activities; parallel specialized linguistic knowledge such as technical vocabulary	Overall reader motivations for text engagement, specialized subject knowledge and specialized subject vocabulary
Epistemology	Disciplinary approaches to and values concerning knowledge, its formation and use	The creation, use and reporting of knowledge within a particular discipline
Writer stance	Attitudinal features of language related to addressing and appealing to the audience	Use of language in terms of interactive and interactional metadiscourse
Schematic Structure	Conventionalized patterns for staging certain types of content	Schematic structure or moves and steps
Use of cognitive genres	Cognitive patterns of textual organization	Cognitive genre knowledge

Compared with this rather open-ended approach to social genres, the previously outlined approach for operationalizing cognitive genres (in Chapters 4 and 5) appears to be more prescriptive in terms of the combinations of organizational knowledge proposed in the cognitive genre model. However, in reality prescriptiveness in relation to the cognitive genre model may be more apparent than real. It is important to remember that the models are proposed as prototypes which, in their actual realizations, may closely resemble or be relatively different from the model. As such, cognitive genres need to be viewed as organizational tendencies rather than as fixed, immutable forms. The purpose in putting forward a model for their prototypical forms is to provide the curriculum designer, materials writer and teacher with frameworks around which they can (a) deconstruct authentic textual segments in systematic ways and (b) organize materials, tasks and pedagogy that have a discoursal focus involving cycles of learning that begin and end with texts. In the social genre/cognitive genre proposal, it is seen that cognitive genres are discoursal building blocks; they operate as a type of default framework that is retrieved to organize the representation of certain types of knowledge within larger, socially organized texts.

A concern often expressed by some educators in relation to genre-based approaches to writing instruction is that they are too prescriptive and do not allow for the development of an individual authorial voice. In addressing this charge of excessive prescriptiveness, it is proposed here that highly competent writers have a well-developed understanding of the prototypical patterns that relate to each of these types of knowledge. Being familiar with such prototypes, experienced writers are able to integrate and exploit them in creative ways to achieve their individualized authorial purposes, appropriate to context and audience.

6.8 Relating social and cognitive genre knowledge to EAP writing courses

Chapter 5 presents a proposal for the incorporation of cognitive genres into the design of general EAP writing courses, such as courses for students preparing for studies in higher education. The following section continues this discussion of genre and pedagogy by including consideration of social genre constructs and the relative roles of social genre and cognitive genre knowledge in academic writing, and approaches to their incorporation into writing course design. Specifically, this discussion examines the inter-relationship of social and cognitive genre knowledge in:

- the creation of discourse;
- developing a discourse competence in learner writers;
- materials design and pedagogy;
- assessment.

Chapter 7, following, further develops the issues raised in this discussion by presenting and providing commentary on a unit from a postgraduate level EAP course that is designed around social and cognitive genre knowledge.

Social and cognitive genre knowledge and the creation of discourse

Since the previous section of this chapter has outlined an approach to describing and deconstructing social genre knowledge and Chapters 4 and 5 presented an approach to cognitive genre knowledge, it is now salient to consider the relative relationship between the two types of genre knowledge in the creation of extended written discourse. Both social genre and cognitive genre knowledge, two sides of the same coin in fact, are critical to the competent and appropriate construction of written academic discourse. However, if the two constructs are to be integrated in genre-based pedagogy, it is important to understand their inter-relationship.

The first key issue in the relative relationship of social genre and cognitive genre knowledge is attempting to understand the level of consciousness at which each type of knowledge appears to operate. At the beginning of Chapter 4, it was proposed that cognitive genre knowledge is procedural knowledge, which among native-speakers of a language is not (generally fully) engaged at a conscious level when encoding extra-linguistic content into extended written discourse in an organized and principled way. Native speakers tend to acquire this type of knowledge from their long experience and continuously developing knowledge of prior texts, and it is usually the case that their formal literacy education has contained little overt focus on the teaching of these forms of discourse structure. Nevertheless, given the requirement to represent certain types of knowledge in written discourse, it seems that native speakers of English will employ, almost in an automatic way, the types of procedural knowledge described in the cognitive genre model. Furthermore, the second study reported in Chapter 4 also appears to indicate that (given a particular rhetorical purpose) more proficient writers will adhere more closely to the features of the model than less proficient or less experienced writers.

Social genre knowledge, on the other hand, tends to be more consciously developed as part of a writer's induction into the genres and conventions of a specific professional, occupational or academic field. For example, the incorporation of communication studies courses into many business studies degrees attests to this more overt focus on social genre knowledge. Business letters, newsletters, memos, evaluative reports and promotional articles are genres that are often the objects of focus in such courses. In relation to genres that are used to report research findings, referencing systems and publication manuals, such as that of the American Psychological Association, and the editorial guidelines for submitters of articles to academic journals provide an increasingly prescriptive framework for the structuring of knowledge, textual organization and aspects of presentation. Similarly, the number of advice books on structuring academic assignment writing (especially dissertation writing) is also constantly increasing. In the case of social genres, it seems that the level of prescriptiveness and the rigidity of this specification seem to be increasing rather than becoming more fluid. Swales (2004), in examining research genres, describes this process in terms of an increasing *generification* in academic and professional communications. As an example, he discusses how academic institutions are increasingly using conventionalized documents to carry out administrative and institutional procedures, such as the increasingly formalized hiring procedures of American universities involving such genres as 'position requests, five-year plans' (p. 5). He notes that transacting within an increasingly 'generified' environment involves the knowledge of networks of related genres: '[t]hese processes of generification require us to pay much closer attention to the operation of genre *systems* (or hierarchies, sets, networks or other kinds of collectivity' (p. 5). However, another aspect of the use of social genres that Bhatia (2004) and others also point to is a tendency for genre mixing and blending leading to the hybrid nature of many social genres, although Bhatia emphasizes that there appear to be definite constraints on the extent to which writers are able to do this.

In relation to their respective influences on linguistic choices, the view taken here is that both social and cognitive genres influence the writer's choice of language, but they influence this choice in different areas. Social genre influences are exerted in relation to context-specific choices, such as the use of the specialized technical vocabulary (relating to a particular field) and the choices of metatextual language relating to the area of writer stance, addressivity and audience. Furthermore, in terms of discourse organization, social genre knowledge relates to the conventionalized structuring of certain genres, such as the Introduction, Methods, Results and Discussion sections of the research article. On the other hand, use of cognitive genres relates to an aim to represent a certain type of knowledge (usually within one section or sub-section of a larger text) and influences linguistic choice in terms of the signalling of local discourse organization and lower-level, more specific aspects of coherence and cohesion. At this more detailed level of discourse organization, it is seen that Crombie's (1985) interpropositional relations provide a more comprehensive approach to identifying the types of lower-level relationships within discourse, and their encodings in language, than the conventional lists of so-called transition markers that are found in many writing textbooks.

Therefore, for designers of academic writing courses that use a whole-text or genre-based approach, the fundamental design choices are twofold. First, the designer has to decide which genre constructs (social or cognitive) should be selected as the basic unit around which the courses are designed. Secondly, the designer has to decide which type of genre knowledge should be included within the course and how it should be arranged. In selecting and arranging genre knowledge within a syllabus or programme, learner language proficiency and learner need will be central guiding factors. These factors are discussed in the following section.

Relating social and cognitive genre knowledge to developing a discourse competence

Deconstructing learner need in relation to academic skills, genre knowledge and the development of a discourse competence must be considered in relation to the stage or level of academic education at which a writing course is located. For adult second-language learners, the teaching of academic writing is an integral part of most English for Academic Purposes (EAP) courses. EAP is essentially taught at three levels: pre-university (often called pre-sessional), in-sessional (undergraduate level) and, increasingly, postgraduate level. At each level, because of different types of learner competence and need, the focus of the course and the discourse requirements will be different.

As stated previously, pre-sessional EAP courses, such as senior secondary school and foundation courses, cannot have a single discipline-specific focus. For example, they cannot, in the first instance, organize pedagogic units around the texts and practices of a single discipline, such as business, humanities or science – unless of course it is known that all of the students within a class group will be studying in only one of those areas. Ensuring the development of a discourse competence through courses at this level, therefore, needs to be achieved in two ways. The first involves making a principled approach to dealing with the more general features of discourse structure that occur in academic texts, and the second involves having a *multi-context* and a *multi-textual* dimension when focusing on discourse structures in different types of EAP course tasks. In the first instance, this can be achieved by approaching discourse knowledge in terms of cognitive genres. (This issue was discussed and developed in considerable detail in Chapter 5.) However, such courses also need to anticipate the future challenge of disciplinary difference in the creation of texts, such as the students' future assignment tasks in various subject or disciplinary areas. The cognitive genre knowledge presented at this level then needs to be taken and used in a multi-context, multi-textual phase of a learning unit, where it is used to examine and deconstruct discourse from a variety of subject areas or disciplines. For example, having presented and practised the discussion cognitive genre, the course could then go on to examine how this structure is used in critique. As part of this focus on critique and using the discussion cognitive genre framework, students could be asked to analyse critique texts from a number of different disciplines and compare their similarities and differences.

The second level of EAP relates to in-sessional EAP courses – such as first- or second-year undergraduate courses. These courses usually aim to further address the language needs (and usually, most urgently, the writing needs) of students at this level. These students will usually have gained entry to higher education on the basis of an overall average IELTS (academic module) score of 6.0 or a TOEFL average score of 550 or higher. However, it is important to realize the limitations of these proficiency levels. The 2005 IELTS Handbook recommends an overall average IELTS score of 6.0 as probably being a suitable entry level to linguistically less demanding vocational training courses, such as in the areas of 'animal husbandry, catering and fire services' (p. 5). Therefore, students entering undergraduate university courses with this proficiency level will still have a range of general language problems.

Of these language needs, usually the most pressing at this level is the need to develop a discourse competence in relation to the writing skill. Students need to have the means to interrogate, deconstruct and appropriately respond to the discourse requirements of undergraduate assignment genres, which, as a number of researchers point out, is not a straightforward issue. As Ann Johns (1997) says, these assignment genres are difficult to pin down and 'are loosely and almost casually named' (p. 23). Furthermore, according to the academic literacies movement (Lea and Street, 1998), assignment genres vary greatly in their expectations because of the particular epistemologies of the different subject areas. This has been illustrated by a number of studies, such as Samraj's (2004) comparison of the genre of research reports from two disciplines. Thus, undergraduate tasks need to be subject to both cognitive and social genre analysis.

In relation to cognitive genre constructs, assignment task prompts need to be interrogated in terms of the scope of types of discourse that they require. For example, students often encounter imperatives like *describe, account for, explain, evaluate, provide a commentary*. Cognitive genre knowledge can be useful in this regard, and can also provide a focused basis for asking clarification questions of a course instructor about their expectations of the assignment tasks. In addition to understanding the cognitive genre requirements of undergraduate assignment tasks, students at this level also need to begin to understand the types of identity, orientation and metadiscourse that their particular discipline requires. To this end, social genre analysis of texts of the discipline can help to answer questions in this area. The issues related to deconstructing the requirements and expectations of disciplinary assignments are multiplied in the case of undergraduates who are taking broad-based degrees and facing courses and assignments in a variety of subject areas.

The third level of EAP of postgraduate courses will usually tend to focus on the written and spoken genres of reporting research and in some ways this area of EAP is the one that is informed by the deepest research base. Genres that are commonly used by researchers and are likely to be included within such courses are: the dissertation, the research article, the conference abstract and the conference paper. Other genres that have been investigated in this area are the reprint request, the grant proposal, and the book review. At this level, the EAP courses may still be interdisciplinary (taken by students from different subject areas), therefore there is a need to constantly alert students to disciplinary differences in the research-reporting genres. Chapter 7 following addresses the issues of incorporating social genre, cognitive genre and linguistic knowledge at this level by presenting and discussing one unit from a postgraduate-level EAP writing course.

Social and cognitive genre knowledge in materials design and pedagogy

In Chapter 5, it was proposed that cognitive genres provide a reasonable basis around which to design a general EAP course, such as a syllabus unit for a pre-sessional writing class. The argument is that cognitive genres provide a basis for cycles of analysis and synthesis in conformity with implementing Widdowson's (1990, pp. 146, 136) approach to Wilkins' (1976) *analytic* syllabus and Skehan's (1996) proposal for incorporating cycles of analysis and synthesis within a modified task-based syllabus.

In approaching the design and delivery of courses that deal with both social and cognitive genres, it is suggested that essentially the same principles apply, and that a top-down approach to examining discourse is used. The framework for analysing social genre presented in Table 6.1 provides the hierarchy of knowledge around which analysis can be organized. The cognitive genre model can be used to examine the lower-level organizational units of the target genre. The cycle of learning proposed for genre-based syllabus design can be based on the approach of Hammond, Burns, Joyce, Brosnan and Gerot (1992). The staging of an EAP syllabus unit incorporating both social genre and cognitive genre knowledge is outlined under the following points:

- A small sample of authentic texts are selected to be used as a basis for examining the social and cognitive elements of the genre.
- The syllabus unit follows top-down principles (social genre before cognitive genre). The enquiry questions proposed in the first section of this chapter could provide a basis for tasks used to deconstruct the different types of social genre knowledge.
- The linguistic features that relate to the more socially constructed elements of the genre are dealt with at the social genre analysis stages. These could include elements such as technical lexis and metadiscoursal features (with the possible exceptions of transition markers, which it is proposed here are dealt with more adequately as part of the cognitive genre focus).
- The sample of texts is examined for its use of cognitive genres.
- One (or more) of the most commonly occurring cognitive genres is deconstructed in terms of its higher-level organizational features, and as a framework around which to practise salient features of grammar and syntax.
- The cognitive genre framework provides opportunities for writing practice, whereby students construct new texts with an intensive focus on organizational and linguistic features.

Chapter 7 following then provides an example of a syllabus unit that incorporates this approach to the staging of both the social and cognitive genre elements.

Social genre and cognitive genre knowledge and writing assessment

The EAP teacher, like teachers in other areas of ELT, needs to have a developed knowledge of approaches to assessing the four language skills, particularly in relation to writing tasks. In particular, it would seem to be important to have knowledge of approaches to assessing the productive skills of speaking and writing in terms of *performance-based* assessment. McNamara (2000, p. 135) defines performance tests as 'a language test in which assessment is carried out in a context where the candidate is involved in an act of communication'. Thus, for example, a performance test of writing would involve the writing of an extended piece of discourse in response to a task involving a specific communicative or rhetorical purpose relating to a context of communication. Using this type of approach to formative assessment of writing (and speaking) can be a vehicle for providing ongoing and cumulative feedback to (EAP) students. In effect, there are two broad ways of scoring writing tasks:

- holistic scoring – assigning a single score for a whole text;
- analytical scoring – assigning a separate score for each of a number of aspects of a task.

In relation to the writing skill, for example, it is proposed here that this type of feedback can be best provided by using *analytical* approaches to assessing the writing skill, along with the use of portfolio assessment. While the advantages of holistic scoring are that it can be done quickly and it can be more easily multi-marked to check reliability, analytical scoring requires the scorers to look at a range of aspects of the writer's performance. Its disadvantages are that it is time-consuming and there are potential problems with the validity of the composite score in measuring the tasks. For example, the weightings within the composite score may reflect the course designer's preferences, but not provide an adequate overall operationalization of the task. The composite score, therefore, needs to relate to an overall theory of discourse in order to overcome these potential problems. However, in terms of providing systematic and ongoing cumulative feedback to writers, analytical scoring can provide types of developmental feedback that are not offered by holistic scoring methods.

To overcome the difficulty of operationalizing a writing task, it is suggested that the social and cognitive genre frameworks proposed here can provide a basis for the analytical assessment of EAP writing. Table 6.3 following provides an example of a cognitive genre assessment feedback form which may be used in the analytical assessment of the report cognitive genre, in this case in relation to describing non-sequential data from a graph or table.

Implementing an analytical marking guide requires discussion, practice and agreement among multiple markers. For example, where the marking

Table 6.3: Analytical marking guide for report cognitive genre

Task Response		
Introduction	The topic is explained in the student's words (1 point)	
	One element of the legend is described (1 point) All the elements of the legend or the axes are clearly described (2 points)	
Ideas	Topic group or paragraph ideas: one point for each significant paragraph idea relevant to the data (maximum 3 points)	
	The development of ideas: one point for additional data or development of the ideas above (maximum 3 points)	
Conclusion	One point for a summary of the data (maximum 1 point)	
Discourse Organization		
Discourse Pattern	Clear evidence of a General-Particular pattern in the staging of the discourse (1 point)	
Organization of paragraph topics	Some evidence of selection and ordering of the paragraph topic ideas (1 point) Selection and ordering of topic ideas follow a clear organizing principle (2 points)	
Paragraph Development	Two points for each paragraph which contains a topic sentence and some clear development of the topic showing inter-sentential cohesion and coherence (maximum 6 points)	
Sentence level cohesion	Half a point for each syntactically correct, appropriately used cohesive device used within sentences (maximum 4 points)	
Language		
Vocabulary	(1 point) limited, insufficient range for the topic (2 points) adequate range for the concepts of the topic (3 points) competent and controlled use of vocabulary	
Sentence Structure	(1 point) weak, little subject/verb agreement, many errors (2 points) considerable number of errors but some sound sentences (3 points) more developed sentences, fewer errors (4 points) competent and controlled	

guide in Table 6.3 is used, there needs to be considerable discussion and negotiated agreement on the awarding of points in the 'Discourse Organization' section, in particular in relation to the sections for

'Paragraph Development' and 'Sentence level cohesion'. An approach that has been followed (in the context where I teach) has been:

- for paragraph development, two points are awarded for highly developed paragraphs in the body of the essay (but not the introduction or the concluding paragraphs), and no single points are given;
- for cohesion, half a point is awarded for the first instance of every correctly used cohesive device used *at sentence level.*

Thus it is possible for writers to gain the full four points for cohesion at sentence level, while receiving no points for paragraph development because of the awkwardness and lack of discoursal cohesion and coherence resulting from the arrangement of the same sentences within paragraphs. In this way, a problem faced by many teachers of academic writing is addressed, that is, the teacher is able to give credit for the writer's ability to create sentences that are, on their own, internally cohesive, but able at the same time to indicate to the writer that there is a lack of cohesion and coherence in the way that the same sentences come together at a discoursal level.

With holistic feedback, the assessment criteria are not transparent, while analytical marking provides more transparent criteria and feedback that can provide the basis for consulting with novice writers. In this way, formative feedback arising from analytical marking (such as the marking guide in Table 6.3) can help to provide a basis for the redrafting of course work and the development of a portfolio of writing during an EAP course.

6.9 Conclusion

This chapter first proposed some of the central types of knowledge drawn upon in the construction of social genres and then provided a brief overview of the social genre/cognitive genre relationship, particularly in terms of its application to the teaching of academic writing. Chapter 7 continues to examine the relationship between cognitive genre and social genre knowledge, particularly in relation to the teaching of academic writing.

Chapter 7: Teaching genre knowledge in an advanced writing course

7.0 Introduction

This chapter illustrates the inter-relationship between social and cognitive genre constructs in the context of one unit of a postgraduate level writing course taught by the writer. This is a non-compulsory course for students who are engaged in research and dissertation writing and who are non-native speakers of English. Students taking the course are studying and performing research in a variety of disciplines. The unit topics of the course are shown in Table 7.1 following.

Table 7.1 Postgraduate level writing course: unit topics

1. Key issues in academic writing: audience, purpose, organization
2. Reporting research: overview and introductions
3. Reporting research: Introductions and the literature review
4. Reporting research: Methods (1)
5. Reporting research: Methods (2)
6. Reporting research: Results
7. Reporting research: Discussions
8. Reporting research: titles, abstracts, acknowledgements and reference lists; conference abstracts
9. Summary, paraphrase and plagiarism
10. Critique
11. Conference posters and conference presentations
12. Grammar review

While much of the course appears to be organized in terms of the conventional IMRD (Introduction, Methods, Results, Discussion) structure that is commonly used in research-reporting genres, such as research articles in academic journals and dissertations, the activities and processes of the course aim to encourage course participants to consider disciplinary differences that occur in the reporting of research. IMRD, therefore, provides a general prototype or baseline against which disciplinary differences and preferences in research reporting can be identified and analysed. As part of this process, course participants then examine the research-reporting genres employed in their own particular disciplines. Thus, the IMRD structure represents a point of departure to examine and practise academic writing as it relates to the research-reporting genres of the writers' own particular disciplines. The rationale for its use in the course is that developing an understanding of the characteristics of research reporting in one's own particular discipline is heightened by awareness of the range of differences that can occur in the research-reporting genres of a range of different disciplines.

7.1 The sample course unit: syllabus

This chapter examines the sixth unit of the course as an example of integrating social and cognitive genre constructs within a course unit that focuses on writing instruction. This unit deals with reporting the results or findings of research, such as in the Results sections in journal articles or dissertations. Table 7.2 following shows an outline of the syllabus for this particular unit of the course.

This syllabus unit is selected for this chapter because the cognitive genre focus that it includes (Report) is the same as that for the sample unit from a general EAP writing course presented in Chapter 5. The reason for selecting a course unit at a more advanced level that includes a focus on the same cognitive genre is to build on the general EAP proposal in Chapter 5 (that focuses more exclusively on cognitive genre knowledge) by illustrating the integration of cognitive and social genre knowledge.

While the organization of this course unit is around the social and cognitive genre constructs presented in earlier chapters, the unit also aims to include the findings of extant research that has examined Results sections in research-reporting texts. The social genre section (the first part of the course unit) includes a focus on research that has examined Results sections in terms of existing social genre approaches. The studies that are included in this section are those of Brett (1994) and Williams (1999). In the second part of the course unit, which involves the cognitive genre focus, some research evidence is provided as a basis for the selection of the content of this section. This is the report of a small-scale study (carried out by the writer) that investigated the use of Report cognitive genres in a small sample of Results sections.

Implementing the dual focus on social and cognitive genre knowledge in this course unit follows the general principle of Johns (1997) that genre knowledge, rather than being prescriptive by offering formulaic patterns or ready-made knowledge to novice writers, should involve providing the tools to investigate the genres of their particular field. Thus, a central aim of the approach here is to encourage novice writers to become discourse analysts as they uncover the attitudes, expectations, conventions and textual patterns that relate to writing within their particular discipline. The genre theory and research drawn upon in this unit are, therefore, used to frame and guide the students' own investigations.

In the sample course unit, it is proposed that novice writers, as discourse analysts, examine the genres of their discipline in terms of the two areas that Bhatia (2004) identifies – *ethnographic* and *textual*. As the ethnographic part of their analysis, novice writers gather information from experienced writers or other non-textual sources in their own fields. In their textual analyses, they examine a sample of Result-reporting texts from their field in terms of the range of the categories of social genre knowledge discussed in Chapter 6, and in terms of one particular cognitive genre (Report) from the model presented in Chapters 4 and 5. To assess this unit of the course, the students' analyses and outcome writing tasks are gathered together as a portfolio that is developed and refined incrementally during the course and submitted at the end of the course.

7.2 Results sections: social genre focus

The approach to analysing Results sections employs the top-down approach of Chapter 6, with the different elements of social genre knowledge discussed in the sub-sections following. Each sub-section considers activities that may be useful in unpacking the enquiry questions that were first presented in Chapter 6, these questions relating to the knowledge areas of context, epistemology, writer stance, schematic structure and, in the second part of the chapter, cognitive genres. Where relevant, existing research on Results sections will also be referred to; this mainly occurs in the third and fourth sections, which consider the writer stance and the schematic organization of Results sections.

In Table 7.2, the activities of the course unit that relate to the social genre focus are briefly summarized as:

- examine the functions and importance of Results sections in reporting research – including their relationship with the other sections of IMRD structure;
- develop enquiry questions relating to the key areas of Results sections and investigate the context and epistemology of Results sections (in a particular discipline);
- review existing research on Results sections and their functions (Brett 1994) and highlight language that relates to these social functions;
- carry out joint textual analyses of three Results sections in terms of Brett's (1994) categories and Swales and Feak's categories (1994, 2nd edn, p. 116), and decide which seems to work best;
- carry out individual analysis of Results sections examining two Results sections from their own discipline using one of the two approaches (used in the joint analyses).

In the following sub-sections, each of these activities is described in more detail following the approach to examining social genres proposed in Chapter 6 and using the learner enquiry questions that were first

Table 7.2: Unit 6 syllabus: reporting Results in research

Aims: Social genre and disciplinary		**Activities**
Contextual and epistemological *Schematic and metatextual*	Students will understand the discoursal functions and rhetorical features of Result sections of research articles/dissertations. These will include: • functional relationship of Results sections to other parts of IMRD structure; • reporting, mextatextual and commentary functions of Reports sections; • integrating graphic data – referring to and highlighting language; • language related to strength of claim/modality.	Students will: • examine the functions and importance of Results sections in reporting research, including their relationship with the other sections of IMRD structure; • develop enquiry questions relating to the key areas of Results sections and investigate the extra-textual context and epistemology of Results sections (relating to a particular discipline); • review existing research on Results sections and their functions (Brett 1994; Williams 1999) and identify features of language that relate to these functions; • carry out joint textual analyses of three Results sections in terms of Brett's (1994) categories and Swales and Feak's categories (1994, 2nd edn, p. 116) and decide which seems to work best; • carry out individual analysis of Results sections, examining two Results sections from their own discipline using one of the two approaches (used in the joint analyses).
Aims: Cognitive genre and linguistic		**Activities**
Overall *Gestalt structure* *Discoursal* *Interpropositional Relations* *Lexical*	Students will be able to write a 200-word data report describing non-sequential data from a line graph, bar graph, pie graph or table. Students will use a WHOLE-PART schematic structure for whole reports and an UP-DOWN schema for the body section of information reports. Students will incorporate a *Preview Details* discourse pattern in writing an information report. Students will have practice in writing topic sentences and developing paragraphs appropriate to this type of writing and the type of content data involved. *Amplification*: Students will focus on the structures of: 1. restrictive and reduced relative clauses (adjectival); 2. object-noun clauses; 3. article use to show specificity. *Simple Contrast:* Students will examine the use of syntactic and lexical markers of contrast. Students will review vocabulary related to statistics and data commentary.	Students will: • consider a guided analysis of one of the three sample Results sections (already examined in the social genre analysis) in terms of the higher-level features of Report cognitive genre – schematic, discourse pattern; • analyse the other two sample texts for occurrences of these higher-level Report cognitive genre features; • analyse the language of the sample Results sections in terms of the use of the definite article as a cohesive device used to indicate specificity, and the specifying structures of restrictive (dependent) and reduced relative clauses, adjectival phrases and object-noun clauses; • perform linguistic analysis and practice tasks; • carry out a joint construction of Report cognitive genre text involving data; • carry out an individual construction of a similar data-reporting text.

presented in that chapter. Essentially the two strands of the genre investigation involve first an ethnographic focus, where novice writers (the students on the course) interview experienced writers in their field, and secondly a textual examination of a sample of Results sections. It is proposed that preparation for the two aspects of the investigation will proceed by students initially developing a schedule of interview questions (from the four areas of social genre knowledge) and by selecting a sample of Results section texts from their particular discipline. Students first carry out the interviews and other extra-textual investigations (using the questions from the four areas of social genre knowledge presented in Chapter 6), and subsequently use their findings as a basis for carrying out the textual investigations. In the explanations of each of these activities that follow, the actual pedagogic order (ethnographic followed by textual analysis) is not followed, but rather the discussion is organized around the four areas of social genre knowledge with their related enquiry questions, as presented in Chapter 6. Following these explanations, the chapter then turns to the cognitive genre focus in relation to Results sections.

The context and purpose of Results sections

In Chapter 6, the possible questions for learner analysis relating to the context and purpose of a social genre were stated:

- *What is the main or overall reason for readers within a particular field wanting to read this type of text?*
- *What (if any) are the types of specialized knowledge necessary to fully understand the content information of this type of text?*
- *What context-specific vocabulary is necessary for processing and understanding this type of text?*

Inducting novice writers into the part genre of Results sections begins with the issue of context. This involves some initial teacher input, such as reviewing the generally accepted functional relationships and roles of Results sections within the IMRD structure in research-reporting texts. Learners are then introduced to the enquiry questions relating to context, and guided towards gathering a sample of four or five Results sections from their own particular disciplines for future textual analysis. For this textual analysis, the students are required to select articles from peer-reviewed journals in their own fields.

In relation to context, the 'ethnographic' or human investigation involves novice writers asking the first two enquiry questions of more experienced writers in the particular discipline as to their expectations of Results sections in their discipline. ('Experienced' here is taken to mean writers who have achieved more than one peer-reviewed publication.) This type of investigation needs to involve gathering and comparing the views of more than one informant in order to develop a balanced view of the field. (Thus, students from the same field each interview a different informant.) Students then try to identify similarities and differences in the informants' views in order to gain an overview or synthesis of ideas from their discipline. Students from the same discipline also then compare their interview information with students from other disciplines in order to identify similarities and differences of approaches to Results sections.

The textual stage of the investigation of context and purpose begins with the novice writers initially examining their sample of texts in terms of their conformity to the findings gleaned from the interview questions relating to context.

Epistemology and Results sections

In Chapter 6, possible questions for learner analysis relating to the epistemology of social genres were listed:

- *How is new knowledge created in this subject area?*
- *How do experts in this subject area view and use knowledge?*
- *How is new knowledge (such as research results/findings) reported in this subject area?*
- *What makes a piece of writing of this type appropriate?*

Trying to uncover the epistemology of a discipline and its influence on writing (in relation to Results sections) involves both ethnographic and textual research activities by novice writers. Yet, as was emphasized in Chapter 6, developing this type of knowledge generally requires a lengthy period of engagement with a particular field, its research activities, processes and research-reporting genres. Nevertheless, the questions above relating to epistemology can lead to some useful consciousness-raising that may help to sharpen the novice writer's awareness of this type of knowledge, and help them consider the influence of such knowledge on research-writing.

In relation to uncovering the epistemology of a particular discipline, the first two questions are really underlying questions that novice writers need to constantly keep before them in developing their understanding of their field. Systematic answers to these two questions come from their gradual development of an in-depth understanding of the approaches, styles and methods of research in the field – this may come partly from a research methods course as well as reading, carrying out and reporting research over a period of time. It is suggested that students begin by considering the first two questions and then write a summary of their current understanding of knowledge-creation in their field. They then apply this summary to their textual analysis, and consider how they see this as being reflected in the Results sections that they are analysing.

The third and fourth questions are used in the ethnographic investigation. Informants are asked how results or findings are reported and what makes this type of writing appropriate within their particular discipline. Again the novice writer needs to gather the views of several informants and try to synthesize their views for common features and areas of agreement. They then compare their informants' views with their currently held view, which they have written in the initial summaries.

Addressivity and audience in Results sections

Research questions seeking to examine writers' stance in a particular disciplinary social genre could be:

- *What parts of the text specifically guide or speak directly to the reader?*
- *What are the features of language that show the writer's attitude towards the text and its content?*
- *What are the features of the language of the text that are trying to influence or persuade the reader in some way?*

Writer stance stems from context and epistemology but is encoded within the discourse, and investigating writer stance relates to the textual aspects of the novice writer's discourse analysis. The types of language that relate to writer stance are sometimes referred to as *metadiscourse,* and the discussion of this in Chapter 6 points to Hyland's (2005, p. 49) model for metadiscourse.

In dealing with writer stance and related language in Results sections, the students examine examples of the types of language that Hyland identifies as metadiscourse in the guided analysis of selected texts. First, as an example of research that examines one aspect of metadiscourse, students examine the study of Brett (1994), who examined the Results sections from 20 sociology research articles employing what he calls three *communicative categories,* one of which he termed *metatextual,* which he says 'defines parts of the text which refer to the data or to other written sections; it is text about the text ... guiding the reader to other parts of the writing' (p. 52). In the sample of sociology examples that he examined, Brett sees what he calls 'metatextual' statements as a recurring pattern in Results sections – something that is addressed in the next section. After examining Brett's earlier approach, students then examine Hyland's model for actual linguistic features of metadiscourse, and specifically the interactional aspects of metadiscourse. This is then exemplified by guided analysis of one or two Results sections to identify their particular use of features of interactional metadiscourse. Students then use this approach to examine their own sample of texts, in order to begin to develop an understanding of writer stance and the use of related metadiscoursal language.

Content schemata and Results sections

Research questions seeking to examine content schemata in particular disciplinary social genres could be:

- *To what extent does this pattern apply to the content of your sample of texts?*

- *Which of your texts vary from the pattern and in what ways?*
- *Where variation from the structure occurs, what are the 'local' reasons for this in the variant texts?*

Carrying out this part of the learner research depends on the types of existing analyses of the genres that have been offered in current research. The teacher, therefore, needs to be familiar with any existing research on the target genre of the learners in order to guide them through this section. If it is the case that no schematic structure or move and step structure has been offered for a particular genre (and this is quite possible), it is useful to look for organizational patterns for the staging of content within their sample of texts, and then pool ideas with students working in the same subject area. Within a novice writer group comprising students from different disciplines, it may be possible to compare findings among disciplines.

In the case of Results sections (like Methods sections), existing research has generally not proposed an organizational structure for the staging of content (such as the CARS move structure that has been proposed for Introductions – see Swales, 1990, p. 141); however, there is in the literature some discussion about the types of information that may or may not be included in Results sections. In published pedagogic materials, Swales and Feak (1994, 2nd edn) discuss this issue of including commentary in Results sections. They say:

> It is traditionally said that the Results section of a RP should simply report the data that has been collected; that is, it should focus exclusively on the 'actual' results. (p. 234)

At this stage in the unit, it is appropriate to review existing research on Results sections (Brett, 1994; Williams 1999) including the increasing role of graphic data (Berkenkotter and Hucken, 1995). Swales and Feak (1994, p. 233) point to corpus research (Thompson, 1993, who examined 20 biochemistry papers) which shows the types of interpretative or commentary statements that can be found in the Results sections of some research. This research has to be treated with caution because of the smallness of the sample (only 20 papers) and the fact that it relates to only one discipline – biochemistry. Also, as noted in the previous section on writer stance, Brett (1994) examined the results sections from 20 sociology research articles employing what he calls three *communicative categories*: *metatextual, presentation* and *comment.* Brett's definitions of parts of Results sections include the following:

> *[M]etatextual* defines parts of the text which refer to the data or to other written sections; it is text about the text ... guiding the reader to other parts of the writing ... *presentation* categories are those which objectively

> and impersonally report, present, or highlight the results or the ways in which they were obtained ... *comment* categories are those in which authors offer their own interpretation of, or comment and opinion about, the results already presented, building up on the presentation categories. (p. 52)

Brett claims that the organizational categories he identifies are cyclical, the most frequent pattern being *pointer* (metatextual) followed by *statement of finding* (presentation), and *substantiation of the finding* (comment). He describes each of the three communicative categories in terms of their linguistic features. In another study, Williams (1999) analysed eight medical research articles using a modified version of Brett's communicative categories. While Williams found Brett's model to be 'an adequate basic model for the rhetorical categories of Results sections for interdisciplinary genre analysis' (p. 362), he observed that the cyclical patterning proposed by Brett for sociology articles was less common in biomedical articles, where the Results section tended to be presented in a more linear way. He therefore suggests that both the type of research (approach, style, method) and the subject-matter influence organization, which may be either *chronological* or *hierarchical.* The problem, however, with both of these studies is that they were only examining Results sections from two disciplines or subject areas – those of sociology and medicine. Furthermore, their analyses of Results sections is descriptive in terms of content categories, rather than structural in terms of internal textual organization.

Following a review of the research on Results sections, course participants undertake guided, joint analyses of several Results sections. First, the class jointly examines two or three pre-selected Results sections in terms of Brett's (1994) categories and Swales and Feak's categories (Swales and Feak, 1994, 2nd edn, p. 116) and then present their views in a discussion about which approach seems to work best. Students then perform the same analysis on the staging of content within their sample texts from their particular discipline and report their findings.

7.3 Results sections: cognitive genre focus

This section consists of two parts. The first outlines a small study that provides the basis for the selection of the cognitive genre focus in the Results section course unit. The second part outlines the pedagogic focus of Unit 6 on cognitive genre knowledge, the activities related to this focus, and their staging.

Analysis of cognitive genres within a sample of Results sections

Introduction

Existing genre analyses (see Brett, 1994; Williams, 1999) propose that Results sections can involve different functional purposes:

- presenting data;
- commenting on or explaining data;
- guiding the reader (metatextual information).

Therefore it seems likely that, in terms of discoursal resources, Results sections will draw upon more than one cognitive genre. However, in this small study, it is proposed that the main cognitive genre employed in Results sections will be Report – the presentation of non-sequential data (see Chapter 4, Table 4.5), which relates to the first of these three types of functional purpose, that of presenting data. Thus Results sections will tend to consistently exhibit many of the features of this cognitive genre structure. In order to investigate this hypothesis relating to the use of cognitive genres in Results sections, a small-scale genre study was carried out in which a sample of Results sections was analysed.

Methods

To select the texts for the sample, academics in one university (in New Zealand) were asked to name the three or four journals in their field to which they most frequently referred, and Results sections from articles published in the year 1999 were selected from the nominated journals. The criteria for the inclusion of a Results section in the sample was that the article from which it was drawn must report an actual research investigation and conform largely to the IMRD (Introduction, Method, Results, Discussion) structure in reporting the research. Results sections were included from the following subject areas:

Table 7.3 Results sections study

Subject	Number of Results sections
Applied Linguistics	2
Education	2
Management	2
Sociology	2
Psychology	2
	10 (total)

The small sample consists of 1,764 words. (The reference list for the sample is shown in Appendix 5.) The Results sections were scanned into plain text files and analysed in two ways: first they were rater analysed in relation to the features of the model for cognitive genres, and secondly using corpus software Oxford WordSmith Tools 4.0 (Scott, 2004). This involved developing a word-list for the sample and performing concordance searches of frequently occurring cohesive devices.

The rater analysis

As the rater, the writer analysed the sample of 10 texts for the occurrence of stretches of discourse that conformed to features of the cognitive genres proposed in the model (Chapter 4, Table 4.5). Analyses of the three levels of knowledge (gestalt structure, discourse patterns and interpropositional relations) were handwritten on each script. This study did not attempt to grade the *degree of conformity* to the model in the analysis of the texts. The benchmark for classification used was: where stretches of text appeared to conform *mainly* to the features of a particular cognitive genre, they were classified in terms of that category.

The corpus analysis

The purpose of the corpus analysis was to provide empirical data to compare with the findings of the rater analysis. Specifically, a comparison was made between the analysis of interpropositional relations and the corpus findings. Using Oxford WordSmith Tools 4.0 (Scott, 2004), a word-list was generated for the sample of Results sections and the most frequently occurring function words (that related to cohesion) were identified. Concordance searches were performed on the salient function words, including scrutiny of the contexts in which they occurred. The frequencies and particular uses of these words were then compared with the rater analysis of interpropositional relations in the whole sample.

Findings: the rater analysis

Using the cognitive genre model as a basis for examining the corpus, Results sections were found to consist of a range of textual resources in terms of the cognitive genre model, but most were found to make some use of the report cognitive genre. This variety of textual resources appears to support the earlier research referred to that proposed Results sections will have a variety of functions, including presenting data, commenting on data, and guiding the reader through linguistic and non-linguistic information such as tables or graphs. Table 7.4 following shows the use of cognitive genres in the sample of Results sections.

The analysis of the sample showed that a salient interpropositional relation was what Crombie calls Amplification, which comprised 23% of the total number of interpropositional relations identified in the sample of 10 texts. (The cognitive genre model proposes that Amplification is a frequent relation in both report and recount cognitive genres.) Table 7.5 following provides an explanation of the Amplification relation.

Table 7.4: The use of cognitive genres in Results sections

Texts	Cognitive Genres
1	Report (4)
2	Report (4)
3	Report (1)
4	Report (1), Explanation (3)
5	Explanation (4)
6	Report (1), Discussion (1)
7	Report (1)
8	Recount (1), Report (2), Discussion (1), Explanation (1)
9	Report (3)
10	Report (1)

The number in parentheses shows number of occurrences of a cognitive genre within a Results section.

Table 7.5: Defining the amplification relation

Interpropositional Relation	Description	Examples: Language features from the corpus
Amplification:	'This relation involves explicit or implicit repetition of the propositional content of one member of the relation in the other member, together with a non-contrastive addition to that propositional content' (Crombie, 1985, p. 26).	'The figures broadly support the informal characterization that softer disciplines tend to employ more citations . . .' (Text 1) *(restrictive and reduced relative clauses)* 'The data from the three groups of learners reveals that the Imperfect was used across all lexical classes.' (Text 2) *(noun clauses as the object of a sentence, reporting verbs and other types of reporting structures)*

Findings: the corpus analysis

The rater analysis showed that subordinate clause structures using 'that' as a cohesive device were important in this type of writing. To provide further data to support the rater analysis, a corpus analysis was performed on the same sample. The software used was Oxford WordSmith Tools 4.0 (Scott, 2004). Table 7.6 following presents data about the first 20 words from the word-list and shows a relatively high frequency of occurrences of 'that' in the sample.

Concordance searches of the 79 occurrences of 'that' found that 38 introduced object noun clauses, 37 introduced relative clauses, and only four occurrences of 'that' were not conjunctions. Clearly these findings

Table 7.6: Results corpus wordlist

Item	Total number	No of texts occurred in
the	642	10
of	380	10
and	263	10
in	243	9
to	181	10
a	140	10
for	126	10
were	104	10
with	82	10
that	79	10
was	74	10
as	72	10
by	65	9
two	53	9
table	49	10
is	47	7
per	45	3
their	45	8
cent	43	3

suggest that these structures are important in this type of writing and should be included in any linguistic focus in relation to Results sections.

Discussion

This small preliminary genre study can only be considered indicative because of the smallness of the sample. But the rater analysis indicates, as suggested by earlier reviewed research, that Results sections use a range of discoursal resources to fulfil different types of rhetorical purpose. However, the central purpose appears to be that of the presentation of data or information, which is borne out by the regular use of report cognitive genre in all ten texts of the sample. This use of report appears to be supported by the high frequency of cohesive elements that are central to report cognitive genre. Therefore, on the basis of these findings it is proposed that for the purposes of a pedagogic focus on discoursal knowledge (such as operationalized here by the cognitive genre model) report cognitive genre is a salient discoursal structure to select for such a focus. Such a focus could relate to the analysis and creation of texts that focus on the representation of data and, in particular, numerical data.

The teaching focus on cognitive genres in Results sections

In Chapter 6, the proposed student enquiry questions relating to uncovering and examining cognitive genre knowledge within a particular social genre were:

- *What are the different micro-level communicative aims of sections of this text?*
- *How is information or argument structured in relation to these aims?*
- *Are there patterns or types of writing which relate to these aims?*

In the social genre focus on schematic structure, it was discovered that extant research on Results sections points to the three functions of Results sections: metatextual segments that guide the reader (called 'pointers' by Brett, 1994), the presentation of data or findings, and explanations of aspects of the findings. The proportions of these types of textual segments appear to vary according to disciplines, but generally it seems that segments of text concerned with the actual presentation of findings tend to occupy the largest part of the Results sections. Clearly the nature of the data reported in Results sections will vary widely between quantitative and qualitative research, yet usually at this point in the research reporting there is an attempt to present findings or results in a compact and principled way for the reader. On the basis of the small study reported in the previous section, it is proposed that in many research articles the presentation of data can be the communicative aim for this part of the Results section, and that this local communicative purpose is often realized by the text segments that realize the features of report cognitive genre.

The syllabus relating to the cognitive genre focus in Unit 6 of the course (Table 7.2) outlines the learner activities that are part of the cognitive genre focus in the unit. Following a top-down approach, students will:

- consider a guided analysis of one of the three sample Results sections (already examined in the social genre analysis) in terms of the higher-level features of report cognitive genre – schematic, discourse pattern;
- analyse the other two sample texts for occurrences of these higher-level report features;
- analyse the language of the sample Results sections in terms of the uses of the definite article as a cohesive device used to indicate specificity, and the specifying structures of restrictive (dependent) and reduced relative clauses, adjectival phrases and object noun clauses;
- perform linguistic analysis and practice tasks;
- carry out a joint construction of report cognitive genre text involving data;

- carry out an individual construction of a similar data-reporting text.

These activities are outlined in further detail in the following sub-sections.

Teacher-guided analysis of a text

This involves identifying a segment of text in one of the three Results sections that is a realization of report cognitive genre. This text segment is isolated, and students are first asked to read it intensively and answer the following questions about the staging of the content:

- *What overall information about the research is included in the introduction?*
- *What are the topics of the subsequent paragraphs?*
- *What rule could you make about information that should be included in the opening section of a section of texts that presents data?*
- *What is the organizing principle for information in the body section of a data presentation section?*

Feedback and discussion of these preparatory questions leads to the presentation of an analysis of the text segment in terms of the three knowledge areas of the cognitive genre. These include the gestalt structure of ideas represented within the text (whole-part, up-down), the discourse pattern of the written text (preview details), and the principal cohesive structures, being those related to the most frequently occurring interpropositional relations. (The study in the previous section identifies these as dependent clause structures, and to this will be added a related focus on definite article use as a cohesive device.)

Student analysis of sample texts

Students then analyse the other two sample texts that have been previously encountered during the social genre analysis for features of the report cognitive genre model. They identify any stretch of text that conforms to the report cognitive genre structure, and the extent to which the textual segment exemplifies the features of the model. They also note the overall amount of the text in each of the two Results sections that is structured by report cognitive genre.

A linguistic focus on cohesive devices

The main cohesive features that promote coherence, as exemplified in the initial sample report text, are then examined more intensively. The small study of Results sections reported in the previous section revealed Crombie's Amplification relation to be a frequent, lower-level organizational device in report texts, and in Results sections where the discourse uses this cognitive genre. Thus the role of hypotactic structures, such as dependent and reduced relative clauses and object noun clauses, are examined as cohesive devices. Also in conjunction with these structures, it seems to be salient to examine the role of the definite article as a central cohesive device for this particular cognitive genre. The following functions of the definite article have been found to provide a useful basis to examine article use in textual segments structured by report cognitive genre:

- Previous mention, e.g. *a questionnaire was employed to gather preliminary data. The questionnaire consisted of ...*
- Uniqueness, only one of its kind, e.g. *the most significant finding...*
- Defined by another noun:
  before the noun, e.g. *the survey findings ...*
  after the noun, joined by 'of/of the', e.g. *the findings of the survey ...*
- Defined by a phrase, e.g. *the responses from the initial sample group indicated ...*
- Defined by a relative clause, e.g. *the responses that emerged from the initial questions indicated ...*

Linguistic analysis and practice tasks

Students then work through practice tasks designed to increase their awareness and accuracy of use of the target cohesive devices. Where possible, such tasks are designed to have a discoursal focus, such as using a cloze or textual format so that the coherence role of the device within discourse is not lost; it is important that the language feature is seen as part of a functioning, operational whole rather than a discrete piece of linguistic knowledge. (Focusing on linguistic features at this stage in the genre-based teaching and learning cycle is intended to support this idea.)

Examination of actual Results sections for occurrences of report

After practice tasks that focus on the salient linguistic features that contribute to cohesion, the other two example Results sections are analysed by students for their use of these linguistic features.

Joint construction of a report

Students are then provided with data that occurs within a hypothetical Results section and jointly construct a small data-reporting text that employs the gestalt structure, discourse pattern and cohesive features of the report cognitive genre. This task can be carried out in a number of ways, such as a partial cloze completion or manipulating the sentence and paragraph elements of a model text response that have been printed on card, cut up and scrambled. Whatever format is selected for the joint construction task should promote a joint discussion and a joint focus on the features of the cognitive genre model.

Individual construction of a report

The final outcome task of the cognitive genre phase is responding to a task that is similar to the task of the joint construction phase, but one that provides less support and requires the students to write their own individual realizations of a report cognitive genre text. The task should provide the opportunity for writers to employ the different aspects of the procedural knowledge that has been presented at this phase in the unit.

Although the social genre focus and the cognitive genre focus are separated and sequential in the organization of this syllabus unit, the underlying idea of the design of the unit is that both aspects are closely inter-related, and that knowledge of both areas is necessary in order for novice writers to develop their discourse competence in relation to the sub-genre of Results sections. By initially addressing the social genre aspects of Results sections, it is possible to establish the disciplinary and discoursal contexts in which the part-genre occurs, and to provide the means to develop a grounded knowledge of its conventionalized forms and functions in different disciplines, such as the different disciplines to which the novice writers belong. Against the socially constructed context of the genre and the related areas of knowledge, the cognitive genre focus considers more abstract procedural knowledge (as well as linguistic knowledge) that enables the writer to deal with the issue of the textual representation of findings in terms of data, and in particular numerical data. Although these two areas are closely inter-related they are concerned with different objects of enquiry and need to be described and introduced in different ways and possibly at different stages in the learning process. This dual focus in the theorizing and model testing of previous chapters which has formed the basis for developing the particular advanced-level academic writing course exemplified in this final chapter.

7.4 Conclusion

This book began by noting the multiplicity of approaches and terminologies that have been proposed to relate discourse classification (in terms of constructs like genre or text type) to pedagogy. In relation to this situation, the aims of this book have been twofold: first to present a critical review of genre theory as it is currently applied to pedagogy, and secondly to present and exemplify a framework for systematizing approaches to genre and their application to the teaching of writing. One of the significant problems with the pedagogic approaches to genre that were reviewed in Chapter 2 is the narrowness of the types of knowledge integrated within existing pedagogic genre constructs, although it has to be conceded that the English for Specific Purposes approach has widened the view of contextual knowledge (Bhatia, 2004; Swales, 1998) and the nature and role of communicative purpose (Askehave and Swales, 2001). However, the knowledge domain that has been largely lacking in both approaches to genre has been the cognitive organizational dimension (operationalized here by cognitive genres), and it is this knowledge area that received considerable focus in the earlier chapters as it is foundational in the development of a discourse competence and genre knowledge by novice writers.

Chapter 1 of this book began by examining a range of pedagogic definitions of the types of knowledge that different theorists propose for the concept of discourse competence. This final conclusion returns to that concept, but in the form of the more recent proposal of Bhatia (2004) for *discursive competence*, which he sees as essential for appropriate use of professional and academic genres. Bhatia proposes that discursive competence includes the three subsuming areas of *textual competence*, *generic competence* and *social competence*:

> Textual competence represents not only an ability to master the linguistic code, but also an ability to use textual, contextual and pragmatic knowledge to construct and interpret contextually appropriate texts ... Generic competence means the ability to identify, construct, interpret and successfully exploit a specific repertoire of professional, disciplinary or workplace genres to participate in the daily activities and to achieve the goals of a specific professional community ... Social competence ... incorporates an ability to use language more widely to participate effectively in a variety of social and institutional contexts to give expression to one's social identity, in the context of constraining social structures and social processes. (pp. 144–5)

As Bhatia proposes, the exercise of a discursive competence involves textual, generic and social knowledge, all of which are drawn upon and converge in the language user's daily output and their participation in a specific academic or professional context. Thus, for pedagogy that aims at teaching novice writers and preparing them to be able to function and transact in such contexts, what is required is an approach to the specification and organization of syllabus, materials and methodology that integrates multiple knowledge areas, which, as proposed in earlier chapters, can be achieved by the use of a genre-based approach. However, to achieve this integration, it is important to establish systematic, analytical approaches to genre constructs and the multiple areas of knowledge that they draw upon.

Bhatia's proposal for discursive competence in effect relates to high levels of writer and speaker competence within specific academic and professional communities - levels of competence that are the endpoint or goal for many of the EAL students whom we teach. Thus, the task of curriculum designers, materials writers and teachers is to facilitate learners to move as closely as possible to the exercise of the full range skills and knowledge that relate to a discursive competence. However, teachers themselves cannot deconstruct and deliver the necessary knowledge and skills that comprise a discursive competence as pre-digested, readily absorbed modules or units that are specific to each discipline (even if our students would prefer such a solution). Nevertheless, what teachers can do is to assist their students to develop their *own capacity* to deconstruct, examine and practise salient discourse features, and to reconstruct discourses within their own particular disciplines. The development of such a capacity requires frameworks, tools and types of expertise that go far beyond what has been conventionally presented in academic writing or study skills textbooks.

In a small way, this book has been an attempt to identify and consider how to develop novice writers' discursive competence by the use of such frameworks, tools and types of expertise. Achieving a discursive competence, in effect, is the ability to deconstruct, understand and reconstruct discourses in ways that are linguistically correct and socially appropriate, but also in ways in which writers as individuals are able to achieve their own communicative purposes through their own authorial voices. Thus, it is the aim of the teacher of academic writing to assist novice writers to achieve this ultimate measure of success, which is the exercise of their own authorial voice within the disciplinary community to which they are bidding for entry.

References

Adam, J.-M. (1985), 'Quels types de textes?' *Le Français dans le Monde*, 192, 39–43.

Adam, J.-M. (1992), *Les Textes: Types et Prototypes.* Paris: Nathan.

Anderson, J. R. (1980), *Cognitive Psychology and its Implications.* San Francisco: W. H. Freeman.

Askehave, I. and Swales, J. M. (2001), 'Genre identification and communicative purpose'. *Applied Linguistics*, 22, 195–212.

Bachman, L. (1990), *Fundamental Considerations in Language Testing.* Oxford: Oxford University Press.

Badger, R. and White, G. (2000), 'A process genre approach to teaching writing'. *ELT Journal*, 54, 153-6.

Bakhtin, M. (1986), *Speech Genres and Other Late Essays* (trans. V. W. McGee). Austin: University of Texas Press.

Barsalou, L. W. (1983), 'Ad hoc categories'. *Memory and Cognition*, 11, 211–27.

Barsalou, L. W. (1992), 'Frames, concepts and conceptual fields', in A. Lehrer and E. Feder Kittay (eds), *Frames, Fields and Contrasts.* Hillsdale, NJ: Erlbaum, pp. 21–74.

Bartlett, F. C. (1932), *Remembering: A Study in Experimental and Social Psychology.* Cambridge: Cambridge University Press.

Beitel, D. A. (1995), 'The embodied schematic approach to the polysemy of spatial prepositions'. Unpublished doctoral dissertation, University of California, Santa Cruz.

Ben-Amos, D. (1976), *Folklore Genres.* Austin: University of Texas Press.

Benesch, S. (2001), *Critical English for Academic Purposes: Theory, Politics and Practice.* Mahwah, NJ: Erlbaum.

Bereiter, C. and Scardamalia, M. (1987), *The Psychology of Written Composition.* Hillsdale, NJ: Erlbaum.

Berkenkotter, C. and Huckin, T. (1995), *Genre Knowledge in Disciplinary Communication: Cognition/Culture/Power.* Hillsdale, NJ: Erlbaum.

Berlin, B., Breedlove, D. E. and Raven, P. H. (1974), *Principles of Tzeltal Plant Classification.* New York: Academic Press.

Berlin, B. and Kay, P. (1969), *Basic Color Terms.* Berkeley: University of California Press.

Bhatia, V. K. (1993), *Analysing Genre: Language Use in Professional Settings.* London: Longman.

Bhatia, V. K. (1998), 'Generic conflicts in academic discourse', in I. Fortanet, S. Posteguillo, J. C. Palmer and J. F. Coll (eds), *Genre Studies in English for*

Academic Purposes. Castello de la Plana: Publicacions de al Universitat Jaume, pp. 15–28.

Bhatia, V. K. (2002), 'Applied genre analysis: analytical advances and pedagogical procedures', in A. Johns (ed.), *Genre in the Classroom: Multiple Perspectives*. Mahwah, NJ: Erlbaum, pp. 279-83.

Bhatia, V. K. (2004), *Worlds of Written Discourse*. London: Continuum.

Biber, D. (1988), *Variation Across Speech and Writing*. Cambridge: Cambridge University Press.

Biber, D. (1989), 'A typology of English text'. *Linguistics*, 27, 3–43.

Biber, D., Conrad, S. and Reppen, R. (1994), 'Corpus-based approaches to issues in applied linguistics'. *Applied Linguistics*, 15, 169–89.

Bloor, M. (1998), 'Variations in the methods sections of research articles across disciplines: the case of fast and slow text', in P. Thompson (ed.), *Issues in EAP Writing, Research and Instruction*. CALS, University of Reading, pp. 84–106.

Bobrow, D. G. and Norman, D. A. (1975), 'Some principles of memory schemata', in D. G. Bobrow and A. Collins (eds), *Representation and Understanding: Studies in Cognitive Science*. New York: Academic Press, pp. 131–49.

Borg, E. (2003), 'Key concepts in ELT: discourse community'. *ELT Journal*, 57, 398–400.

Braine, G. (1989), 'Writing in science and technology: an analysis of assignments from ten undergraduate courses'. *English for Specific Purposes*, 8, 3–15.

Brett, P. (1994), 'A genre analysis of the results section of sociology articles'. *English for Specific Purposes*, 13, 47–59.

Brooks, L. R. (1968), 'Spatial and verbal components of the act of recall'. *Canadian Journal of Psychology*, 22, 349–69.

Brown, R. (1958), 'How shall a thing be called?' *Psychological Review*, 65, 14–21.

Brown, R. (1965), *Social Psychology*. New York: Free Press.

Burke, K. (1950), *A Rhetoric of Motives*. Berkeley: University of California Press.

Burns, A. and Joyce, H. (1997), *Focus on Speaking*. Sydney: National Centre for English Language Teaching and Research.

Bush, D. (1994), 'Writing at university: what faculty require'. *EA Journal*, 13, (2), 16–28.

Butt, D., Fahey, R., Feez, S. Spinks, S., and Yallop, C. (2000), *Using Functional Grammar: An Explorer's Guide*. (2nd edn). Sydney: National Centre for English Language Teaching and Research.

Canale, M. (1983), 'On some dimensions of language proficiency', in J. R. Oller, Jr (ed.), *Issues in Language Testing Research*. Rowley, MA: Newbury House, pp. 333-42.

Canale, M. and Swain, M. (1980), 'Theoretical bases of communicative approaches to second language teaching and testing'. *Applied Linguistics*, 1, 1–47.

Canseco, G. and Byrd, P. (1989), 'Writing required in graduate courses in business administration'. *TESOL Quarterly*, 23, 305-17.

Carr, T. and Curren, T. (1994), 'Cognitive factors in learning about structured sequences: applications to syntax'. *Studies in Second Language Acquisition*, 16, 205-30.

Carrell, P. L. (1981), 'Culture-specific schemata in L2 comprehension', in R. Orem and J. Haskell (eds), *Selected Papers from the Ninth Illinois TESOL/BE Annual Convention, First Midwest TESOL Conference*. Chicago: TESOL/BE, pp. 123-32.

Carrell, P. L. (1987), 'Content and formal schemata in ESL reading'. *TESOL Quarterly*, 21, 461–81.

Celce-Murcia, M. and Dornyei, Z. (1995), 'Communicative competence: a pedagogically motivated model with content specifications'. *Issues in Applied Linguistics*, 6, 5–35.

Chafe, W. (1972), 'Discourse structure and human knowledge', in J. B. Carroll and R. O. Freedle (eds), *Language, Comprehension and the Acquisition of Knowledge*. Washington: Winston.

Chafe, W. (1994), *Discourse, Consciousness and Time*. Chicago: University of Chicago Press.

Christie, F. (1990), *Literacy for a Changing World*. Hawthorn, Victoria: Australian Council of Educational Research.

Cohen, L., Manion, L. and Morrison, K. (2000), *Research Methods in Education* (5th edn). London: Routledge Falmer.

Conley, T. M. (1990), *Rhetoric in the European Tradition*. Chicago: University of Chicago Press.

Connor, U. and Mauranen, A. (1999), 'Linguistic analysis of grant proposals: European Union Research Grants'. *English for Specific Purposes*, 18, 47–62.

Corbluth, J. D. (1975), 'English? – or "Special English"?' *English Language Teaching Journal*, 24, 277-86.

Council of Europe (2001), *Common European Framework of Reference for Languages: Learning, Teaching, Assessment*. Cambridge: Cambridge University Press.

Crombie, W. H. (1985), *Process and Relation in Discourse and Language Learning*. Oxford: Oxford University Press.

Crombie, W. H. (1987), *Free Verse and Prose Style: An Operational Definition and Description*. London: Routledge and Kegan Paul.

Crombie, W. H. and Rika-Heke, P. (1991), 'ESP: fact or fiction'. *Revista Alicantina de Estudios Ingleses*, 4, 25–36.

Crookes, G. (1986), 'Towards a validated analysis of scientific text structure'. *Applied Linguistics*, 7, 57–70.

Crowhurst, M. (1990), 'The development of persuasive/argumentative writing', in R. Beach and S. Hynds (eds), *Developing Discourse Practices in Adolescence and Adulthood*. NJ: Ablex Publishing, pp. 200-23.

Davidson, D. (1978), 'What metaphors mean'. *Critical Enquiry*, 5, 47.

Derewianka, B. (1990), *Exploring How Texts Work*. Sydney, Australia: Primary English Teaching Association.

Devine, J. (1993), 'The role of metacognition in second language reading and writing', in J. G. Carson and I. Leki (eds), *Reading in the Composition Classroom: Second Language Perspectives*. Boston: Heinle and Heinle, pp. 105–27.

Devitt, A. J. (2004), *Writing Genres*. Carbondale: Southern Illinois University Press.

Dudley-Evans, A. (1986), 'Genre analysis: an investigation of the introductions and discourse sections of MSc dissertations', in M. Coulthard (ed.), *Talking About Text*. Discourse Analysis Monographs No. 13: English Language Research. Birmingham: University of Birmingham, pp. 128–45.

Dudley-Evans, T. (1989), 'An outline of the value of genre analysis in LSP work', in C. Laurén and M. Nordman (eds), *Special Language: From Humans Thinking to Thinking Machines*. Clevedon, UK: Multilingual Matters, pp. 72–9.

Dudley-Evans, T. (1993), 'Variation in communication patterns between discourse communities: the case of highway engineering and plant biology', in G. M. Blue (ed.), *Language, Learning and Success: Studying Through English*. London: Macmillan, pp. 141–7.

Dudley-Evans, T. (1994), 'Genre analysis: an approach to text analysis for ESP', in M. Coulthard (ed.), *Advances in Written Text Analysis*. London: Routledge, pp. 219–28.

Dudley-Evans, T. and St John, M. J. (1998), *Developments in English for Specific Purposes: A Multi-Disciplinary Approach*. Cambridge: Cambridge University Press.

Eggins, S. (1994), *An Introduction to Systemic Functional Linguistics*. London: Pinter.

Eggins, S. (2004), *An Introduction to Systemic Functional Linguistics* (2nd edn). London: Continuum.

Eggins, S. and Martin, J. R. (1997), 'Genre and registers of discourse', in T. Van Dijk (ed.), *Discourse as Structure and Process*. London: Sage Publications, pp. 230-56.

Fauconnier, G. (1985), *Mental Spaces: Aspects of Meaning Construction in Natural Language*. Cambridge, MA: MIT Press.

Feez, S. (1998), *Text-Based Syllabus Design*. Sydney: National Centre for English Language Teaching and Research, Macquarie University.

Feez, S. (2002), 'Heritage and innovation in second language education', in A. Johns (ed.), *Genre in the Classroom: Multiple Perspectives*. Mahwah, NJ: Erlbaum, pp. 43–69.

Ferris, D. (2001), 'Teaching writing for academic purposes', in J. Flowerdew and M. Peacock (eds), *Research Perspectives on English for Academic Purposes*. Cambridge: Cambridge University Press, pp. 298–314.

Fillmore, C. J. (1968), 'The case for case', in E. Bach and R. T. Harms (eds),

Universals in Linguistic Theory. New York: Holt, Rinehart and Winston, pp. 1–88.

Fillmore, C. J. (1975), 'An alternative to checklist theories of meaning'. *Berkeley Linguistics Society*, 1, 123–31.

Fillmore, C. J. (1976), 'Frame semantics and the nature of language', in S. R. Harnad, H. D. Steklis and J. Lancaster (eds), *Origin and Evolution of Language and Speech*. New York: Academy of Science, pp. 20–32.

Fillmore, C. J. (1977), 'Scenes-and-frames semantics', in A. Zampolli (ed.), *Linguistic Structures Processing*. Amsterdam: North Holland, pp. 55–80.

Fillmore, C. J. (1985), 'Linguistics as a tool for discourse analysis', in T. A. Van Dijk (ed.), *Handbook of Discourse Analysis*; Vol. 1. London: Academic Press, pp. 11–39.

Firth, J. R. (1957), *Papers in Linguistics, 1934–1951*. London: Oxford University Press.

Firth, J. R. (1968), 'A synopsis of linguistic theory, 1930–1955', in F. R. Palmer (ed.), *Selected Papers of J. R. Firth 1952–1959*. London: Longman, Green, pp. 168-205 (original work published in 1957).

Flowerdew, J. (1993), 'An educational, or process, approach to the teaching of professional genres'. *ELT Journal*, 47, 305–16.

Fowler, A. (1982), *Kinds of Literature: An Introduction to the Theory of Genres and Modes*. Cambridge, MA: Harvard University Press.

Gimenez, J. C. (2000), 'Business e-mail communication: some emerging tendencies in register'. *English for Specific Purposes*, 13, 237–51.

Gledhill, C. (2000), 'The discourse function of collocation in research article introductions'. *English for Specific Purposes*, 19, 2, 115–35.

Gosden, H. (1992), 'Discourse functions of marked theme in scientific research articles'. *English for Specific Purposes*, 11, 207–24.

Grabe, W. (2002), 'Narrative and expository macro-genres', in A. Johns (ed.), *Genre in the Classroom: Multiple Perspectives*. Mahwah, NJ: Erlbaum, pp. 249–67.

Grabe, W. and Kaplan, R. B. (1996), *Theory and Practice of Writing: An Applied Linguistic Perspective*. New York: Longman.

Gunawardena, C. N. (1989), 'The present perfect in the rhetorical division of biology and biochemistry journal articles'. *English for Specific Purposes*, 8, 265–73.

Halliday, M. A. K. (1978), *Language as a Social Semiotic*. London: Edward Arnold.

Halliday, M. A. K. (1985), *An Introduction to Functional Grammar*. London: Edward Arnold.

Halliday, M. A. K. and Hasan, R. (1989), *Language, Context and Text: Aspects of Language in a Social-Semiotic Perspective*. Oxford: Oxford University Press.

Hammond, J., Burns, A., Joyce, H., Brosnan, D. and Gerot, L. (1992), *English for Social Purposes: A Handbook for Teachers of Adult Literacy*. Sydney, Australia, NCELTR, Macquarie University.

Hasan, R. (1978), 'Text in the systemic functional mode', in W. Dressler (ed.), *Current Trends in Text Linguistics.* Berlin: Walter Gruyter, pp. 51–72.

Hasan, R. (1989), 'The identity of a text', in M. A. K. Halliday and R. Hasan, *Language, Text and Context.* Oxford: Oxford University Press, pp. 97-118 (original work published in 1985).

Hinkel, E. (2002), *Second Language Writers' Text: Linguistic and Rhetorical Features.* Mahwah, NJ: Erlbaum.

Hoey, M. (1979), 'Signalling in discourse'. *Discourse Analysis Monograph No. 6.* Birmingham: English Language Research, University of Birmingham.

Hoey, M. (1983), *On the Surface of Discourse.* London: George Allen and Unwin.

Hoey, M. (1994), 'Signalling in discourse: a functional analysis of a common discourse pattern in written and spoken English', in M. Coulthard (ed.), *Advances in Written Text Analysis.* London: Routledge, pp. 26–45.

Hoey, M. (2001), *Textual Interaction: An Introduction to Written Discourse Analysis.* London: Routledge.

Holmes, R. (1997), 'Genre analysis and the social sciences: an investigation of the structure of the research article discussion sections in three disciplines'. *English for Specific Purposes,* 16, 321–37.

Hopkins, A. and Dudley-Evans, T. (1988), 'A genre-based investigation of the discussion section in articles and dissertations'. *English for Specific Purposes,* 7, 113–22.

Hutchinson, T. and Waters, A. (1987), *English for Specific Purposes: A Learning-Centred Approach.* Cambridge: Cambridge University Press.

Hyland, K. (1994), 'Hedging in academic writing and EAP textbooks'. *English for Specific Purposes,* 13, 239–56.

Hyland, K. (2000), *Disciplinary Discourses: Social Interactions in Academic Writing.* London: Longman.

Hyland, K. (2002a), 'Genre: language, context, and literacy'. *Annual Review of Applied Linguistics,* 22, 113–35.

Hyland, K. (2002b), 'Specificity revisited: how far should we go now?' *English for Specific Purposes,* 21, 385–95.

Hyland, K. (2003), 'Discourse analysis in L2 writing research'. *Journal of Second Language Writing,* 12, 165–70.

Hyland, K. (2005), *Metadiscourse.* London: Continuum.

Hymes, D. (1972), 'On communicative competence', in J. B. Pride and J. Holmes (eds), *Sociolinguistics.* Harmondsworth: Penguin, pp. 269–93.

Hyon, S. (1996), 'Genre in three traditions: implications for ESL'. *TESOL Quarterly,* 30, 693–722.

Jacoby, S., Leech, D. and Holte, C. (1995), 'A genre-based developmental writing course for undergraduate ESL science majors', in D. Belcher and G. Braine (eds), *Academic Writing in a Second Language: Essays on Research and Pedagogy.* Norwood, NJ: Ablex, pp. 351–73.

Johns, A. M. (1997), *Text, Role and Context: Developing Academic Literacies.* Cambridge: Cambridge University Press.

Johns, A. M. (2001), 'The future is with us: preparing diverse students for the challenges of university texts and cultures', in M. A. Hewings (ed.), *Academic Writing in Context: Implications and Applications.* Birmingham: University of Birmingham Press, pp. 30–42.

Johns, A. M. and Swales, J. M. (2002), 'Literacy and disciplinary practices: opening and closing perspectives'. *Journal of English for Academic Purposes,* 1, 13–28.

Johnson, M. (1987), *The Body in the Mind: The Bodily Basis of Meaning, Imagination, and Reason.* Chicago: University of Chicago Press.

Johnson, P. (1981), 'Effects on reading comprehension of language complexity and cultural background of a text'. *TESOL Quarterly,* 15, 169–81.

Jones, C., Turner, J. and Street, B. (eds) (1999), *Students Writing in the University: Cultural and Epistemological Issues.* Amsterdam: John Benjamins.

Jordan, R. R. (1997), *English for Academic Purposes: A Guide and Resource Book for Teachers.* Cambridge: Cambridge University Press.

Kant, I. (1998), *Critique of Pure Reason* (trans. P. Guyer and A. W. Wood). Cambridge: Cambridge University Press (original work published 1781).

Kaplan, R. B. (1987), 'Cultural thought patterns revisited', in U. Connor and R. B. Kaplan (eds), *Writing Across Languages: Analysis of L2 Text.* Reading, MA: Addison Wesley, pp. 9–21.

Knapp, P. and Watkins, M. (1994), *Context–Text–Grammar: Teaching the Genres and Grammar of School Writing in Infant and Primary Classrooms.* Broadway, NSW, Australia: Text Productions.

Knott, A. (1996), 'A data-driven methodology for motivating a set of coherence relations'. Unpublished PhD thesis, Department of Artificial Intelligence, University of Edinburgh.

Knott, A. and Sanders, T. (1998), 'The classification of coherence relations and their linguistic markers: an exploration of two languages', *Journal of Pragmatics,* 30, 135–75.

Knott, A., Sanders, T. and Oberlander, J. (2001), 'Levels of representation in discourse relations'. *Cognitive Linguistics,* 12, 3, 197–209.

Kroll, B. (1979), 'A survey of the writing needs of foreign and American college freshmen'. *English Language Teaching Journal,* 23, 219–27.

Kroll, B. (ed.) (2003), *Exploring the Dynamics of Second Language Writing.* Cambridge: Cambridge University Press.

Lackstrom, J., Selinker, L. and Trimble, L. (1973), 'Technical rhetorical principles and grammatical choice'. *TESOL Quarterly,* 15, 51-7.

Lakoff, G. (1987), *Women, Fire and Dangerous Things: What Categories Reveal About the Mind.* Chicago: Chicago University Press.

Lakoff, G. and Johnson, M. (1980), *Metaphors We Live By.* Chicago: University of Chicago Press.

Langacker, R. (1987), *Foundations of Cognitive Grammar,* Vol. 1. Stanford: Stanford University Press.

Lave, J. and Wenger, E. (1991), *Situated Learning: Legitimate, Peripheral Participation.* Cambridge: Cambridge University Press.

Lea, M. R. and Street, B. (1998), 'Student writing in higher education: an academic literacies approach'. *Studies in Higher Education*, 23, 157–72.

Lea, M. R. and Street, B. (1999), 'Writing as academic literacies: understanding textual practices in higher education', in C. N. Candlin and K. Hyland (eds), *Writing: Texts, Processes and Practices*. London: Longman, pp. 62–81.

Leki, I. (2000), 'Writing, literacy and applied linguistics'. *Annual Review of Applied Linguistics*, 20, 99–115.

Logan, G. D. (1988), 'Towards an instance theory of automatisation'. *Psychological Review*, 95, 492–527.

Love, A. (1993), 'Lexico-grammatical features of geology textbooks: process and product revisited'. *English for Specific Purposes*, 12, 197–218.

Luke, A. (1996), 'Genres of power? Literacy education and the production of capital', in R. Hasan and G. Williams (eds), *Literacy in Society*. London: Longman, pp. 308–38.

Luzon Marco, M. J. (2000), 'Collocational frameworks in medical research papers: a genre-based study'. *English for Specific Purposes*, 19, 63–86.

Macken, M., Kalantzis, M., Kress, G., Martin, J. R., Cope, W. and Rothery, J. (1989), *A Genre-Based Approach to Teaching Writing, Years 3–6*, Book 4. *The Theory and Practice of Genre-Based Writing*. Sydney, Australia: Directorate of Studies, NSW Department of Education in association with the Literacy and Education Research Network.

MacLaughlan, G. and Reid, I. (1994), *Framing and Interpretation*. Melbourne: Melbourne University Press.

Malinowski, B. (1923), 'The problem of meaning in primitive languages', in C. K. Ogden and I. A. Richards (eds), *The Meaning of Meaning*. London: Routledge and Kegan Paul, pp. 296–336.

Malinowski, B. (1935), *Coral Gardens and Their Magic*, Vol. II. London: George Allen and Unwin.

Mann, W. C. and Thompson, S. A. (1988), 'Rhetorical structure theory: a theory of text organization'. *Text*, 8, 3, 243–81.

Marmor, G. S. and Zaback, L. A. (1976), 'Mental rotation by the blind: does mental rotation depend on visual imagery?' *Journal of Experimental Psychology: Human Perception and Performance*, 2, 515–24.

Martin, J. R. (1984), 'Language, register and genre', in F. Christie (ed.), *Language Studies: Children's Writing: Reader*. Geelong, Australia: Deakin University Press.

Martin, J. R. (1986), 'Intervening in the process of writing development', in C. Painter and J. R. Martin (eds), *Writing to Mean: Teaching Genres Across the Curriculum*. Applied Linguistics Association of Australia, Occasional Paper 9, 11–43.

Martin, J. R. (1989), *Factual Writing: Exploring and Challenging Social Reality*. Oxford: Oxford University Press.

Martin, J. R. (1992), *English Text: System and Structure*. Amsterdam: John Benjamins.

Martin, J. R. (1994), 'Macro-genres: the ecology of the page'. *Network*, 21, 29–52.

Martin, J. R. (1995), 'Text and clause: fractal resonance'. *Text*, 15, 5–42.

Martin, J. R. (1997), 'Analysing genre: functional parameters', in F. Christie and J. Martin (eds), *Genre and Institutions: Social Processes in the Workplace and School*. London: Cassell, pp. 3–39.

Martin, J. R. (2000), 'Design and practice: enacting functional linguistics'. *Annual Review of Applied Linguistics*, 20, 116–26.

Martin, J. R. (2001), 'Language, register and genre', in A. Burns and C. Coffin (eds), *Analysing English in a Global Context*. London: Routledge, pp. 149–66.

Matsumoto, Y. (1997), 'From attribution/purpose to cause: image schema and grammaticalization of some cause markers in Japanese', in M. Verspoor, K. D. Lee and E. Sweetser (eds), *Lexical and Syntactical Constructions and the Construction of Meaning: Proceedings of the Bi-Annual ICLA Meeting in Albuquerque, July 1995*. Amsterdam: John Benjamins.

Matthews, R. C., Buss, R. R., Stanley, W. B., Blanchard-Fields, F., Cho, J. R. and Druhan, B. (1989), 'Role of implicit and explicit processes in learning from examples: a synergistic effect'. *Journal of Experimental Psychology: Learning, Memory and Cognition*, 15, 1083–1100.

McNamara, T. F. (1995), 'Modelling performance: opening Pandora's Box'. *Applied Linguistics*, 16, 159–79.

McNamara, T. F. (2000), *Language Testing*. Oxford: Oxford University Press.

Meyer, B. J. F. (1977), 'The structure of prose: effects of learning and memory and implications for educational practice', in R. C. Anderson, R. J. Spiro and W. E. Montague (eds), *Schooling and the Acquisition of Knowledge*. Hillsdale, NJ: Erlbaum, pp. 179–200.

Miller, C. R. (1984), 'Genre as social action'. *Quarterly Journal of Speech*, 70, 151–67.

Miller, C. R. (1994), 'Rhetorical community: the cultural basis of genre', in A. Freedman and P. Medway (eds), *Genre and the New Rhetoric*. London: Taylor and Francis, pp. 67–78.

Minsky, M. (1975), 'A framework for representing knowledge', in P. Winston (ed.), *The Psychology of Computer Vision*. New York: McGraw-Hill, pp. 211–77.

Minsky, M. (1985), *The Society of Mind*. New York: Simon and Schuster.

Moore, T. and Morton, J. (1999), *Authenticity in the IELTS Academic Module Writing Test: A Comparative Study of Task 2 Items and University Assignments*. International English Language Testing System: Research Rep. No. 2. 64–106. IELTS Australia.

Moore, T. and Morton, J. (2005), 'Dimensions of difference: a comparison of university writing and IELTS writing'. *Journal of English for Academic Purposes*, 4, 1, 43–66.

Morrow, P. R. (1989), 'Conjunct use in business news stories and academic journal articles: a comparative study'. *English for Specific Purposes*, 8, 239–54.

Norman, D. A., Rumelhart, D. E. and the LNR Research Group (1975), *Explorations in Cognition*. San Francisco: Freeman.

Nunan, D. (1993), *Discourse Analysis*. London: Penguin.

Nunan, D. (1998), 'Teaching Grammar in Context'. *ELT Journal*, 52, 2, 101–9.

Nunberg, G. (1978). *The Pragmatics of Reference*. Bloomington: Indiana University Linguistics Club.

Nwogu, K. N. (1991), 'Structure of science popularisations: a genre-analysis approach to the schema of popularised medical texts'. *English for Specific Purposes*, 10, 111–23.

Oller, J. W. (1995), 'Adding abstract to formal and content schemata: results of recent work in Peircean semiotics'. *Applied Linguistics*, 16, 273–306.

Paltridge, B. (1993a), 'A challenge to the current concept of genre: writing up research'. Unpublished thesis, University of Waikato, Hamilton, New Zealand.

Paltridge, B. (1993b), 'Writing up research: a systemic-functional perspective'. *System*, 21, 175–92.

Paltridge, B. (1994), 'Genre analysis and the identification of textual boundaries'. *Applied Linguistics*, 15, 288–99.

Paltridge, B. (1995a), 'Genre and the notion of prototype'. *Prospect*, 10, 3, 28–34.

Paltridge, B. (1995b), 'Working with genre: a pragmatic perspective'. *Journal of Pragmatics*, 24, 393–406.

Paltridge, B. (1996), 'Genre, text type, and the language learning classroom'. *ELT Journal*, 50, 237–43.

Paltridge, B. (1997), *Genre, Frames and Writing in Research Settings*. Amsterdam: John Benjamins.

Paltridge, B. (2001), *Genre and the Language Learning Classroom*. Ann Arbor: University of Michigan Press.

Paltridge, B. (2002), 'Genre, text type, and the English for Academic Purposes (EAP) Classroom', in A. Johns (ed.), *Genre in the Classroom: Multiple Perspectives*. Mahwah, NJ: Erlbaum, pp. 73–90.

Paris, S. G., Lipson, M. and Wixon, K. K. (1983), 'Becoming a Strategic Reader'. *Contemporary Psychology*, 8, 293–316.

Pawley, A. and Syder, F. H. (1983), 'Two puzzles for linguistic theory: nativelike selection and nativelike fluency', in J. C. Richards and R. W. Schmidt (eds), *Language and Communication*. New York: Longman, pp. 191–226.

Pearson Casanave, C. and Hubbard, P. (1992), 'The writing assignments and writing problems of doctoral students: faculty perceptions, pedagogical issues, and needed research'. *English for Specific Purposes*, 11, 33–49.

Peng, J. (1987), 'Organisational features in chemical engineering research articles'. *ELR Journal*, 1, 79–116.

Pica, T. (1985), 'The selective impact of classroom instruction on second language acquisition'. *Applied Linguistics*, 6, 3, 214–22.

Pienemann, M. and Johnston, M. (1987), 'Factors influencing the development of language proficiency (the multi-dimensional model – summary)', in D. Nunan (ed.), *Applying Second Language Acquisition Research*. Adelaide: National curriculum Resource Centre, pp. 89–94.

Pilegaard, M. and Frandsen, F. (1996), 'Text type', in J. Verschueren, J.-O. Ostaman, J. Blommaert and C. C. Bulcaen (eds), *Handbook of Pragmatics 1996*. Amsterdam: John Benjamins, pp. 1–13.

Popken, R. L. (1993), 'An empirical study of indirect speech acts in résumés'. *English for Specific Purposes*, 12, 239–49.

Price, R. (1997), 'An analysis of stylistic variables in electronic mail'. *Journal of Business and Technical Communication*, 11, 5–23.

Putnam, H. (1981), *Reason, Truth and History*. Cambridge: Cambridge University Press.

Quinn, J. (1993), 'A taxonomy of text types for use in curriculum design'. *EA Journal*, 11, 2, 33–46.

Reed, S. K. (1972), 'Pattern recognition and categorization'. *Cognitive Psychology*, 3, 382–407.

Reid, J. (2001), 'Academic EAP writing and curriculum design', in Silva, T. and Matsuda, P. K. (eds), *On Second Language Writing*. Mahwah, NJ: Erlbaum, pp. 143–60.

Richards, J. C., Platt, J. C. and Platt, H. (1992), *Longman Dictionary of Language Teaching and Applied Linguistics*. Essex, England: Longman.

Richgels, D. J., McGee, L. M., Lomax, R. G. and Sheard, C. (1987), 'Awareness of four text structures: effects on recall of expository text'. *Reading Research Quarterly*, 22, 177–96

Robinson, P. C. (1991), *ESP Today: A Practitioner's Guide*. New York: Prentice Hall.

Robinson, P. J. and Ha, M. A. (1993), 'Instance theory and second language rule learning under explicit conditions'. *Studies in Second Language Acquisition*, 15, 4, 413–38.

Rosch, E. (1973), 'Natural categories'. *Cognitive Psychology*, 4, 328–50.

Rosch, E. (1975), 'Cognitive representations of semantic categories'. *Journal of Experimental Psychology: General*, 104, 192–233.

Rosch, E. (1978), 'Principles of categorisation', in E. Rosch and B. B. Lloyd (eds), *Cognition and Categorization*. Hillsdale, NJ: Erlbaum, pp. 27–47.

Rosch, E. and Mervis, C. (1975), 'Family resemblances: studies in the internal structure of categories'. *Cognitive Psychology*, 7, 573–605.

Rosch, E., Mervis, C., Gray, W. D., Johnson, D. M. and Boyes-Braem, P. (1976), 'Basic objects in natural categories'. *Cognitive Psychology*, 8, 382–439.

Rumelhart, D. E. (1975), 'Towards an interactive model of reading', in S. Dornic (ed.), *Attention and Performance VI*. Hillsdale, NJ: Erlbaum, pp. 573–603.

Rumelhart, D. E. (1976), 'Understanding and summarizing brief stories', in D. LaBerge and S. J. Samuels (eds), *Basic Processes in Reading: Perception and Comprehension*. Hillsdale, NJ: Erlbaum, pp. 265–303.

Rumelhart, D. E. and Ortony, A. (1977), 'The representation of knowledge in memory', in R. C. Anderson, R. J. Spiro and W. E. Montague (eds),

Schooling and the Acquisition of Knowledge. Hillsdale, NJ: Erlbaum, pp. 99–135.

Salies, T. M. G. (1998), 'Texts as image-schemas: a cross-linguistic analysis of discourse in the light of cognitive linguistics'. Unpublished dissertation, Oklahoma State University.

Samraj, B. (2002), 'Introductions in research articles: variations across disciplines'. *English for Specific Purposes* 21, 1–18.

Samraj, B. (2004), 'Discourse features of the student-produced academic research paper: variations across disciplinary courses'. *Journal of English for Academic Purposes*, 3, 5–22.

Sanford, A. J. and Garrod, S. C. (1981), *Understanding Written Language*. Chichester, England: John Wiley.

Schank, R. C. (1975), 'The structure of episodes in memory', in D. G. Bobrow and A. Collins (eds), *Representation and Understanding: Studies in Cognitive Science*. London: Academic Press, pp. 237–72.

Schank, R. C. and Abelson, R. P. (1977), *Scripts, Plans, Goals and Understanding*. Hillsdale, NJ: Erlbaum.

Scott, M. (2004), WordSmith Tools version 4. Oxford: Oxford University Press.

Searle, J. R., (1979), *Expression and Meaning: Studies in the Theory of Speech Acts*. Cambridge: Cambridge University Press.

Selinker, L., Todd-Trimble, M. and Trimble, L. (1978), 'Rhetorical function-shifts in EST discourse'. *TESOL Quarterly*, 12, 311–20.

Sengupta, S., Forey, G. and Hamp-Lyons, L. (1999), 'Supporting effective English communication within the context of teaching and research in a tertiary institute: developing a genre model for consciousness raising'. *English for Specific Purposes*, 18, 1, 7–22.

Serra-Borneto, C. (1997), 'Two-way prepositions in German: image and constraints', in M. Verspoor, K. D. Lee and E. Sweetser (eds), *Lexical and Syntactical Constructions and the Construction of Meaning: Proceedings of the Bi-Annual ICLA Meeting in Albuquerque, July 1995*. Amsterdam: John Benjamins.

Shalom, C. (1993), 'Established and evolving spoken research process genres: plenary lecture and poster session discussions at academic conferences'. *English for Specific Purposes*, 12, 37–50.

Silva, T. (1990), 'Second language composition instruction: developments, issues and directions in ESL', in B. Kroll (ed.), *Second Language Writing: Research Insights for the Classroom*. Cambridge: Cambridge University Press, pp. 11–23.

Sionis, C. (1995), 'Communication strategies in the writing of scientific research articles by non-native users of English'. *English for Specific Purposes*, 14, 2, 99–113.

Skehan, P. (1996), 'A framework for the implementation of task-based instruction'. *Applied Linguistics*, 17, 38-62.

Spiro, R. and Taylor, B. (1987), 'On investigating children's transition from narrative to expository discourse: the multi-dimensional nature of psychological text classification', in R. Tierney, P. Anders and J. Mitchell (eds), *Understanding Readers' Understanding*. Hillsdale, NJ: Erlbaum, pp. 77–93.

Stierer, B. (2000), 'Schoolteachers as students: academic literacy and the construction of professional knowledge within master's courses in education', in M. R. Lea and B. Stierer (eds), *Student Writing in Higher Education*. Buckingham, UK: SRHE and Open University Press, pp. 179–95.

Stross, B (1969), '*Language acquisition by Tenejapa Tzeltal children*'. Unpublished PhD dissertation: University of California, Berkeley.

Swales, J. M. (1981), *Aspects of Article Introductions* (Aston ESP Research Rep. No 1). Birmingham, England: Language Studies Unit, University of Aston.

Swales, J. M. (1986a), 'A genre-based approach to language across the curriculum', in M. L. Tickoo (ed.), *Language Across the Curriculum*. Anthology. Series 15. Singapore: SEAMEO Regional Language Centre.

Swales, J. M. (1986b), *English for Specifiable Purposes*. Singapore: SEAMEO Regional Language Centre.

Swales, J. M. (1988), 'Discourse communities, genres and English as an international language'. *World Englishes*, 7, 211–20.

Swales, J. M. (1990), *Genre Analysis: English in Academic and Research Settings*. Cambridge: Cambridge University Press.

Swales, J. M. (1998), *Other Floors, Other Voices: A Textography of a Small University Building*. Mahwah, NJ: Erlbaum.

Swales, J. M. (2002), 'On models in applied discourse analysis', in C. N. Candlin (ed.), *Research and Practice in Professional Discourse*. Hong Kong: City University of Hong Kong Press, pp. 61–77.

Swales, J. M. (2004), *Research Genres: Exploration and Applications*. Cambridge: Cambridge University Press.

Swales, J. M. and Feak, C. B. (1994), *Academic Writing for Graduate Students: A Course for Non-native Speakers of English*. Ann Arbor: University of Michigan Press.

Tannen, D. (1993) (ed.), *Framing in Discourse*. Oxford: Oxford University Press.

Tapper, J. (1994), 'Directives used in college laboratory oral discourse'. *English for Specific Purposes*, 13, 205–22.

Tarone, E., Dwyer, S., Gillette, S. and Icke, V. (1981), 'On the use of the passive in two astrophysics journal papers'. *English for Specific Purposes*, 1, 123–40.

Thomas, S. and Hawes, T. P. (1994), 'Reporting verbs in medical journal articles'. *English for Specific Purposes*, 13, 129–48.

Thompson, S. (1994), 'Frameworks and contexts: a genre-based approach to analysing lecture introductions'. *English for Specific Purposes*, 13, 171–86.

Trimble, L. (1985), *English for Science and Technology: A Discourse Approach*. Cambridge: Cambridge University Press.

Van Dijk, T. A. (1977), *Text and Context: Explorations in the Semantics and Pragmatics of Discourse*. London: Longman.

Van Dijk, T. A. (1980), *Macrostructures: An Interdisciplinary Study of Global Structures in Discourse, Interaction and Cognition.* Hillsdale, NJ: Erlbaum.

Van Dijk, T. A. (1993), 'Generalising about genre: new conceptions of an old concept'. *College Composition and Communication,* 44, 573–86.

Ventola, E. (1984), 'The dynamics of genre'. *Nottingham Linguistics Circular,* 13, 103–23.

Ventola, E. (1985), 'Orientation to social semiotics in foreign language teaching'. *Applied Linguistics,* 5, 275–86.

Ventola, E. (1987), *The Structure of Social Interaction: A Systemic Approach to the Semiotics of Service Encounter Interaction.* London: Pinter.

Virtanen, J. (1992), 'Issues of text typology: narrative – a "basic" type of text?' *Text,* 12, 292–310.

Wenden, A. L. (2001), 'Metacognitive knowledge in SLA: the neglected variable', in M. P. Breen (ed.), *Learner Contributions to Language Learning.* Harlow, Essex: Pearson Education, pp. 44–64.

Wenger, E. (1998), *Communities of Practice.* Cambridge: Cambridge University Press.

Werlich, E. (1974), *Typologie der Texte.* Heidelberg: Quelle and Meyer.

Werlich, E. (1976), *A Text Grammar of English.* Heidelberg: Quelle and Meyer.

Whately, R. (1826/1975), *Elements of Logic.* Scholars Facsimiles and Reprints.

Widdowson, H. C. (1983), *Learning Purpose and Language Use.* Oxford: Oxford University Press.

Widdowson, H. G. (1989), 'Knowledge of language and ability for use'. *Applied Linguistics,* 10, 128–37.

Widdowson, H. G. (1990), *Aspects of Language Teaching.* Oxford: Oxford University Press.

Widdowson, H. G. (2004), *Text, Context, Pretext: Critical Discourse in Discourse Analysis.* Oxford: Blackwell.

Wilkins, D. (1976), *Notional Syllabuses: A Taxonomy and its Relevance to Foreign Language Instruction.* London: Oxford University Press.

Williams, I. (1996), 'A contextual study of lexical verbs in two types of medical research reports: clinical and experimental'. *English for Specific Purposes,* 15, 175–97.

Williams, I. (1999), 'Results sections of medical research articles: analysis of rhetorical categories for pedagogical purposes'. *English for Specific Purposes,* 18, 347–66.

Winograd, T. (1975), 'Frame representations and the declarative/procedural controversy', in D. G. Brobrow and A. Collins (eds), *Representation and Understanding.* London: Academic Press, pp. 185–210.

Winograd, T. (1977), 'Representation: formalisms for knowledge', in A. Zampolli (ed.), *Fundamental Studies in Computer Science,* Volume 5: *Linguistic Structures Processing.* Amsterdam: North-Holland Publishing, pp. 459–79.

Wittgenstein, L. (1953), *Philosophical Investigations.* Oxford: Blackwell.

Appendices

Appendix 1: Crombie's interpropositional relations

Process	Relation	Definition
Associative	Simple Contrast	Involves the comparison of two things, events or abstractions in terms of some particular in respect of which they differ.
	Comparative Similarity (Simple Comparison)	Involves the comparison of two things, events or abstractions in terms of some particular in respect of which they are similar.
	Statement – Affirmation	The truth of a statement is affirmed.
	Statement – Exception	Involves a statement and an exception to that statement.
	Statement – Exemplification	The first member provides a general statement and the second adds a proposition which is presented as an exemplification of the general statement in the first member.
	Statement – Denial	Involves the denial of the truth of a statement or validity of a proposition.
	Denial – Correction	Involves a corrective non-antonymic substitute for a denial.
	Concession – Contra-expectation	Involves direct or indirect denial of the truth of an inference.
	Supplementary Alternation	Involves two or more non-antithetical choices.
	Contrastive Alternation	Involves a choice between antitheses.
	Paraphrase	Involves the same proposition expressed in different ways.
	Amplification	Involves implicit or explicit repetition of the propositional content of one member of the relation in the other, together with a non-contrastive addition to that propositional content.
Logico-deductive	Condition – Consequence	Involves a consequence which depends upon a realizable or unrealizable condition or hypothetical contingency.
	Means – Purpose	Involves an action that is/was/will be undertaken *with the intention of* achieving a particular result.
	Reason – Result	Involves the provision of a reason *why* a particular effect came about or will come about.
	Means – Result	Involves a statement of *how* a particular result is/was/will be achieved.
	Grounds – Conclusion	Involves a deduction drawn on the basis of an observation.
Tempero-contigual	Chronological Sequence	Provides the semantic link between event propositions one of which follows the other in time.
	Temporal Overlap	The relation of temporal overlap links two events which overlap, either wholly or partly, in time.
	Bonding	This is a non-elective, non-sequential relation between two conjoined or juxtaposed propositions. The second member adds at least one new proposition to the first and the members are not connected in an elective, comparative or sequential way.

(Based on Crombie, 1985, pp. 18-28, 1987, p. 102)

Appendix 2: Corpus study: selection method, population and sample

The aim of the study was to gather a small corpus of 20 academic texts from a range of academic disciplines and examine them for instances of the cognitive genres.

Requests were made (personally and by email) to 15 academic staff, each teaching in a different academic discipline at a New Zealand university. Staff were asked to name the four or five academic journals that they were most likely to refer to. Reponses were received from 11 staff from the subject areas of: applied linguistics, biology, computer science, education, English, general linguistics, history, law, business management, psychology and sociology.

From the journal titles (or other periodical publications) named by staff members, two or three articles (or book chapters) were gathered from each of the journals named, from issues for the year 1999 or years closest to that year. Altogether the titles for nine articles were gathered for each of the eleven subject areas, making a total population of 99 articles which were numbered 1 to 99. Using the random number function of a scientific calculator, articles from the population were selected as the corpus. These articles are listed in the table following.

Study 1: Randomly selected corpus

Corpusitem number	Subject	Journal or edited book	Volume,issue, pages	Article title	Author
1	Psychology	*Journal of Experimental Psychology*	(1999), 25, 4 pp. 965–75.	'Infants' and adults' perception of scale structure'.	Sandra E. Trehu, E. Glenn Schellenberg and Stuart B. Kamenetsky
2	Applied Linguistics	R. Hasan and G. Williams (eds), *Literacy in Society*	(1996)	'Technology and/or weapon: the discipline of reading in the secondary English classroom'.	Ann Cranny-Francis
3	Computer Science	*Communications of the ACM*	(1999), 42, 2 pp. 74–79	'The realities of software technology payoffs'.	Robert L. Glass
4	English Literature	*The Journal of Commonwealth Studies*	(2000), 35, 1, pp. 121–129	'Children's literature and British child emigration schemes: a missed opportunity'.	Elwyn Jenkins

5	Population Studies (Geography)	*New Zealand Population Review*	(1997), 23, 1/2, pp. 19–44.	'English language requirements and immigration policy in New Zealand'.	Anne M. Henderson, Andrew D. Trilin, Regina Pernic and Nicola North
6	Applied Linguistics	*Applied Linguistics*	(1999), 20, 4, pp. 460–480	'Item versus system learning'.	Rod Ellis
7	Biological Sciences	*Science*	(1999), 284, 5,417, pp. 1177–79	'Net primary production of a forest ecosystem with experimental CO2 enrichment'.	E. H. Delucia, J. G. Hamilton, S. L. Haidu, R. B. Thomas and J. A. Andrews
8	English Literature	*The Review of English Studies*	(1999), 50, 198, pp. 155-165	'French and Italian sources for Ralegh's "Farewell false love"'.	Jonathon Gibson
9	Business Management Communication	*Business Communication Quarterly*	(1999), 62, 1, pp. 10–28	'Writing and other communication standards in undergraduate business education'.	Melinda Knight
10	Education	*Research in Science Education*	(1999), 29, 1, pp. 69–88	'Educating science teachers for the sociocultural diversity of urban schools'.	Kenneth Tobin, Gale Seiler and Mackenzie W. Smith
11	Education	*International Journal of Science Education*	(1999), 21, 11, pp. 1169–85	'Empirical evaluation of an educational conservation programme introduced in Swiss secondary schools'.	Franz X. Bogner
12	Applied Lingusitics	*Applied Linguistics*	(1999), 20, 2, pp. 237–64	'Small Cultures'.	Adrian Holliday
13	Applied Linguistics	*ELT Journal*	(1998), 52, 2, pp. 140–145	'ELT project planning and sustainability'.	Alastair Sharp
14	Law	*Harvard Journal of Law and Public Policy*	(1999), 23, 1, p. 159	'Regulating network industries: a look at Intel'.	Randal C. Picker
15	Law	*Human Rights Quarterly*	(1999), 21, 2, pp. 342–63	'The African Human Rights Court: a two-legged stool'.	Makau Mutua

16	Computer Science	*Software: Practice and Experience*	(2000), 30, 9, pp. 973–1002	'An index allocation tool for object-oriented database systems'.	B. Bertin, B. Catania and A. Filippone
17	Applied Linguistics	*ELT Journal*	(1998), 52, 3, pp. 235–42	'Towards more humanistic English teaching'.	Jane Arnold
18	Business Management	*Asia Pacific Journal of Management*	(2000), 17, 62, p. 83	'Performance of US FDI in different world regions'.	G. Qian
19	Business Management	*Academy of Management*	(2000), 43, 4, pp. 681–687	'Managerial interpretations and organizational context as predictors of corporate choice of environmental strategy'.	S. Sharma
20	Computer Science	*International Journal of Human–Computer Interaction*	(1999), 11, 4, p. 185	'Cognitive walkthroughs: understanding the effect of task description detail on evaluator performance'.	Andrew Sears and David J. Hess

Appendix 3: Instructions for the administration of the four writing tasks

Instructions for supervisors of the writing tasks

Please issue the scripts, and then read the following instructions

- You will have 30 minutes to write an essay response to the task you have in front of you.
- Please write your response to the task on the lined paper attached.
- If you complete the writing task early, please indicate by raising your hand and both papers will be collected.
- Your essay will remain anonymous, but if you wish to claim your essay back in the future, please detach and keep the fold-out number tab on the lined answer paper which you will need to show the researcher to claim back your script. He will retain a photocopy for his analysis.
- Please start now, you have 30 minutes.

After allowing 30 minutes to perform the writing task, please say:

- Please stop writing and fill in the questionnaire. When you have finished the questionnaire please hand in your papers.

Appendix 4: Example of an analysed script from Study 2

Task 3 (Relating to Discussion Rhetorical Type):
The New Zealand government should restrict the number of admissions of New Zealanders to university degree programmes as there are insufficient employment opportunities for university graduates in New Zealand today.

Analysed Script:

B32

There are a number of arguments for both restricting the number of admissions of New Zealanders to university degree programmes because of the lack of suitable job opportunities available, and for allowing free admission of suitably qualified students to those same degree programmes, despite the apparent lack of employment opportunities.

The main reason that restrictions should be imposed is that of taxpayer contributions to the considerable expense of educating a New Zealand student to degree level. Whereas the student is required to contribute a substantial amount of the cost of tertiary education, it is only in the vicinity of 20% of the total cost incurred. The balance is funded by the government directly from taxpayer contributions. This would appear to be a rather inappropriate use of the country's finances if there are not likely to be sufficient employment opportunities available at the completion of such study.

A further reason for restricting entry into degree programmes when the certainty of suitable jobs is absent, is the increasing accumulation of student debt from years of tertiary study, and the subsequent consequences which this is bringing to a generation of New Zealanders n their future lives. Their lack of ability to borrow to buy houses businesses and cars, as well as the stress engendered by their indebtedness over a life time, will undoubtedly cause a number of social problems for an entire generation.

In direct contrast to the above arguments, it could be considered that the government should allow free access to degree programmes to all suitably qualified New Zealanders as education can be considered an investment for life and eventually there will be a payback in the form of entrepreneurialism, burgeoning business, and innovative developments of other commercial enterprises, many of which will add to the health of the economy.

In addition, well qualified New Zealanders are able to travel overseas and find placement in appropriate fields of employment out of New Zealand. Eventually these people return and bring skills and experience back to New Zealand, thus contributing to the country in the long term.

On balance then it can be seen that there are compelling reasons for both restricting entry to University degrees as well as allowing free access by all qualified New Zealanders. Eventually the country should benefit in different ways from whichever policy is pursued.

386 words

Appendix 5: Results sections corpus

Corpus item number	Subject	Journal	Volume, issue, pages	Article title	Author
1	Applied Linguistics	*Applied Linguistics*	(1999), 20, 3, 341–67	'Academic attribution: citation and the construction of disciplinary knowledge'.	Ken Hyland
2	Applied Linguistics	*Applied Linguistics*	(1999), 20, 2, 151–78	'The development of past tense verbal morphology in L2 Spanish'.	M. R. Salaberry
3	Education	*International Journal of Science Education*	(1999), 21, 5, 499–514	'Global environmental priorities of secondary students in Zabrze, Poland'.	Michael Robinson and Piotr Kalta
4	Education	*Journal of Research in Science Teaching*	(1999), 326, 4, 455–73	'Factors associated with students' intentions to engage in science learning activities'.	Malcolm B. Butler
5	Management	*International Journal of Intercultural Relations*	(1999), 23, 3, 387–409	'Communicating information in conversations: a cross-cultural comparison'.	Han Zao Li
6	Management	*Asia Pacific Journal of Management*	(2000), 17, (1), 67–83	'Performance of US FDI in different world regions'.	G. Qian
7	Psychology	*Journal of Experimental Psychology*	(1999), 25, 6, 1625–40	'Action planning and the temporal binding of response codes'.	Gijsbert Stoert and Bernhard Hommel
8	Psychology	*Psychological Review*	(1999), 106, 3, 491–528	'Phonology, reading acquisition and dyslexia: insights from connectionist models'.	Michael W. Harm and Mark S. Seidenberg
9	Sociology	*Social Policy Journal of New Zealand*	(1999), 13, 115–35	'Healthcare needs for older adults'.	R. A. Flett, N. Kazantsis, N. R. Long, M. A. Millar and C. Macdonald
10	Population Studies	*New Zealand Population Review*	(1999), 25, 119–32	'Cultural resources of immigrants and international business in New Zealand'.	N. Watts and A. Trlin

Index

abductive inferences 49
academic literacies movement 133, 146
accommodationist *see also* assimilative or pragmatic pedagogy 2, 9–10
Askehave I 30, 33, 89, 95, 132, 167

Bachman L 3
Bakhtin M 81
Bereiter C 82
Berkenkotter C 134–5, 158
Bhatia V K 7 13, 29, 33–4, 36, 117, 130–2, 139, 144, 153, 167–8
Biber D 7, 35–36, 77, 83–5, 91–4, 96, 106, 130,140
Braine G 87–9
Bush D 87

Canale M 3
Canseco G 88, 90
Carrell P 20, 31–2, 34, 51
categories
  basic level categories 44–47, 56, 67, 70, 72, 75
  subordinate categories 45–47, 50, 62, 67, 75
  superordinate categories 43–7, 50, 56, 67, 70, 73, 75–6
Celce-Murcia M 3
Christie F 13
cognitive processes 97, 100, 103, 127
coherence 3–4, 36, 60, 121, 125, 140, 144, 149–50, 165–6
coherence relations 98
cohesion 3–4, 13, 36, 111, 121, 125, 140, 144, 149–50, 161, 166
Common European Framework of Reference for Languages 4, 8
communicative competence 2–5, 109–10
community of practice 30–1
Conrad S 28
content schemata *see* schemata
criterial attribute 23, 26
critical pedagogy 10
Crombie W H 28, 97–8, 103, 125, 137, 161–2
Crowhurst M 85
cue validity model 44

Derewianka B 13–14, 86–7
Devine J 111–12
discourse communities 30–3, 35, 76, 95
  place discourse communities 31
discourse competence 1–6, 9–10, 45, 47, 80, 94
discourse patterns 7, 95, 97–8, 100, 103, 118, 120–1, 127, 140, 161
Dŏrnyei Z 3
Dudley-Evans T 13–14, 27, 29, 32–3, 127, 138

Eggins S 13, 16–18, 20, 24–5, 132
English for Specific Purposes 14, 24, 26–7, 113, 130, 138, 167
epistemology 36, 131–5, 141, 153–4, 156–7

family resemblances 40–2, 44, 91
Fauconnier G 64–6, 71

field *see also* field tenor mode 15, 17–21, 24, 82
field tenor mode 16, 23
Flowerdew J 112
foregrounded and background information 80
Fowler A 7, 23
frame semantics 52,56,71,74
frame theory 39, 56, 63–4, 76
frames 52 56–64, 74–6
Frandsen F 7–8, 35–6, 91, 94, 129

Garrod S 20, 31, 52, 54–6, 66, 75–6, 80–1
gestalts 68, 73, 76, 97–8
goals *see also* scripts and plans 39, 52–4, 75

Halliday M A K 15–6, 24
Hasan R 7, 13, 16–9, 21–4, 131
hierarchy 39–40, 45–6, 54, 58, 61, 75, 82–3, 147
Hoey M 7, 97–8, 123, 125
Hopkins A 14, 29, 33, 138
Hutchinson T 26–7
Hyland K 7, 29, 37, 81, 98, 127, 131, 134, 136–7, 157
Hyon S 29, 138

iconic and non-iconic distinction 21
ID principle 65
idealized cognitive models 39, 64, 71–3, 75
interpropositional relations 97–100, 103, 106, 111, 118, 121–7, 137, 144, 154, 161, 165, 185

Johns A 10, 13, 89, 90, 146, 152
Johnson M 20, 37, 39, 51, 67–73, 75, 81, 97, 123
Jordan R R 7

Kaplan R 82–3, 85
Knapp P 13–14, 18, 24, 86
Kroll B 81, 87

Lakoff G 20, 39, 46, 70–3, 75, 98, 123
Luke A 35, 130

macrofunctions 8
macro-propositions 60
macrostructures 7, 22, 60–1, 64
Malinowski B 14
Martin J 7, 13, 15–18, 21–2, 26, 82, 85–6, 132
mental space theory 64
mental spaces 39, 64–5, 71
Mervis C 23, 42, 44–5, 74–5
metadiscourse 36, 98, 131, 137–8, 141, 146, 157
meta-genres 85
metaphor 64–5, 67, 69–72
metonymy 71
Meyer B 50, 85
Miller C 82–3, 129
mode *see also* field tenor mode 15–16, 18–20, 23, 31, 82
mood 24–5

Moore T 88–91
Morton J 88–91

narrow angle courses 113

Oller J 20, 49–50, 75–6, 81

Paltridge B 6, 21–2, 24–6, 35–6, 77, 86, 115, 130, 139
Pearson Casanave C 87
Pilegaard M 7–8, 35–6, 91, 94, 129
plans *see also* scripts and goals 52–4, 75
pragmatic functions 65
procedural knowledge 11, 36, 56, 64, 76–7, 79–81, 96, 104, 109, 112, 114, 116–18,121–2, 125, 127, 143, 166–7
process genre approach 112
prototype theory 37, 42
prototypes 42, 44–5, 59–60, 64, 71, 73–4, 79, 86, 94, 141–2

reasoning
  abductive 49
  deductive 49–50, 100
  inductive 49
Reppen R 28
rhetorical functions 7, 89–91
rhetorical moves 31–2
Rosch E 23, 37, 42–5, 60, 74–5, 80, 103, 140
Rumelhart D 48–9, 52, 68, 75–6

Sanford A 20, 31, 52, 54–6, 66, 75–6, 80–1
Scardamalia M 82
scenarios 31, 39, 52, 54–6, 63, 74–5
schema theory 37, 39, 47–8, 51–2, 74–5
schemata
  abstract schemata 49–50, 52
  content schemata 31, 34, 49, 51–2, 76, 131, 139, 157
  formal schemata 31–2, 34, 49–51, 76
  image schemata 39, 64, 67–8, 70–3, 97–8, 100
  rhetorical schemata 49, 52
  transcendental schemata 68
schematic structure 13, 16–17, 19, 21–2, 24, 26, 36, 77, 114, 120, 122, 130–2, 138, 141, 153–4, 158, 164
scripts *see also* goals and plans 31, 39, 52–3, 55, 61, 74–5, 103
Skehan P 110
social-semiotic 15, 19
space builders 65
spatialization of form hypothesis 71–3, 98
Swales J 31–3, 36, 89–90, 95, 130–2, 138, 143, 153–4, 158–9, 167
syllabus
  analytic syllabus 115, 147
  relational syllabus 116
  synthetic syllabus 114–15
systemic functional linguistics 9, 14, 18–19, 21, 25, 82, 130, 132, 138

tenor 15–16, 19–20, 23, 25
text type 7–9, 35–6, 84–5, 96, 167
theme *see also* theme rheme 24–5, 28, 92

theme rheme 25, 92
transitions 137
transitivity *see also* transitivity system 20, 24–6
transitivity system 24–26

Van Dijk T 7, 22, 56, 60–1, 63–4, 66, 73, 75–6, 97
Ventola E 13–14

Waters A 26–7
Watkins M 13–14, 18, 24, 86
Wenden A 111
Werlich E 7
Widdowson H 109–10, 112–17, 122, 131–2
wide angle courses *see also* narrow angle courses
Wittgenstein L 23, 40–2, 73–4
writer stance 136, 141, 144, 153, 157–8

Lightning Source UK Ltd.
Milton Keynes UK
UKOW031600090413

208950UK00003B/8/P